MW00826264

TRIAL ADVOCACY BASICS

SECOND EDITION

TRIAL ADVOCACY BASICS

SECOND EDITION

Molly Townes O'Brien

Australian National University
ANU College of Law

Gary S. Gildin

Dickinson Law
Pennsylvania State University

NATIONAL INSTITUTE FOR TRIAL ADVOCACY

© 2016 National Institute for Trial Advocacy

No part of this work may be reproduced or transmitted in any form or by any means, electronic or mechanical, including photocopying and recording, or by any information storage or retrieval system without the prior written approval of the National Institute for Trial Advocacy unless such copying is expressly permitted by federal copyright law.

Address inquiries to:

Reprint Permission
National Institute for Trial Advocacy
1685 38th Street, Suite 200
Boulder, CO 80301-2735
Phone: (800) 225-6482
Fax: (720) 890-7069
Email: permissions@nita.org

ISBN 978-1-60156-563-1
eISBN 978-1-60156-564-8

FBA 1563

Library of Congress Cataloging-in-Publication Data

Names: O'Brien, Molly Townes, 1959- author. | Gildin, Gary S., author.
Title: Trial advocacy basics / Molly Townes O'Brien, Australian National University, ANU College of Law, Gary S. Gildin, Dickinson Law, Pennsylvania State University.
Description: Second edition. | Boulder, Colorado: National Institute for Trial Advocacy, [2016]
Identifiers: LCCN 2016025518 | ISBN 9781601565631
Subjects: LCSH: Trial practice—United States. | Trial practice.
Classification: LCC KF8915.O24 2016 | DDC 347.73/75—dc23 LC record available at https://lccn.loc.gov/2016025518

Printed in the United States.

CONTENTS

Chapter Eleven: Making and Responding to Objections

CHAPTER TWELVE: CLOSING ARGUMENT

CHAPTER THIRTEEN: GETTING READY FOR TRIAL

ACKNOWLEDGEMENTS

The authors would like to acknowledge the contribution of Professor Dent Gitchel, who was a co-author of the first edition of this book.

Chapter One

Introduction to the Courtroom

She had everything she needed, didn't she? Three years of law school study, many months of preparation, a new suit, and a briefcase full of files and notes. So why was her stomach churning as she stepped through the metal detector into the courthouse? Had she done enough? Had she forgotten anything? This would be no law school exercise. This time the stakes were real.

1.1   Welcome to the Courtroom

Almost everyone feels a sense of awe and reverence upon entering a courtroom. Courtrooms are impressive places. They are the arenas in which the essential rights of individuals and society are asserted, vindicated, defined—and sometimes taken away. The American people trust their most important public problems to the jury trial process. Juries are called on to decide all kinds of issues, including which company will clean up a polluted site, how much money is needed to compensate for an injury, whether someone committed a terrible crime, and even whether a person will live or die. The American people rely on the jury trial system to decide what happened and to resolve disputes on a just basis. The jury trial system, in turn, relies on lawyers to bring their clients' issues, information, and causes before the court and to present them in a legally and morally compelling way.

The design of the courtroom itself reflects the importance society places on the function of the lawyer in resolving human conflict. Every courtroom has a "bar" separating litigants and counsel from the public. Parties to litigation may come before the bar only when their cases have been scheduled to be heard and are "at bar." Witnesses may come before the bar only when they are called to testify. Lawyers, and only lawyers—those who have passed the bar examination and have become members of the bar—have the right by virtue of their standing as members of the profession to come before the bar any time they are in a courtroom.

Society grants the privilege of representing others in court only to lawyers. This is both a rare privilege and an awesome burden. When a lawyer enters the court, it is not her own life, liberty, or property that is at stake: it is her client's. For a young lawyer, the knowledge that the client's real interests are at stake is enough to cause a serious case of pretrial jitters.

This book is designed to serve as a practice manual, a pretrial companion, and a mentor for the lawyer who is relatively new to the trial process. We hope that even experienced lawyers will find the tactics and techniques captured in the book to be a valuable refresher. It will provide straightforward explanations of the processes and skills that are required to be successful at trial. It will also explain the reasons behind these recommendations. The book is intentionally general in its approach so that the methods discussed will apply to virtually any trial of any kind of case before a jury.

1.2   The Nature of Trial

The great English barrister, Sir Edward Marshall Hall, said:

> A lawyer and an actor are akin. It is true I have no mask, I have no set lines, I have no black cloth and I have no floodlights to help bring illusion. But out of the miseries and the joys and experience of men I must create an atmosphere of living reality so that it may be felt and understood by others, for this is advocacy.

Although the issues and problems confronting a jury are weighty and real, in one sense there is nothing real about the trial itself. A trial is a dramatic recreation of disputed past events, a drama staged in the courtroom to reconstruct for a jury a scenario that occurred in the past and now exists only in its consequences and in memory. A jury does not see the events that fostered a legal dispute; it merely witnesses a reenactment. Therefore, the jurors' perception of what occurred, rather than what actually happened, is the decisive element in determining the outcome of a trial. Only what the jurors are persuaded to believe matters. The difficult job of the advocate at trial is to use evidence, or "proof," to create a coherent narrative that jurors will accept as The Truth. The advocate must create that "atmosphere of living reality" using all of her dramatic and storytelling skills, and she must do so in such a way that the story is accepted as the true version of events. The lawyer must use the evidence to tell a story that not only addresses the legal elements of the case, but also is logical, simple, believable, and morally compelling. The advocate must tell this story within the confines of the rules of evidence and professional responsibility, and the conventions of trial practice.

At the end of the trial, the court instructs the jury to apply the law as if the trial had been a scientific experiment, i.e., to apply the law to the facts that have been presented and, by a process of deductive reasoning, reach a logical decision. However, as every experienced trial lawyer knows, the system does not operate by the scientific method. The jury's acceptance or rejection of facts depends in large measure on the manner in which the lawyer presents and argues the evidence.

Jurors often decide cases on general impressions. Like most of us, they ultimately want to do what is fair. They try hard to apply the law as it is explained by the judge to the evidence they hear and see. However, in virtually every case that goes to the jury, the law and facts will support more than a single result. Therefore, the version of the facts that the jury accepts is usually the set of facts that is most persuasively presented. The difference between winning and losing often depends upon the manner of presentation. We lawyers have no control over what evidence exists. However, we have enormous control over what evidence to present and how to present the available evidence.

A trial lawyer's job is often analogized to directing a play, painting a picture, or constructing a building. All these analogies have one thing in common: they involve creative activity. The theatrical director, painter, and building contractor all put raw materials together in a way that produces a final, unified product. So it is with trial lawyers. We take the raw materials we are furnished—the facts and the law—and arrange them in a way that constitutes the story, the picture, or the structure that will justify a verdict in our client's favor. A lawyer may not create facts or manufacture evidence. As someone once said, "We cannot invent our facts. Either Elvis Presley is dead or he isn't."[1] The essence of the trial lawyer's job is to marshal and present the available facts in a way that is most likely to persuade the jury to find in his client's favor.

The way facts are presented can be at least as important as the facts themselves. Small things can sometimes have a profound impact on the perception of the jurors. For example, assume that one of your opponent's witnesses tells a bald-faced lie on the stand. You know that the witness, who sounds quite credible in the courtroom, made a glaringly inconsistent statement in his deposition. You also know that you have the right to impeach this witness with his prior statement so that jurors can accurately assess his credibility. Your knowledge of the prior inconsistent statement is of no use, however, unless you are able to drive it home forcefully to jurors. Consequently, you must be able to find it quickly, a feat that can only be accomplished if you have suffered the drudgery of painstaking preparation. When you find the statement, you must then know how to examine the witness about it effectively, a feat you can accomplish only if you have mastered basic, practical trial techniques. If either lack of preparation or lack of skill prevents you from creating in the jurors' minds a perception that the witness is a liar, it does not matter whether he is, in fact, a liar. In court, the only facts that exist are those that are in the jurors' minds through their own experience or common sense and those that are introduced into evidence and believed by the jurors.

1.3   What Makes a Good Trial Lawyer?

A trial lawyer works hard. She practices one of the world's most intense, challenging, stressful, and rewarding professions. No one becomes a competent trial lawyer without untold hours of work. Burning the midnight oil, weekends at the

---

1. Eric Hobsbawm, *The New Threat to History*, 62–63 (1993).

office, and sleepless nights are part of the job. Therefore, at the core of every trial lawyer is a person with a great capacity for work.

A trial lawyer concentrates on the client and the case. An advocate is defined as "a person who argues for the cause of another person in a court of law."[2] Consequently, a trial lawyer acts on behalf of others, not himself.

The lawyer's role in an adversarial system of justice is to present evidence and argument in a way that will enhance his client's likelihood of winning the case. An effective trial lawyer concentrates completely on the case during trial—the witnesses, the jury, the exhibits—and thinks hardly at all about himself. As a trial lawyer, you are an advocate for your client and a fiduciary of both your client and the court.[3]

To succeed, the trial lawyer must become selfless. For the lawyer, the trial becomes an out-of-body experience. Every successful trial lawyer sooner or later learns the great truth that the less you think about yourself in the courtroom, the better job you do. You only have a finite amount of mental energy. Every ounce of that energy you expend thinking about yourself is wasted. Of course, you must constantly remain aware of the personal impression you are making on the jurors, but there is a vast difference between self-awareness and self-absorption. You must train yourself to focus on your client's case rather than your own performance. That does not mean you should shrink into the background. You should project confidence.

Recent psychology and business studies have shown that spending a few minutes by yourself, posing in open, expansive postures can cause increased feelings of power and tolerance for risk. Power posing in private—even for two short minutes—can have advantages that are both psychological and physiological. Both men and women may experience hormonal changes and enhanced feelings of confidence and communication ability.[4]

A trial lawyer plays by the rules. Every lawyer's conduct is restricted by rules of evidence and procedure, by the solemn obligation as an officer of the court to uphold the judicial system,[5] by rules of ethics,[6] and by considerations of simple courtesy and professionalism. These boundaries circumscribing the conduct of lawyers are

---

2. *Merriam-Webster Dictionary*, http://www.merriam-webster.com/dictionary/advocate (last viewed May 11, 2016).
3. *See* MODEL RULES OF PROFESSIONAL RESPONSIBILITY 1.7(b) Conflict of Interest; 3.3 Candor toward Tribunal; 8.4(d) Misconduct (conduct prejudicial to the administration of justice).
4. Carney, Dana R., Amy J. C. Cuddy, & Andy J. Yap. "Power posing brief nonverbal displays affect neuroendocrine levels and risk tolerance," *Psychological Science* 21.10 (2010): 1363–1368.
5. On being sworn in as attorneys, most states require an oath of office that includes allegiance to the Constitution of the United States and the state. *See, e.g.*, a group of New York attorneys being sworn in. https://www.youtube.com/watch?v=3wSFvOu4u0o (last viewed May 11, 2016).
6. *See* MODEL R. PROF. CONDUCT 3.3 Candor toward Tribunal; 8.4(d) Misconduct (conduct prejudicial to administration of justice).

what distinguish an adversarial, common-law trial from a brawl. Adherence to these boundaries is always wise as a matter of tactics as well as a matter of ethics.

A trial lawyer organizes and disseminates information. To be effective, a trial lawyer must master three elements of advocacy and utilize them to maximum advantage in each case. First, the trial lawyer must have a thorough understanding of the applicable law. Second, the trial lawyer must have a complete mastery of the facts. Third, the trial lawyer must have a manner of presenting the facts to the jury in a way that both fulfills the requirements imposed by the law and persuades the jurors that the lawyer's side of the case should prevail. A trial lawyer, then, must be student, investigator, organizer, and rhetorician. Your job as a trial lawyer is to present the facts from a perspective that is most favorable to your client. You must analyze the facts, focus attention on those that are advantageous to your client, and simplify the presentation of the facts into a story that jurors will be able to comprehend and accept.

A trial lawyer is an artist. There are no natural trial lawyers. To be sure, some people are born with aptitudes most of us do not possess, but natural talent is not a prerequisite to becoming an effective trial lawyer. It helps, but it is not essential. Hard work to develop whatever abilities you have is far more important than the measure of talents you were born with. On the other hand, a lawyer blessed with great natural ability who relies on that ability to serve as a substitute for diligent preparation is doomed to failure.

Becoming a trial lawyer is not unlike becoming an athlete. Lawyers and athletes are artists, and no art can be produced without sound technique. Very few young-sters shooting baskets on the school playgrounds of America will become NBA stars, no matter how hard they try. That level of success is dependent upon inborn athletic ability. Nevertheless, many of those kids who have little natural ability will become proficient players through diligent practice. On the other hand, some who have great natural ability will never fulfill their potential because they are unwilling to put in the years of endless practice in the fundamentals of dribbling, passing, shooting, and defense that are necessary to achieve stardom. We cannot all be superstars, but every lawyer can be a proficient, effective trial advocate.

A trial lawyer is an authority figure in the courtroom. A trial lawyer's every move should be calculated to convey the subtle impression that she is in command of the courtroom. She must assume the role of leader and make the jury comfortable following her. She must exercise the gentle art of persuasion, not the rough craft of dictation. Everything a lawyer says or does should be directed toward softly selling her theory of the case to jurors.

A trial lawyer is sincere. One of the wonderful things about the profession of trial lawyer is that people of all descriptions can be successful at it. Outstanding trial lawyers come in every size, shape, gender, and color. Be yourself. You cannot be anyone else even if you try. Furthermore, each of us is endowed with a lovable essence to which others will respond favorably if we just let it shine through. If you open your heart honestly and sincerely to others, they will respect you. If jurors respect you, they will follow you.

A trial lawyer diligently prepares. Every experienced trial lawyer agrees on one thing: the most essential factor in a lawyer's success is preparation. There is no substitute for it. In every sort of case, time after time, year after year, the most prepared lawyer usually wins. You cannot delegate preparation. You may delegate tasks in order to free your time for other, more important, responsibilities involved in preparing your case. However, the ultimate job of rolling up your sleeves, studying the law, learning the facts, and preparing the witnesses is yours if you aspire to be a real trial lawyer. Those who wing it may fool their clients and win some cases, but enduring success belongs to the lawyers who toil in the trenches of trial preparation.

A trial lawyer teaches. To some degree, a courtroom is like a classroom and the trial lawyer, like a teacher, imparts knowledge to the trier of fact. But experienced lawyers have a broader obligation as educators. Every trial lawyer has learned his skills from other lawyers. We drink from wells we did not dig and warm our hands at fires we did not build. One of the many traditions of our profession is sharing our knowledge with other members of the bar. As officers of the court and members of a highly select and learned circle, we have an obligation to improve the quality of trial practice by teaching less experienced lawyers the finer points of the art of advocacy.

1.4 The Basic Outline of a Jury Trial

Every American jury trial proceeds in a similar way. Differences do exist between jurisdictions, and indeed, from courtroom to courtroom within each jurisdiction, but the broad procedural outlines are the same.

1) Jury selection

2) Opening statements

3) The prosecutor's or plaintiff's case-in-chief

4) The plaintiff or prosecution rests

5) Motions are made and argued

6) The defendant's case-in-chief

7) The defense rests

8) Motions are sometimes made and argued

9) The plaintiff's or prosecution's case in rebuttal

10) The plaintiff or prosecution again rests

11) Motions are renewed

12) Jury instruction conference

13) Closing arguments

14) The court instructs the jury

15) The jury retires to deliberate

16) The jury returns its verdict

Jury Selection.[7] The process of jury selection must occur before the trial can begin. Many lawyers consider jury selection to be the most important step in the trial process.

The questioning of prospective jurors to determine if they are qualified to serve is known as voir dire.[8] The way voir dire is conducted varies widely from judge to judge, but the following is a fairly typical format. First, the judge asks general questions of the jury panel to determine whether they know the lawyers or parties or are familiar with the facts of the case. Next, the lawyer for the prosecution or plaintiff gets to question the panel, followed by the lawyer for each of the defendants.[9]

As the voir dire examination proceeds, each lawyer may move the court to strike prospective jurors for cause if information comes to light indicating that a juror may be biased, prejudiced, distracted, or for any reason unable to hear the evidence and render a fair, impartial verdict. Following voir dire, each lawyer may exercise a prescribed number of peremptory challenges.[10] Lawyers do not have to state the reasons for their peremptory challenges and may exercise them for almost any reason.[11]

Many judges allow jurors to take notes during the trial. Some jurisdictions actually encourage judges to permit jurors to take notes.[12] Where notes are allowed, the jurors may be handed small notebooks and pencils to take notes if they choose to as the trial proceeds. In some courts, the notebooks are organized in the same manner as the trial, with headings on the top of each page outlining the trial proceedings. The judge may give jurors some instructions on note-taking

---

7. *See* chapter four.

8. The term "voir dire" also is used to describe the limited cross-examination as to the admissibility of evidence that is allowed at the time the evidence is presented.

9. In many federal courts and some state courts, lawyers are only permitted to submit questions to the court, to be asked by the judge, rather than directly questioning the panel themselves. See FED. R. CRIM. P. 24(a) and FED. R. CIV. P. 47(a), which give the court discretion either to allow direct questioning by lawyers or to restrict the lawyers to submitting questions to be asked by the court.

10. *See* FED. R. CRIM. P. 24(b); FED. R. CIV. P. 47(b).

11. A peremptory challenge may not be based solely on the basis of race, Batson v. Kentucky, 476 U.S. 79 (1986), or gender, J.E.B. v. Alabama, 511 U.S. 127 (1994). This rule applies in both criminal and civil cases. Edmonson v. Leesville Concrete Co., 500 U.S. 614 (1991) (and was upheld in Snyder v. Louisiana, 552 U.S. 472 (2008)).

12. *See, e.g.,* U.S. v. Causey, 748 F.3d 310 (7th Cir. 2014).

and may direct them on what to do with the notebooks at the end of the day. Note-taking can help jurors to recall the evidence presented.

As a lawyer involved in presenting the evidence, you should be aware of how and when jurors are taking notes. You should talk to the jury about note-taking during the jury voir dire, demonstrate good note-taking during your trial presentation, and consider mentioning whether a point may be important enough to write down. Jurors' notebooks present a terrific tool for communication and memory.

Opening Statements.[13] After the jury is empaneled, the lawyers give opening statements. The lawyer for the prosecution or plaintiff goes first. These statements are intended to give the jury a broad overview of the position of each party and of the evidence that will be presented. During opening statements, lawyers are not allowed to argue which inferences should be drawn from the evidence. However, in reality, the opening statement is a critical persuasive moment of the trial.

The Prosecutor's or Plaintiff's Case-in-Chief. As the party with the primary burden of proof, the prosecution or plaintiff presents its evidence first. The evidence consists of the oral testimony of witnesses and usually of exhibits such as photographs, diagrams, and documents.

The questioning of each witness begins with direct examination. The party that called the witness asks questions first. Direct examination questions, which should generally be open-ended and non-leading,[14] are designed to facilitate the witness telling his story.

When the direct examination is concluded, the lawyer for each opposing party has an opportunity to cross-examine the witness. Cross-examination is designed to place the witness's direct testimony in its proper perspective. Cross-examination questions, which are generally leading, may elicit admissions from the witness that support the cross-examiner's story of the case. Cross-examination also may be designed to point out weaknesses in a witness's ability to perceive or remember, some bias or prejudice of the witness, or the witness's untruthful character. Cross-examination is limited to the scope of direct examination plus matters going to the witness's credibility.[15]

The lawyer who conducted the direct examination is allowed to ask more questions after the cross-examination for the purpose of giving the witness an opportunity to explain or rebut any matters brought out on cross-examination. This stage of questioning is called redirect examination. Recross-examination, which is usually not

---

13. *See* chapter five.
14. *See* chapter six.
15. *See* FED. R. EVID. 611(c). Some state courts do not limit the scope of cross-examination in the same way. *See, e.g.,* Givens v. State, 264 Ga. 522, 523(2), 448 S.E.2d 687 (1994) (every accused has a right to a thorough and sifting cross-examination); OHIO RULES OF EVIDENCE 611(B), Scope of cross-examination ("Cross-examination shall be permitted on all relevant matters and matters affecting credibility.").

advisable, may be utilized in an attempt to re-inflict damage that has been repaired during redirect examination.

The Plaintiff or Prosecution Rests. When the plaintiff or prosecution has presented all of the evidence that comprises its case-in-chief—in other words, when that party feels it has presented a *prima facie* case—it states to the court that it "rests." Before resting, you should confirm that the court's view of which exhibits have been admitted into evidence squares with your exhibit chart.

Motions are Made and Argued. At this point in the trial, the defendant should move for full or partial "judgment as a matter of law" or "judgment of acquittal" (as it is now called in federal court[16] and many state courts) or "directed verdict" (as it is more traditionally denominated). This motion is absolutely necessary in a civil case if the defendant is to preserve any argument as to the sufficiency of the evidence.[17] These motions are made outside the hearing of the jurors and are transcribed by the court reporter and argued to the court.

If the defendant's motion is granted as to all issues, the trial is over. Assuming that the motion is denied on at least one issue, the trial proceeds.

The Defendant's Case-in-Chief. The defense now has the opportunity to present any witnesses or other evidence in support of its position, as well as in support of any affirmative defenses it has raised. The examination of each witness proceeds in the same manner as it did during the plaintiff's or prosecution's case-in-chief.

The Defense Rests. After the defense has presented whatever evidence it has, it "rests."

Sometimes Motions Are Made and Argued. If the defendant has raised affirmative defenses, the plaintiff may make motions for full or partial judgment as a matter of law (directed verdict) at this point.[18] These motions are critical if the plaintiff is to preserve for appeal the issue of sufficiency of the evidence as to any affirmative defense.[19]

The Plaintiff's or Prosecution's Case in Rebuttal. The plaintiff or prosecution now has an opportunity to offer additional evidence to rebut evidence that the defendant has introduced. Examination of witnesses proceeds in the same orderly fashion as during other stages of the trial. The scope of the plaintiff's or prosecutor's evidence in rebuttal is limited to matters raised by the defense.

---

16. FED. R. CRIM. P. 29.
17. FED. R. CRIM. P. 29(a); FED. R. CIV. P. 50(a).
18. FED. R. CIV. P. 50(a); "Judgment as a matter of law" or a directed verdict of guilty is not available to the prosecution in a criminal case.
19. FED. R. CIV. P. 50(e).

The Plaintiff or Prosecution Again Rests. When the plaintiff or prosecution has completed the presentation of its evidence in rebuttal, it again rests.[20]

Motions Are Renewed. At the close of all the evidence, each party may renew its motions for judgment of acquittal or judgment as a matter of law (directed verdict). In civil cases, renewal of the motion is required to preserve the issue of sufficiency of the evidence for posttrial motions and appeal.[21]

Jury Instruction Conference. After the evidence is concluded and the court has ruled on all motions, the court holds a conference with the lawyers outside the hearing of the jurors, usually in chambers, during which counsel argue and the court decides how to instruct jurors. The lawyers will have previously submitted proposed jury instructions to the court. As the court goes through the proposed instructions, the lawyers must make appropriate objections on the record as to both instructions that are refused and instructions that are approved in order to save the issues for appeal.

During this conference the court will also decide the verdict form—whether to submit the case to the jury on specific interrogatories or on a general verdict. Some judges give jurors a written copy of the instructions to take into their deliberations. This decision by the judge may be governed by statutory or case law in the jurisdiction.[22]

Closing Arguments.[23] Closing arguments are the lawyers' opportunity to sum up the evidence and attempt to persuade jurors to find in their respective clients' favor. The party with the ultimate burden of persuasion (almost always the prosecution or plaintiff) goes first.[24] Then the opposing party (usually the defense) presents its closing. After the defense closing, the prosecution or plaintiff has an opportunity to get in the last word by giving a brief rebuttal argument in response to matters argued by the defense.[25]

The Court Instructs the Jury. The judge now reads the jury instructions to jurors.[26] These instructions advise jurors of the law applicable to the case. In some jurisdictions, jury instructions are given before closing arguments.

---

20. Sometimes the defendant may also present a surrebuttal case.

21. FED. R. CIV. P. 50(a).

22. In Arkansas, for example, the court may give the jury a typewritten copy of the instructions to take into the jury room during deliberations. Gambill v. Stroud, 258 Ark. 766, 531 S.W.2d 945 (1976). If all counsel request, the court must give the jury a typewritten copy. ARK. CODE ANN. 16-64-114.

23. *See* chapter twelve.

24. *See* FED. R. CRIM. P. 29.1.

25. *See* FED. R. CRIM. P. 29.1. In some jurisdictions, the defense closes first, followed by the closing of the plaintiff or prosecutor. Because the party with the burden of persuasion gets the final word, there is no defense rebuttal.

26. This is when it is normally done in federal court, though the timing of jury instructions is discretionary with the court. *See* FED. R. CIV. P. 51.

The Jury Retires to Deliberate. The jury is conducted into the jury room. The jurors normally take the exhibits with them,[27] along with written jury instructions if the court has provided them. The door is locked and the jurors deliberate in private until they have either reached a verdict or reported that they are unable to do so. Sometimes the jurors submit written questions to the judge. If the judge chooses to answer, everyone is called back into the courtroom. This is the time when lawyers twiddle their thumbs, pace, make small talk, and grow grey hair.[28]

The Jury Returns Its Verdict. Finally, a knock is heard from the inside of the jury room door. The bailiff answers it and reports that the jury has reached a verdict. The lawyers and parties scurry to counsel table and stand expectantly. The judge throws on the robe and ascends the bench. The bailiff leads jurors into the jury box. The court asks, "Ladies and Gentlemen, have you elected a foreperson? Madame Foreperson, have you reached a verdict? Would you please hand your verdict form to the bailiff?" The bailiff hands the verdict form to the judge, who reads it aloud. "Ladies and gentlemen, is this your verdict? Does either side wish to poll the jury?"

1.5   Differences between Bench and Jury Trials

Bench trials proceed in the same general order as jury trials. And in general, the techniques of persuasion are the same. Of course, since there is no jury, there is no process of jury selection and there are no jury instructions. Some judges prefer to dispense with opening statements, closing arguments, or both in bench trials. The judge will usually tell you how he intends to proceed. The judge may say, "Counsel, I've read the pleadings and understand the respective positions of the parties. I don't think opening statements would be of any value. Does either side wish to make any opening remarks?" In this case, you should follow the judge's wishes and forego opening statement. However, if the judge simply asks, "Does either counsel wish to make an opening statement?" an effective reply is, "Your Honor, if the court feels that opening statements would be helpful, I'm prepared to make one." Since the court is not only referee but also fact-finder and arbiter, it is important to establish early on that your objective is to deliver to the court exactly what it wants.

Obviously, since the court hears and sees all evidence in a bench trial, there is a tendency for the court to "let it all in for what it is worth." Nevertheless, objections should be interposed to inadmissible evidence in bench trials, just as in jury trials, when that evidence is important and its admission may be reversible error. The rules of evidence are equally applicable in bench trials, and if no timely, specific objection is made, there can be no appeal based on the improper admission of evidence.[29]

---

27. The trial court is usually authorized by statute to send all exhibits to the jury room during deliberations. The court generally has discretion to determine which exhibits to send into the jury room. *See, e.g.*, Patterson v. State, 742 N.E.2d 4 (Ind. 2000).

28. Or lose whatever hair they have.

29. Fed. R. Evid. 103(a)(1).

Chapter Two

Analyzing the Case for Trial

"Professor, I have a case that really might go to trial. Discovery is complete. The case is on the judge's trial calendar. Everybody has complied with the court's pretrial order. I don't think there is much chance for a settlement. I have to get ready to take up my briefcase, go to the courthouse, and present the case. Do you have any advice for me? How should I go about getting ready for trial?"

"John," I said. "The process of preparing for trial is like rowing a boat upstream from a dock. You begin at the ending point of your journey—your dock—your closing argument to the jury."

"Begin at the end? This sounds like advice from Alice in Wonderland."

"It does sound backwards. Remember, when you row a boat, you move backwards through the water. You have to pull hard to move upstream, but as you row, your goal is still ahead of you. Gradually, the scene in front of you changes. Finally, the whole river lies before you and you can see every rock and deep place in the route."

"Are you telling me to move backwards through the entire case, Professor?"

"Yes, John, but now that you have rowed upstream, your trip back to the dock will be an easy slide down river."

2.1   The Theory of Your Case

As you prepare to present your case at trial, start by thinking about the end of the trial and your closing argument. The closing argument is your guiding star throughout the trial preparation and presentation process. Your every action while preparing the case and during trial must be taken with the eventual closing argument in mind. Closing argument, or "summation" as it is sometimes called, will be the culmination of all your work on the case. In it, you will pull together the facts and the law, tell your client's story, and demonstrate to the jury why your client's cause is right and just. You will persuade jurors why they should accept your version of the events and draw the inferences you want them to draw from the evidence, rather than drawing the inferences your opponent wants them to draw.

The closing argument presents a clear, complete, and compelling account of your theory of the case. The case theory is the combination of law and facts that justifies a verdict in your client's favor. Notice that the case theory has both a *legal* and a *factual* aspect.

The *legal* aspect of the case theory describes the legal framework that will support a decision for your client. Every cause of action or defense is composed of "elements." These elements are points that must be proved if the cause of action or defense is to prevail. Whoever has the burden of proving a cause of action or defense must introduce admissible evidence to prove *every one* of its elements or the cause or defense will fail.

The factual aspect of the case theory is the story of the case established by the evidence admitted at trial. The story of the case must be consistent with the elements prescribed by the legal aspect of your theory. However, as will be more fully discussed, the factual aspect of the theory of the case is not founded in, nor organized around, the legal elements.

If you have handled the case from its inception you should have developed the theory of the case, at least generally, long before the time for final trial preparation. But you will often find that two or more theories of liability or defense flow from the facts. You will not use every conceivable theory at trial. Though you almost certainly pleaded all possible theories, you will probably emphasize only one during trial. Moreover, as you have worked with the case, your theory of the case will not have remained static. As your investigation of the law and the facts proceeded, you may have had to alter your theory. You may have thought of several different possible ways of accounting for certain developments or events. Some things you initially thought were true now do not seem plausible. You may be convinced of some matters that you cannot prove because witnesses or documents are not available. Now, as you prepare for trial, you must exercise your judgment and choose a theory or theories that are both provable and plausible. You must develop both the legal and factual aspects of a *winning* theory of the case.

In every case—from your first trial as a rookie lawyer to your final trial before retiring as a seasoned veteran of the courtroom—you must conduct two independent analyses to choose the theory of the case. Faithful execution of these analyses is necessary to develop a theory of the case that satisfies the separate requirements to prevail at trial: 1) presenting a case that is *legally* sufficient, and 2) persuading jurors that your client's account of the disputed facts giving rise to the trial is the true version of what occurred.

2.2 Developing the Legal Aspect of Case Theory

As a general rule, the reason your case proceeded to trial is because there are disputes of fact to be resolved by a jury. In civil cases, if the material facts are not in dispute a trial is unnecessary; instead the judge will grant a pretrial motion for summary judgment in favor of plaintiff or defendant. While the accused has a constitutional right to trial by jury, where there is no disagreement as to the relevant facts, most criminal cases will be resolved by a plea agreement.

Even though the animating purpose of the trial is to have the jurors determine which party's version of what occurred is true, defendant may prevail at trial before the case is submitted to the jury. As noted in chapter one, once plaintiff/prosecutor rests its case, defendant—before calling its first witness—may ask the judge to enter judgment for the defense. The grounds for the motion is that even if the court accepts the entirety of the testimony of the plaintiff's/prosecution's witnesses, that evidence does not establish *all* the elements that the law requires in order to prove the civil wrong or crime.[1]

To present a legally sufficient case and avoid a judgment for the defense at the close of the case-in-chief, plaintiff/prosecutor must successfully execute the following three-part protocol in every case:

Protocol for Presenting a Legally Sufficient Case

- Identify *each and every* element of the cause of action/crime

- Present sufficient evidence to *each and every* element of the cause of action/crime

- Present sufficient evidence to establish *each and every* element of the cause of action/crime during the plaintiff's/prosecutor's case-in-chief

---

2.2.1. Identify Each and Every Element of the Cause of Action/Crime

Your initial task as a trial lawyer occurs outside the courtroom: conducting thorough legal research regarding the legal elements of your case. You must continue researching until you are confident that you have identified every element that the law requires to establish each cause of action/crime you will pursue at trial. Should your legal research fail to identify a required element, it is quite unlikely that you will choose to ask questions of any of your witnesses to establish that element—

---

1. Defense counsel also may raise the motion for judgment at the close of all the evidence, and in some jurisdictions must do so to preserve the ability of the trial judge to enter judgment for the defense after the jurors return a verdict for the plaintiff or the prosecution. *See* FED. R. CIV. P. 50. In civil cases, the plaintiff similarly may move for judgment at the close of the evidence. *Id.* Because the defendant has the constitutional right to trial by jury, the prosecutor may not ask the judge to enter a guilty verdict. *See* chapter one.

leaving the court no choice but to grant a motion for judgment at the close of the case-in-chief.[2]

2.2.2. Present Sufficient Evidence to Establish Each and Every Element of the Cause of Action/Crime

To survive a defense motion for judgment, you must offer sufficient evidence to establish each and every element of the cause of action or crime. In planning what witnesses to call, as well as deciding what questions to ask each witness, you must verify that you will elicit sufficient testimony from at least one witness for each and every legal element.

While perhaps self-evident, it is worth mentioning that the burden of proof does not relieve plaintiff/prosecutor of the obligation to offer evidence at trial supporting each and every element. The government will not satisfy the requirement that it prove defendant's guilt beyond a reasonable doubt if the prosecution offers evidence of seven of the eight legal elements required to establish a particular offense; to convict the defendant, the prosecution must offer evidence supporting each of the eight elements. Similarly, the plaintiff will not meet the more relaxed burden of proof in civil cases by offering evidence that establishes a preponderance of the elements. As in the criminal case, plaintiff's counsel must present evidence of each and every element of the cause of action.

2.2.3. Present Sufficient Evidence to Establish Each and Every Element of the Cause of Action/Crime during the Plaintiff/Prosecutor's Case-in-Chief

In planning the case for trial, the plaintiff/prosecutor must assume that the defendant will move for judgment at the close of the case-in-chief. In ruling whether the plaintiff/prosecutor has presented a legally sufficient case, the judge must look only to the testimony and exhibits that have been presented through the witnesses who have testified. You will not survive a motion for judgment by representing to the court that you will prove an element during the cross-examination of witnesses you expect to be called by the defense. In a civil case, if the defendant is the only person with knowledge of facts proving a required element, plaintiff's counsel must call the defendant during its case-in-chief or offer into evidence excerpts of the deposition of the defendant that establish the element. Of course, given the constitutional privilege against self-incrimination, the prosecution can never call the defendant as a witness to establish an element (although the prosecutor may offer into evidence prior statements of the defendant that were obtained in conformity with established limits on interrogation). But the prosecutor may and must call other witnesses

---

2. As the lawyer for the defendant, you must do the same research for affirmative defenses and, in civil cases, any counterclaims or cross-claims you have pleaded.

aligned with the defense when they are the only persons who can offer evidence to support one of the elements of the crime.

The plaintiff/prosecutor also must offer evidence of those elements she believes will not be disputed by the defense. If you conclude the defendant does not contest an element because of an admission made in a pleading, response to a discovery request, or a stipulation, you must formally move that pretrial admission into evidence at trial during the case-in-chief.

As defense counsel, you must conduct the same three steps of the protocol to be prepared to make a motion for judgment at the close of the plaintiff/prosecutor's case-in-chief. You should have a proof checklist—a document that lists the required elements—next to you at counsel table. Place a checkmark next to an element when the plaintiff/prosecutor elicits testimony supporting that element. Once the plaintiff/prosecutor rests, you should move for judgment if there is any element on the proof list without a checkmark.

2.2.4. Applying the Protocol to Remedies

Much of the time, the material, factual disputes giving rise to the trial relate to whether the defendant committed the underlying civil wrong or crime. However, you must also adhere to the three-step protocol for the remedies your client is seeking.

Even where you have properly offered sufficient evidence to establish each and every element of liability in a civil case, defense counsel may move for *partial* judgment at the close of the case-in-chief as to any remedy—legal or equitable—whose elements you have not fully established. Accordingly, for each remedy that your client is seeking, you must offer evidence in your case-in-chief sufficient to prove each and every element of that remedy. For example, if the law permits recovery of "reasonable and necessary medical expenses" in a personal injury case, you may not recover those losses merely by offering the medical bills into evidence. You also must offer testimony (or a stipulation) that the 1) medical care afforded was necessary for treatment of the plaintiff's injuries, and 2) the charges for the treatment were reasonable. For tangible damages, the plaintiff typically must not only prove that he suffered the harm, but also must offer evidence that allows jurors to calculate the amount of the loss without engaging in mere speculation. Consequently, to recover damages for future wage loss, you may have to call an expert economist, a doctor, and a vocational rehabilitation expert to establish 1) the plaintiff's life expectancy; 2) work life expectancy; 3) functions he will no longer be able to perform; 4) the difference in wages and benefits he would have received over his lifetime if uninjured, compared to the reduced wages and benefits he will earn in light of his injuries;

5) increase in future wages and benefits due to inflation and productivity; and 6) the reduction to present value of future wage loss and medical expenses.[3]

To execute the first step of the protocol—identifying each and every element of the cause of action—your legal research as to remedy must unearth the answer to three questions:

1) What are the categories of damages (or equitable relief) recoverable for the particular cause of action?

2) For each category, what are the elements that must be proven to recover damages (or equitable relief) for that category?

3) For each category, what type of evidence is required, permitted or prohibited to prove each element?

Your law school may have offered a course titled "Remedies," which suggests that there is a generic body of law applicable to all civil wrongs. To the contrary, you must research the relevant statutes and case law that define the damages (and/or equitable relief) that are recoverable for the particular cause of action you are asserting. If you are bringing a lawsuit on behalf of a victim of police misconduct, the damages recoverable for the officer's commission of a common law tort are different than the damages you may recover for the "constitutional tort," the deprivation of constitutional rights redressed under the cause of action created by federal statute, 42 U.S.C. § 1983.

Second, your research into the elements required to recover a category of damages must extend to the legal standard governing each element. As noted earlier, the law may permit recovery of "reasonable and necessary," as opposed to "actual," medical expenses.

Finally, you must continue researching until you have learned the type of evidence that is required, permitted, or prohibited in proving an element. Is proof of past profits sufficient to recover future lost profits in a breach of contract case? Or must the plaintiff present an expert witness to project and calculate future profits that would have been earned had the defendant not breached the agreement?

While less frequent in criminal cases, a statute may provide that the sentence may be enhanced where at trial the prosecution proves an element beyond the proof required to establish the underlying crime.[4] In such cases, as the prosecutor,

---

3. Some jurisdictions treat the rise in wages and benefits due to inflation and reduction to present value as a "total offset." The plaintiff may still recover an increase in future wages due to enhanced productivity. *See* Kaczkowski v. Bolubasz, 421 A.2d 1027 (Pa. 1980).

4. *See* 18 U.S.C. § 924(c) (increasing mandatory minimum sentence depending on whether a firearm was possessed (five years), brandished (seven years), or discharged (ten years) during, in relation to, or in furtherance of crime of violence or drug trafficking crime).

you must offer such evidence in your case-in-chief to procure the longer sentence following conviction.

2.2.5 Legal Research Tips

Your ability to successfully raise and defend the motion for judgment at trial demands thorough legal research to accurately identify each and every element of the cause of action/crime and the remedy. In criminal cases and civil actions for violation of a statute, the elements are set forth in the language of the statute, as well as case law interpreting that language. The following statute is annotated (with brackets) to highlight the eight elements the prosecution must prove to convict the defendant of first-degree murder:

> A person commits the crime of first-degree murder if [1] after delibera-tion [2] and with the intent [3] to cause the death [4] of a person [5] other than himself, [6] he or she [7] causes the death [8] of another person.

Some of the elements are unambiguous on the face of the statute. For other ele-ments, such as deliberation and intent, you will have to research case law interpreting the statute to know what evidence you must offer to prove the element.

In common law causes of action, the elements are a product of the cumulative body of case law defining the conduct that gives rise to liability and the remedies that are available. It is quite likely that no single case will address or apply the full set of elements. Consequently, you must continue to research cases until you are confident you have discovered all of the elements. For example, in a garden-variety action for recovery of damages arising out of an automobile accident, you may have to read multiple cases to learn that the plaintiff must prove the following elements:[5]

1) Negligence, which can be either a violation of a common law duty to use reasonable care or breach of a duty imposed by statute;

2) Causation, which may require proof of both proximate cause and cause in fact;

3) Where the defendant is an employer, that the person who was driving the car was acting in the scope of his employment;

4) Reasonable and necessary past medical expenses;

5) Expenses that the plaintiff will incur in the future for medical care;

6) Wages and benefits lost between the time of the accident and trial;

---

5. *See* Penn. Suggested Standard Civil Jury Instr. §§ 7.00–7.40, 7.110–7.130, 8.00, 13.10, 13.20, and 13.100.

7) Impairment of future earning capacity (the difference between wages and benefits the plaintiff would have earned over his lifetime if uninjured less the wages and benefits he will earn);

8) Past intangible damages (which may include physical pain and suffering, mental pain and suffering, embarrassment, humiliation, disfigurement, loss of life's pleasures);

9) Future intangible damages (which may include physical pain and suffering, mental pain and suffering, embarrassment, humiliation, disfigurement, loss of life's pleasures);

10) If the defendant's actions were not only negligent but also reckless, punitive damages designed to punish and deter, which may allow or require introduction of evidence of the defendant's net worth.

Certain research strategies will help you determine the elements. In researching case law, you should look for cases whose procedural posture requires the court to apply the elements. You are most likely to find the elements discussed in rulings on motions to dismiss, motions for judgment on the pleadings, motions for summary judgment, and motions for judgment at and after trial.

The most direct embodiment of the elements is the court's instructions to the jury. In addition to researching case law adjudging the accuracy of instructions to the jury, you should investigate whether your jurisdiction has an approved or suggested set of standard jury instructions.[6]

Finally, you should consult respected secondary sources, such as hornbooks and practice guides. While never a sufficient basis for determining elements, these works provide an excellent starting point to identify the spectrum of potential elements for the cause of action/crime. You then must conduct subsequent research into primary authorities in your jurisdiction to verify the governing elements.

The elements dictate the evidence you must offer in the case-in-chief to present a legally sufficient case. However, you must fully research the elements of the cause of action/crime to ethically determine what claims you may include in the complaint initiating a civil lawsuit[7] or in the information or indictment that commences a criminal case. At trial, you will use a proof checklist to guide you in raising and defending motions for judgment.[8] At the end of the trial, the judge will give the jury a series of instructions on the law that applies to the case. These instructions

---

6. In some jurisdictions like California, the state supreme court has approved the jury instructions as an accurate statement of the law. In other jurisdictions like Pennsylvania, a committee composed of judges, lawyers, and law professors issues and updates suggested standard jury instructions that it believes reflect the current state of the law.

7. *See* FED. R. CIV. P. 11(b).

8. See section 2.2.3, *supra.*

summarize all of the legal principles that are necessary to reach a verdict. Every "element" of the case, every presumption, even the permissible modes of reasoning and the burden of proof, are explained in the jury instructions. You should create a draft set of jury instructions when you have finished your initial legal research.[9] You may revise this initial set of instructions as you learn more facts through investigation and discovery. Nevertheless, creating it early gives you a frame of reference for everything else you do to prepare for trial.

2.3   Developing the Factual Aspect of Case Theory

The protocol for presenting a legally sufficient case ensures that you offer evidence supporting a legal theory that will survive motions for judgment and be submitted to the jury. However, satisfying that protocol will not achieve the second requirement to prevail at trial: persuading the trier of fact that your client's version of the disputed facts is truly what occurred. The elements of the cause of action/crime are legal constructs, categorizing and objectifying when behavior is wrongful so members of society can conform their conduct to predictably avoid liability or punishment. The elements are not designed to help a jury choose between conflicting testimony about the events allegedly giving rise to culpability. Consequently, you also must choose a factual story of the case.

Trial lawyers traditionally have used the "CPR" method to advocate their client's version of the facts. Focusing on accounts of the moment of the crime/civil wrong, we bolster the veracity of our witnesses' testimony and undermine the testimony of our adversary's witnesses by comparing 1) the *credibility* of the witnesses, 2) the ability of the witnesses to *perceive* the event, and/or 3) the accuracy of the witnesses' *recollection* of the event.

Spurred by newer scientific understanding of how the brain makes decisions, the "story method" has emerged as the preferred mode of factual persuasion. All humans—including judges and jurors—resolve conflicting information by automatically creating a coherent story of what occurred and why. Perhaps the most important book on trial advocacy written in the past fifty years is a work not addressed to lawyers: Daniel Kahneman's *Thinking Fast and Slow*.[10] Summarizing the findings of cognitive psychology, Kahneman explains that the brain has two functional operations: System 1 and System 2. System 1, the "fast" part of thinking, operates instinctively and subconsciously, associating newly received information with established patterns of how the world and its inhabitants typically operate. System 2 of the brain, the "slow" part of thinking, synthesizes vast amounts of information, comparing and contrasting data, and applying known rules. Law schools train their students to hone the type of analysis typical of System 2 brain function.

---

9. *See* chapter thirteen.
10. Daniel Kahneman, *Thinking Fast and Slow*, Farrar, Straus and Giroux (2011).

However, System 2 thinking draws heavily on the body's glucose supply. Consequently, if the jurors' System 1 is satisfied that it has associated new information with a predictable pattern, their brains will not activate the System 2 function.[11]

The CPR method of arguing how the jury should resolve fact disputes is a quintessential appeal to System 2 of the brain. We ask the jurors to compare the credibility, perception, and recollection of the array of witnesses, guided by the judge's instructions on credibility and burdens of proof. Kahneman's work, and the neuroscience and social science that underlie his findings, counsel that we should instead be pressing System 1 arguments. We must tell a story—one that begins long before the moment of the cause of action/crime—that fits a recognized pattern of how the world works. Properly constructed, the story makes our client's version of what occurred entirely predictable, and in the jury's mind even inevitable.

While lawyers only recently have embraced the persuasive role of story, most other disciplines have long recognized its power. As a result, there is near-universal agreement as to the three central elements of story—character, motive, and plot—the second protocol you must follow in analyzing the case for trial.

2.3.1 Character

The first decision you must make is to determine which *one* person's story will occupy the center of the trial's factual narrative. Other parties and witnesses of course will enter that narrative. However, to maintain the appeal to System 1 reasoning, you must unmistakably tell one person's story.

You will have several choices as to whose story to tell: that of your client, the opposing party, one of the non-party witnesses, even on some occasions that of an inanimate object. In making the selection, you should be animated by the first, indispensable, and arguably most important element of story: the character of that person.

The jurors' instinctive System 1 prediction of what occurred will be launched by the character traits of the subject of the story. On a daily basis, we conduct ourselves based upon instantaneous judgments about how others in our orbit will act or react. These judgments are often based on the most slender shards of information about character. Consequently, it is vital that you identify the character traits of the subject

---

11. The jurors' System 1 analysis will be validated by the judge's instruction that the jurors should apply their experience in the ordinary affairs of life to the facts. E.g., "In deciding whether to draw an inference you must consider all the facts in the light of reason, common sense and experience." 9TH CIR. CRIM. JURY INSTR. § 3.8 (2000). "You are permitted to draw, from the facts which you find have been proved, such reasonable inferences as you feel are justified in the light of your experience." Devitt, Edward J., et al., *Federal Jury Practice and Instruction: Civil*, § 70.03 (4th ed. 1987). "You are entitled to consider [the] evidence in the light of your own observations and experiences in the affairs of life." 8TH CIR. MODEL CIV. JURY INSTR. 1.0-1 (1992).

of your story—traits formed and displayed long before the moment of the crime/civil wrong—that will cause the jury to automatically predict and accept his subsequent motive and actions.

Because of our argumentative nature and reluctance to concede any turf to our adversary, trial lawyers are prone to categorize people as uniformly saintly (our client) or irredeemably evil (the opposing party). In reality, most people are not so one-dimensional. Perhaps the most powerfully predictive character trait is that of a fundamentally decent person who, through the hand that life dealt, may be motivated under particular circumstances to act against his inherently better self. Most of the stories we have read—fiction and non-fiction alike—depict a basically good person whose life journey renders him especially vulnerable to succumbing to competing forces of temptation, anger, jealousy, longing for a better life, greed, lack of self-confidence, entitlement, or regret.

The law of evidence generally rules out one trait of character—the propensity to do the very act that is at issue at trial. While logically relevant, there is a risk that the jury will give undue weight to prior similar acts (good or bad). With some exceptions in criminal cases, most jurisdictions preclude introduction of testimony regarding a party's character for engaging in the very conduct giving rise to the trial.[12]

2.3.2 Motive

The second element of the trial story is motive: what subjectively caused the subject of the story to act in a particular way in the particular situation. Interestingly, motive is rarely an element of the cause of action or crime. Yet unless you can explain why the person whose story you are telling was motivated to behave as he did, the jury will not intuitively find the story to rest comfortably in a pattern of how life generally works. While not a legal requirement, motive is an essential ingredient of the believability and predictability of the story of the case.

Motive must be a by-product of the chosen character trait(s) of the subject of the story. Indeed, "story character" is not precluded by the law's general preclusion of character evidence precisely because character is not used to establish a propensity to engage in conduct similar to the events at trial. Rather, story character makes it more probable that the subject of the story would harbor the motive to act as he did at the moment of the cause of action or crime.[13]

If you cannot explain why, because of his character, the person whose story you are telling would be motivated to do what she did, you need to find a different story (or settle the case). You could choose a different character trait or find a different

---

12. *See* FED. R. EVID. 404.

13. Although precluding prior similar acts to prove propensity, the law of evidence permits introduction of past conduct to prove motive. FED. R. EVID. 404(b).

person whose story to tell. Conversely, if you identify the motive that ordinarily follows from the selected character trait, the trier of fact will instinctively predict and understand how that person acted.

Like the element of character, introducing motive requires you to pull the story further back in time from the moment of the civil cause of action/crime. And, unlike the actions necessitating the trial, the facts that prove character and motive often are undisputed, further increasing their persuasive force.

2.3.3 Plot

The third element of the story is the plot, advancing the narrative of character and motive to the moment of the civil cause of action/crime. Properly constructed, the plot must include not only the physical actions of the subject of the story, but also describe what he was thinking at the time he acted.

Plot ostensibly is the easiest component of the story for lawyers because it typically coincides with the central legal elements. However, determining the plot requires the trial lawyer to shed a mainstay of legal advocacy: the alternate argument. In drafting legal briefs, we further our cause when we supply the court with three independent bases for a ruling—only one of which the judge need accept. Offering alternate versions of what occurred, however, will undermine our attempt to persuade jurors. We carefully chose the character trait and motive to cause jurors' System 1 brains to instinctively predict the ensuing behavior. If we then suggest alternative versions of what actually happened, we make the jurors question the validity of that prediction. We move the jury's decision process to a System 2 analysis, opening the jurors' minds to opposing counsel's version of events in the now-expanded catalogue of plot alternatives.

Upon modest reflection, it should not be surprising that jurors will want to find a single version of what occurred. We could dispense with trials if technology permitted us to transport jurors back in time to witness the wrong; upon their return to the present, the jurors would report exactly what they saw, not alternative accounts. The trial is the law's approximation of the time machine. Unable to beam the jurors back in time, we summon those persons who witnessed that past event to presently share their observations with the jury. As was true of their hypothesized time travel, the jurors will expect to return with a singular version of what occurred.

2.3.4 The Character–Motive–Plot Continuum

In sum, before uttering a single word in the courtroom, you must find the factual story whose elements line up in a continuum:

Character ↔ Motive ↔ Plot

The character trait(s) of the person whose story you are telling must naturally give rise to his motive. That motive must be the animating cause of the very thoughts harbored and actions taken at the moment of the cause of action/crime. Unless and until you have found a story that fits the continuum, you will not be able to successfully tap into the trier of fact's System 1 brain that in most instances will instinctively decide whose version of facts is correct.

The story of the case drives the substance of every portion of the trial. During voir dire, you will de-select those jurors whose unique life experiences would inhibit them from accepting the story. In the opening statement, you simply tell the story of the case—not just the single plot, but also the character and motive that makes that plot inevitable. Your direct examinations should elicit the facts that evidence the chosen character, motive and plot; equally important, you must refrain from presenting testimony that could support alternative versions of what occurred. You likewise must plan the cross-examination of each witness in light of the chosen story of the case, often using adverse witnesses to bolster the character, motive, or plot of your story. In closing argument, you must continue to use the story form, showing jurors that the (often undisputed) evidence established the character and motive that make your version of the disputed facts inevitable.

By disposition and training, lawyers are System 2 creatures. Therefore, we need all the help we can get at trial to resist the constant temptation to offer evidence of alternate stories that, if accepted, would result in a favorable verdict. The most useful device is a written statement of our factual theory of the case—a paragraph that identifies 1) whose story we are telling, 2) the character trait(s) of that person, 3) his motive and 4) the single plot. The theory statement literally must be in our line of vision whenever we are preparing for trial. Seeing the theory statement will remind us to prune from our presentations any information that does not contribute to the factual story of our case.

2.3.5 Stakes and Theme

You should use two additional devices to increase the jury's ability to understand and be persuaded by the story of the case: stakes and theme.

Stakes

The story of the case causes the jurors System 1 brains to automatically predict and accept your version of the disputed facts. The stakes of the case will cause jurors, on an emotional level, to root for your client to win because of the effect the verdict will have on someone's life.

Every trial has legal consequences that follow from the verdict. While second nature to the lawyers, the legal stakes are policy-driven outcomes that rarely will ignite a juror's emotional attachment to the outcome. In most civil cases, the aftermath of a plaintiff's verdict is the forced transfer of money from the defendant. However, jurors may not readily see how requiring the defendant to give money to the plaintiff—especially for damages for intangible injuries like pain, suffering, embarrassment, humiliation, and loss of life's pleasure—will in any way restore the injured party to his previous condition. Conversely, a defense verdict ensures that a person who is not negligent (or in many cases, his insurance company) will be excused from paying for the injuries to the plaintiff, even where the defendant's action caused the harm. This policy judgment is not likely to induce jurors to root for denying compensation to the catastrophically injured party.

In a criminal case, the legal stakes are punishment and deterrence of a guilty defendant. While a sufficient motivator for particularly heinous offenses, some jurors may have difficulty seeing how either the victim's or the defendant's life will be meaningfully improved by incarceration in less egregious instances. A verdict of not guilty—particularly one premised upon the existence of reasonable doubt—advances the policy that it is better that ninety-nine guilty persons be freed than one innocent person be wrongfully convicted. This is hardly a compelling reason to root for exoneration in those cases in which the jury believes the accused is likely guilty, but the prosecution has fallen shy of its burden of proof.

Instead of relying upon the rational stakes of the law to motivate the jurors, you must identify what is to be gained on an emotional, non-intellectual level by the verdict. Great stakes must have three attributes:[14]

1) They must not be purely material or monetary;

2) They must be relatable to the audience and connected to universal human experience; and

3) They must be irreplaceable and not easily quantifiable.

Often the stakes may be the favorable resolution of the very conflict in character that motivated the subject of the story to act. A verdict against the defendant in a civil or criminal case represents the consensus of the community that may jar the defendant to finally confront and address the competing forces that caused him to act against his true, good nature. A defense verdict in a civil case may cause the plaintiff to mature and improve his life by accepting responsibility for his own actions, or may be the only means to liberate the defendant from the plague of unwarranted fear and self-doubt that he had carelessly caused injury to another. A not guilty verdict in a criminal case may be the only means of providing true safety, security, and closure to the victim by inducing the police to continue their search for the real criminal.

---

14. Thanks to documentary filmmaker Joseph Meyers, a principal in Trial Story, www.trialstory.com, (last visited May 11, 2016), for making us aware of the concept of stakes and identifying its attributes.

Theme

The theme is a rhetorical device that frames the central issue of the trial or that acts as a memory cue for your most important trial idea. In the world of popular music, this concept is called a "hook." A song's hook is the play on words, catchy phrase, or melodic twist that grabs the listener's attention—the one you cannot get out of your mind and still remember decades later. Baby boomers nearing retirement can still muster the refrain, "I can't get no satisfaction." In advertising, the hook is the phrase that is used over and over in different advertisements so that it becomes associated with the product. For example, Nike uses the phrase "Just do it" to promote its sporting goods. Like a great song or a memorable ad, your trial should have a theme that sums up your story of the case in a way that will implant itself in the minds of the jurors and serve as the lens through which the jury sees individual pieces of evidence.

There are four ways to find a theme. First, borrowing from the world of music and advertising, we can find a catch phrase that captures the essence of our case. The most famous example is Johnnie Cochran's theme in his closing argument in the O.J. Simpson case, "If the glove does not fit, you must acquit." That theme not only focused the jury's attention on the most visible weakness in the prosecution's case, but also was "catchy and melodic." Far less successful was defense counsel's attempt to pirate that theme in the Galleon insider trading prosecution, arguing "If the information was public, you must acquit."

Secondly, the theme may be a universal principle of human behavior represented by your story of the case. From the time we were young, our parents and teachers cautioned us to "look both ways before crossing the street." That phrase may serve as a theme where the theory of the case is that harm was caused because of a party's failure to check for dangers before acting.

A third source of theme is words uttered from the mouth of the opposing party. Political consultants are expert in exploiting this device, evidenced by the Obama campaign's repeated incantation of Mitt Romney's "47 percent" remark[15] surreptitiously recorded at a private fundraiser in Boca Raton, Florida. Just as that phrase captured what the Democratic Party viewed as the central reason to reject the opposing candidate, words from the mouth of the opposing party may crystallize the essence of the story of your case.

---

15. "There are 47 percent of the people who will vote for the president no matter what . . . who are dependent upon government, who believe that they are victims. . . . These are people who pay no income tax . . . and so my job is not to worry about these people. I'll never convince them that they should take personal responsibility and care for their lives," said Romney.

The Yale Book of Quotations, which selects quotes that "are famous, important or revealing of the spirit of the times," crowned Romney's "47 Percent" remark the 2012 quote of the year.

Finally, because they are relatable and connected to universal human experience, the stakes of the case are a fertile source of themes. "Please ask the police to find the real murderer, who continues to roam the streets" may serve as the hook that not only compels the jury to root for acquittal, but unifies the story of the defense.

Choose something simple, but not foolish or trite. Make sure that your theme passes the "gag and giggle" test: make sure that it is something you are comfortable using repeatedly throughout your trial without making yourself or the jury gag or giggle. As will be discussed in subsequent chapters, once you decide on a theme for your case, you will invoke the theme strategically throughout the trial.

CHAPTER THREE

THE LAWYER'S COURTROOM DEMEANOR

Knowing that this had been his first trial, the judge invited the young lawyer into her chambers after the verdict. She did not want to volunteer an unwanted critique, so she asked for his thoughts on the trial. Was there anything about the trial he had questions about? Anything he had not expected?

"I guess the biggest surprise, Judge," he responded, "was how physically demanding the trial was for me. Every night, my legs have been as tired and sore as if I ran ten miles."

"Son," the judge smiled, "you paced at least ten miles around the courtroom every day you were on trial. You never stood still. We all felt worn out just watching you."

"Did I really, Judge?" He was genuinely astonished. "I had no idea."

3.1 The Trial Lawyer on Trial

Painstaking preparation, though absolutely essential to a successful trial, is not enough. Presentation is equally important. And make no mistake about it: the jurors' eyes will be on you every moment. The way you act may be as important as anything you say. Every time a juror sees you, that juror will assess your behavior, consciously or unconsciously, and form impressions about the merit of your case. Your behavior will have a profound impact on the outcome of every case you try.

Every law student learns that a witness's demeanor is one of the factors the jury may take into account in assessing that witness's credibility.[1] If a witness fidgets, looks away, or hesitates too long before answering, jurors may decide that the witness is lying and discount her testimony. The law, being eminently practical, allows jurors to consider demeanor because they will do it anyway. It is human

---

1. *See, e.g.*, NINTH CIRCUIT CIVIL JURY INSTRUCTION 3.6, § 1.11 (2007) ("In considering the testimony of any witness, you may take into account: . . . [t]he witness's manner while testifying;"); *Manual of Model Civil Jury Instructions for the District Courts of the Eighth Circuit* 3.4 (2014) ("In deciding what testimony to believe, consider . . . how a witness acted while testifying. . . ."); ARK. MODEL INSTRUCTION (Civil) 105 ("In determining the credibility of any witness and the weight to be given the witness's testimony, you may take into consideration the witness's demeanor while on the witness stand. . .").

nature. Consciously or unconsciously, we base our acceptance or rejection of others partly on how we see them act. To quote an old but true cliché: "Actions speak louder than words." Consequently, everything each witness says and does during the trial, in or out of the witness box, may have a profound effect on any juror who oversees or overhears it. Likewise, every move you make will have an impact on the jury because jurors will draw conclusions about your credibility from their observations of your demeanor.

But what about the court's boilerplate instruction to the jurors that they must base their verdict only on the evidence?[2] Technically, a lawyer's demeanor is not something that jurors should consider. Basic legal ethics teach us that a lawyer may not testify in a case he is trying.[3] Nothing that the lawyers say is evidence in the case. Therefore, in theory, the lawyer's credibility is not an issue before the jury. But, as Yogi Berra noted, "In theory, there is no difference between theory and practice. In practice, there is." Though the rules of evidence and ethics dictate that the lawyer's credibility is not an issue in the trial, the rule of human nature is otherwise. In a very real sense, a lawyer is an unsworn witness in every case he tries. The lawyer's credibility is as much in the balance as that of any sworn witness.

Regardless of how you feel inside, always try to look like a winner. Even if you are behind, a sustained look of control and confidence can give you a mental edge that results in victory.

—Arthur Ashe

One of the authors remembers talking to several jurors after a particularly difficult trial. The evidence favoring her client's affirmative defense was very thin and she had been surprised to win an acquittal. She asked one of the jurors whether the jury was concerned about how little evidence there was on the affirmative defense. "Well, we were," came the response, "but we figured you must have known about a lot more that you just couldn't bring into court. We thought you were telling the truth, so we voted with you."

If you can present yourself as the trustworthy leader the jurors can follow confidently to a just result, you will greatly improve the chances of winning your case.

---

2. *See, e.g.,* Devitt, Edward J., *Federal Jury Practice and Instructions: Civil,* § 70.03 ("You are to consider only the evidence in the case."); Ark. Model Instr. (Civ.) 101 ("You are to decide this case fairly, based only on the evidence I allow to be presented in this courtroom and the law as instructed by me. You are not to consider information from any other source. . . . And do not allow sympathy, prejudice, or like or dislike of any party or any attorney in this case to influence your decision."); *Manual of Model Civil Jury Instructions for the District Courts of the Eight Circuit 2014,* 1.3 ("Do not let sympathy, or your own likes or dislikes, influence you. The law requires you to come to a just verdict based only on the evidence, your common sense, and the law that I give you in my instructions, and nothing else.")
3. Model Rule of Professional Conduct 3.7.

The jurors are looking for a leader. They have been sworn to do justice (an awesome responsibility) and must find their way through what appears to them to be an impenetrable thicket of confusing, contradictory facts and indecipherable law. They are likely to follow the lawyer who best gains their confidence by coolly guiding them through the evidentiary undergrowth. Many jurors believe that the lawyers know what really happened in the case. They think that the lawyers know the Truth about the events at issue in the trial. In the eyes of these jurors, the trial pits one lawyer who is fighting a just cause against another who is trying to use the law's technicalities to pull the wool over the jurors' eyes. If they believe that you are the lawyer who is fighting for a just cause, they will be more forgiving in their assessment of the evidence in favor of your client. If they believe and trust you, they will want to do what you ask them to do. The jurors will judge your case and client, to a large extent, on your integrity and credibility. They will judge your integrity and credibility by everything you say and do, in and out of the courtroom.

3.2 Effective Courtroom Behavior

3.2.1 Before You Get to Court

From the moment you park your car or leave your office to walk to the courthouse on the morning of trial until the moment the jury retires, you must assume that the jurors are listening to your every word and watching your every move. Look purposeful. Walk briskly and eagerly. Put on your game face. You never know who may be listening and watching. You want any jurors who observe you to see a lawyer heading confidently to the courtroom to take care of her client's serious business.

If you meet another lawyer, be courteous, but be careful not to appear too casual or lighthearted. Be aware that a juror may overhear anything you say. One of the authors, on his way to defend a case, got onto a crowded elevator with the lawyer representing the plaintiff. They exchanged greetings, then the plaintiff's lawyer actually said, "This little case shouldn't take too long. We ought to be out of here by three." Two future members of the jury were on that elevator. That lawyer's remark, more than anything said or done during the trial itself, may have been responsible for the jury's verdict in favor of the defendant. The unguarded remark destroyed the lawyer's credibility, and anything the plaintiff or her witnesses said in trial in support of her claim for $50,000 went unheeded. That lawyer's case was as good as over when he made that remark that belittled his case. After hearing such a remark, what credit could a juror possibly give to the lawyer's oration about how important the case was and the substantial amount of damages his client ought to get?

Remain equally aware of your conduct during recesses. When you speak to your client during recesses, whether in the courtroom, the hallway, or the restroom, remain conscious that others are probably observing you. Do not make the tragic mistake of assuming that you are offstage whenever the court is in recess. A trial lawyer walks out onto center stage when he leaves for the courthouse and remains there until jurors are led away to the deliberation room.

3.2.2 At Counsel Table

Jurors will be watching you even when you are seated at counsel table. As you sit there, try to appear alert and interested, pleasant but not flippant. You must try to project the image of calm assurance even when you are not speaking. When you rise, rise confidently. When you stand, stand tall. When the judge walks in and says, "Good morning," be the first to rise and say, "Good morning, Your Honor." When the judge asks if the parties are ready for trial, stand proudly and state with assurance, "The defense is ready, Your Honor." These will probably be the first words you have an opportunity to utter, and by saying them confidently, you telegraph an initial impression of calm, courteous control. The sooner you seize the high ground of the courtroom battlefield, the better. As one trial lawyer puts it:

> I try to act as if I were in my home and the parties, witnesses, judge, and jury are my guests. I'm always courteous, but I try to create the impression that I'm establishing the boundaries, that I'm the one who's making the rules.

In the heat of courtroom combat, you must always remember that you are a professional and act accordingly. Use your manners. Try every case as if your parents were sitting in the front row.

Always show proper respect for the court. Stand every time you address the court and always call the judge "Your Honor." The judge is neither a "sir" nor a "ma'am." (Outside the courtroom, you should address the judge as "Judge." Do this even if you and the judge are close friends, except when you are alone or in a social setting where everyone present is a close friend.)

As for opposing counsel, every lawyer is entitled to be treated with respect and courtesy. Return rudeness with civility and the jurors will reward you. The opposing lawyer is your professional adversary, not your enemy. The trial must not become a personal matter between you. When the trial is over, win or lose, shake hands with your opponent.

As a general rule address every witness as "Mr." or "Ms." First names are normally inappropriate in court. If a witness has a title such as "Doctor," "Reverend," or "Captain," use the title, as it demonstrates respect. In limited situations, such as when your client is a youngster, it may be appropriate to call a witness by first name, but do so only with caution and forethought (and make sure the judge does not mind).

3.2.3 While Making and Responding to Objections

An article of faith among trial lawyers is that making too many objections offends the jurors. We are taught from early childhood that it is rude to interrupt and each objection is necessarily an interruption. Nevertheless, there are times when you must object. When improper questions are asked and they are hurting your case, you must interpose an objection. Any argument concerning the admissibility of evidence is foreclosed if you do not make a timely and specific objection.[4]

When you must object, you should do it in a way that communicates knowledge, confidence, and authority. First, state your objection clearly and simply. Do not make any statement that focuses negative attention on yourself instead of the evidence. For example, time and time again you will hear lawyers say something like, "Your Honor, I just don't see the relevance of . . . ." You should simply rise calmly, say "Objection," and state the grounds. Act like you know what you are doing, and do not make self-deprecating comments. Never say "I don't understand . . . ," "I don't see . . . ," or "I'm confused." You are not seeking education: you are objecting. Say so.

When your opponent objects, respond in a calm, self-assured voice that everyone in the courtroom can hear. State simply why the item of evidence is admissible. Be sure to respond to the ground stated in the objection. Too often, you will hear eloquent explanations of why a statement is not hearsay when the objection was based not on hearsay, but on relevance.

When one of your questions draws an objection, do not withdraw the question before the judge has an opportunity to rule. Your opponent may be wrong. Even if your opponent's objection is correct, the court may overrule it. The law of evidence vests enormous discretion in the trial judge and many evidentiary questions are not clear-cut. When you withdraw your question, you admit to the jury that your opponent was correct and that you were wrong. When an objection is sustained, move on to another question as if nothing had happened. If the judge overrules the objection, repeat the question that drew the objection.

Do not react with visible emotion to judicial rulings during the trial, particularly when things go against you. For example, after the court overrules one of your objections, do not slump in your chair or shake your head in disbelief, no matter how bad the ruling was. The jurors probably think the judge is always right, so do not place yourself in a position antagonistic to the court. Remember that the jurors may not know the difference between "sustained" and "overruled." Or, they may not have been tracking which side made the objection. So, if you do not frown or sigh or do anything else to indicate your disappointment with the ruling, jurors may

---

4. Fed. R. Evid. 103(b).

think you won the point. If you never look as if you are losing, jurors will probably believe you are winning.

Remember also that jurors appreciate good sportsmanship. Shaking your head after an adverse ruling is the courtroom equivalent of throwing down your bat after a strikeout in baseball. Everybody knows that an umpire in baseball can make a bad call once in a while. The best baseball players accept it and move on. The best lawyers do the same.

3.2.4 *While Addressing the Jury—The Importance of Eye Contact*

You must assume that the jurors' attention is focused on you every minute. During the trial, you become an important person to the jurors. You can, in turn, express your respect for the jurors by the way you address them. During voir dire, opening statement, and closing argument, look at the jurors. Establish eye contact with each juror. The eyes really are the windows to the soul. When you gaze through a person's eyes into the depth of his being, you tell him he is the most important person in your universe at that moment.

Give each juror (or potential juror during voir dire) your undivided attention for at least a moment. Do not allow your attention to be distracted by your notes. Do not read while you talk to jurors.

You have a great opportunity to express respect and enhance the appearance of control simply by looking the jurors in the eye and speaking from the heart. You may need a checklist of points you must cover. But that is all the paper you need, and you should not look at it while you speak.

3.2.5 *While Examining Witnesses*

Eye contact is just as important when you are examining witnesses as when you are addressing the jury. Good eye contact during witness examinations has several beneficial effects. First, it has a reassuring effect on your witnesses. Second, it forces you to listen to the witnesses' answers. You can miss some important information while you are checking your next question. Third, it makes you appear interested in what your witnesses are saying. Jurors will look at you from time to time as a witness answers. If you are not looking at a witness and listening attentively to her answer, the jurors may assume, at least subconsciously, that the testimony is not very important. But if they see you standing attentively, they will return their attention to the place it belongs: on your witness. People naturally follow another person's gaze. If you stand on the street and start looking up at the sky, other people will look up at the sky. If you look at the wall, other people will check the wall to see what is so interesting about it. In trial, your focus on the witness will put the jury's focus where you want it to be.

You will probably need to have some notes with you when you conduct direct examinations. You should refer to them as seldom as possible and never while a witness is answering a question. Just carry on a friendly conversation with each witness. Act interested in what the witness has to say. You should appear to be hearing each witness's testimony for the first time.

Eye contact is equally crucial during cross-examination. It is a powerful instrument to control witnesses. Stare them down. When a witness averts his gaze during your cross-examination, you are usually damaging his credibility.

3.3   Managing Your Body

Each of us is trapped inside a body with upper appendages that long to flap, feet that long to pace, a mind that becomes uncomfortable with silence, and a voice that tries desperately to whisper when we speak in a large room. These unruly body parts will, if untamed, distract mightily from an otherwise impressive courtroom performance. Part of becoming a polished trial lawyer involves becoming aware of and learning to control the way you move and speak in the courtroom. The goal is to achieve a physical presentation that puts the jurors at ease and allows them to focus on your message.

From studies of public speaking, we know that audiences naturally feel empathy for the person speaking to them. If a speaker is nervous or upset, the audience will sense it and feel uncomfortable too. The audience in a trial—the jury—wants you to put them at ease. Your confidence reassures them. You put them at ease by using a presentation style that appears self-assured and controlled, but relaxed and conversational.

Of course, during a trial you are not likely to feel perfectly confident or relaxed, so you must learn and practice ways to make yourself appear calm and in control. Effective public speaking begins with your state of mind. The quest for perfection and desire for approval may have provided the extra motivation and incentive that inspired you to fully prepare for trial. Without lowering your standards, once in the courtroom, 100 percent of your focus must be on giving jurors the information they need to decide the case. While always mindful to behave in a way that portrays our trustworthiness and professionalism, at no time should we be thinking about how successfully we are performing. Inside the courtroom, evaluating our performance will cause us to adhere to scripted presentations rather than respond to the inevitable twists and turn of the trial. And when we invariably pause or stumble, we will make matters worse by mentally berating ourselves for falling shy of perfection. The antidote is to place our entire focus on the message, and none on how well the messenger is doing.

The second ingredient of effective public speaking is breathing. Every lawyer is, and should be, nervous before standing to speak at trial. That nervousness is not a character defect, but rather is the adrenaline produced by the body to prepare you for trial. In fact, if you are not nervous, you do not care enough about your client and should not be trying the case. You can control the anxiety produced by the adrenaline by taking slow, deep, calming breaths.

The final step in the process is to identify the specific things that you do that are distracting or that communicate that you are ill at ease. As you prepare for trial, have a friend or relative videotape part of your trial presentation. Watch the videotape with someone you trust. Notice your posture, your gestures, speed of your delivery. Do you have distracting habits? Try to see yourself as others see you. You may be one of those lucky people who have a perfectly natural, spontaneous style that immediately communicates self-assurance. You may have been a high school forensics champion or a television newscaster in a previous career. If, like most of us, you were not, you may consider the following suggestions to cure some of the most prevalent presentation problems.

3.3.1 *Hands*

What do you do with your arms and hands? They are there, so learn to manage them. Of course, it is anatomically possible simply to let them hang limply at your sides. They will not fall off, but most of us feel quite foolish and uncomfortable if our arms are unused for long.

Let us first examine several things you should not do.

Do not shove both hands in your pockets. That posture looks entirely too casual for the courtroom. The conventional wisdom teaches us never to place a hand in a pocket.

Do not clasp your hands in front of your groin in the posture sometimes known as "the fig leaf." That posture is defensive and conveys fear and apprehension. If you must clasp your hands together, do it behind your back in a "parade rest" position.

Do not cross your arms over your chest. That is a covering-up gesture and your body language should convey openness.

Do not put your hands on your hips. That is a posture of aggression, and an aggressive stance is really another manifestation of fear. On the other hand, you can and should practice some power posing while you are alone (at home, in the restroom stall, or in your office). Even for one minute, power posing—that is, standing in open, expansive postures—can help make you become more powerful in the real world.[5] Of course, you won't use the power pose in the courtroom, but your manner will convey a sense of confidence.

---

5. Carney, Dana R., Amy J. C. Cuddy, & Andy J. Yap. "Power posing brief nonverbal displays affect neuroendocrine levels and risk tolerance," *Psychological Science* 21.10 (2010): 1363–1368.

The basic courtroom position of each arm should be either hanging at your side or held with the elbow bent at no more than a right angle. From that position it is easy to gesture comfortably and naturally. One hand may rest on a lectern. Practice standing and talking without moving your hands. When you become comfortable doing so, you can then begin to gesture purposefully.

3.3.2 Legs and Feet

Legs and feet present as daunting a problem as hands. They want to move constantly. The goal is to walk around the courtroom only when you have a purpose for doing so.

Do not pace. First, practice standing rooted in one spot as if you were a tree. After you have mastered this, you can start to move when you have a reason to move. Movement adds interest to your presentation and can be used to focus attention on important points. You may stand near one end of the jury box while arguing one point and move to the other end when you begin arguing the next point. But take steps only when you have a purpose for doing so.

Stand with your weight distributed evenly on both feet and with more of your weight on the balls of your feet than the heels. Even if you are not pacing around the courtroom, a trial can be an exhausting physical ordeal. This position, in the long run, is the least tiring way to stand. Besides, it looks good. It looks solid. It looks confident.

Do not lock your knees. It restricts circulation. If you are standing with your weight distributed evenly on both feet, it will prevent you from crossing your legs or cocking your hip to one side.

3.3.3 Voice

Most of us are terribly uncomfortable with silence. When we are alone we feel compelled to fill the air with sounds from a radio, stereo, iPod, or television set. When we are with others, we find it almost impossible to sit quietly without talking. When there is a pause in conversation, our natural reaction is to search for something to say. We feel compelled to fill every unfilled pause. When examining witnesses, because of our discomfort, most of us unconsciously tend to insert an "um," "and," or "and, uh," or repeat the witness' previous answer before asking the next question. Try to eliminate these distracting habits from your witness examination technique.

Do not fear silence. Once we overcome our discomfort with silence, we can utilize silence as a valuable tool to add impact to our courtroom presentations. A pregnant pause before a question can add impact to the question when it finally comes. A dramatic pause before making a point during closing argument can create anticipation. Do not be afraid of silence. Instead, use it to your advantage.

Do not speak too softly. In tense situations, our voices often tend to become tiny. A trial is certainly a tense situation, and if you are not careful, your voice will turn inward and you will begin to mutter. Anything you or your witnesses say that is not heard is wasted. You must be sure everyone in the courtroom hears your every word. Courtrooms are typically large spaces with poor acoustics, so speak at a volume that seems very loud to you. You cannot maintain the necessary volume by shouting because it will wear out your vocal cords. You must project your voice by maintaining good posture and breathing deeply from your diaphragm. Open your throat and aim your voice toward the witness or the most distant juror.

3.3.4 Attire

It should go without saying, but unfortunately does need to be said, that you should dress professionally. You are there solely as an advocate for someone else and, as such, it is your professional responsibility to look the part of a professional lawyer. You should take care, however, to wear clothes that are comfortable so that you do not have to tug on them or readjust them each time you stand up. Wear comfortable shoes so that your walk is natural.

Do not wear anything that will distract jurors from your message. One of the authors once saw a lawyer go into court wearing what appeared to be a perfectly acceptable jacket and tie. The lawyer kept his jacket buttoned most of the day, which did not seem strange. As the afternoon wore on, however, and the courtroom grew somewhat hot, he unbuttoned his jacket, revealing a naked lady sitting in a martini glass painted on his tie. The jurors laughed. The judge was not amused.

3.3.5 Let the Jury Know You

Even if you have mastered your voice and your gestures and you have dressed for success, you may still be wondering how you can project an aura of calm assurance when you are terrified and shaking in your boots. One way is to remind yourself that you are human and admit it publicly. You will make mistakes. Everybody does. If you are scared or go blank or slip up, admit it. You will probably be surprised how admitting your imperfection will relax you. Moreover, the jurors are human beings, with all the frailties and imperfections that go with that condition. Your frank confession of your fear and mistakes will cause them to identify with you and like you.

3.4 The Gentle Art of Persuasion

As you consider what you can do to make the jury trust you and make your presentation more persuasive, bear in mind the following guidelines for effective courtroom behavior.

No one likes a know-it-all. Few things drive us away quicker than a person who is always telling us what he knows and who refuses to acknowledge that another point of view may be worthy of consideration. Such behavior in the courtroom is not only annoying, but it also subtly contradicts the court's instruction to jurors to be fair and impartial to all parties.

Do not be overly aggressive when arguing your case. Suggestions are more pleasantly received than commands. For example, the lawyer for a plaintiff in a personal injury suit, when arguing pain and suffering as an element of damages, will be well advised, after reviewing the evidence, to respectfully suggest that, "An appropriate amount of compensation for the pain and suffering Mr. Anderson has endured as a result of the defendant's negligence would be *x*-dollars."[6]

But don't be wishy-washy. Do not explain why you think your side is stronger. Eliminate qualifying phrases such as "I think . . . ," "We believe . . . ," and "It is our position that . . ." from your courtroom vocabulary. They convey a lack of confidence in your position.

On the other hand, do be wary of using too many intensifying adjectives. They often subtly communicate the impression that you lack confidence in your position and are therefore "puffing." It is usually less persuasive to say, "The car was really, really old," than to say simply, "The car was old." Even more persuasive would be to say, "The car was a 1997 Pontiac with rust on the bottom of the doors, one broken window, and no muffler." Use specific details rather than intensifying adjectives to make your points more persuasively. Make your points simply, confidently, and forcefully.

---

*While one should always study the method of a great artist,
one should never imitate his manner. The manner of an artist
is essentially individual, the method of an artist is absolutely universal.
The first is personality, which no one should copy;
the second is perfection, which all should aim at.*

—*Oscar Wilde*

Be honest. If an issue has two sides, admit that it does and explain why your side is the stronger one. Jurors will appreciate an honest lawyer.

Be fair. Do not ever try to pull cheap tricks. They are rude, improper, and will offend the jury. Jurors try to be fair and they appreciate fairness on the part of lawyers. Jurors will detect exaggeration or misstatements of the evidence. If you are not fair in your assessment of the evidence, the jurors will not trust you.

---

6. Some jurisdictions prohibit the lawyer from suggesting a dollar figure for intangible damages.

Be yourself. Let your own personality shine through. Though you should always incorporate other lawyers' techniques into your repertoire, never try to imitate another lawyer's style.

Be sincere. Find something about your case that you can believe in and communicate your belief in that something to jurors from your heart. Jurors, like all people, are moved to pull for someone who sincerely puts his heart into a task. If you are not willing and able to leave a little bit of your heart in the courtroom on behalf of a client, you should not represent that client.

CHAPTER FOUR

JURY SELECTION

The young lawyer was tired and frustrated. She had been reading about voir dire techniques all afternoon and was feeling overwhelmed. She called on an old friend who was an experienced trial lawyer. "Boil it down for me. What am I trying to accomplish here?" she asked.

"Voir dire may be the most important part of the trial," her old friend responded. "During voir dire, you establish your personal credibility with the jury. You inform the jury of the key elements of your theory of the case. You also find out who the jurors are and you uncover and deal with their prejudgments about the case."

"Well, I guess it makes sense to make a good first impression," the young lawyer mused, "but does it really matter which jurors are stricken? Whoever the jurors are, they will all have the same evidence in front of them."

Her friend shook his head. "The same evidence will be understood differently by different people," he explained. "Voir dire gives you a chance to assure yourself of a jury of people who can be persuaded by what you have to say. It is important because, as Oliver Wendell Holmes said, 'What lies behind us and what lies before us are tiny matters compared to what lies within us.'"

4.1   Jury Selection Basics

The jury selection process is governed by statute and varies among the jurisdictions. Indeed, the specifics of the process may vary from courtroom to courtroom within one jurisdiction. Nevertheless, all systems have many characteristics in common. The following discussion fairly summarizes the practice in a typical American court.

The first step is the assembly of a venire panel of prospective jurors. The United States Constitution requires that the procedure followed in selecting venire panels be such that no ethnic, racial, religious, or gender group be excluded.[1] The process of assembling the venire is generally governed by statute and carried out by court staff.

---

1. U.S. Const. amends. VI & XIV.

The process should be designed to ensure that each venire panel represents a cross-section of the community.[2] Commonly, names are drawn from voter registration lists, automobile registration lists, or even telephone directories. Jurors typically receive a summons that tells them what day or days to appear at the courthouse. Jury service is both a right and duty of citizenship, and jurors must set aside their own business and personal lives to attend the trial.

Although jury service is a right and most people are eligible to serve,[3] not everyone is qualified or suitable to serve on the jury of a particular case. Jurors are qualified to serve only if they can listen to the evidence fairly and impartially and follow the judge's instructions on the application of the law. The process used for discovering if there is any reason why a member of the venire should not serve on the jury is a question-and-answer session called voir dire. During this session, the potential jurors are given some information about the case and asked questions by the lawyers or the court. Based on what the potential jurors say in response to those questions, the lawyers will "select"—or more accurately "deselect"—the jury by exercising "challenges" to eliminate some of them.

Challenge for Cause. A challenge for cause is designed to remove an unqualified juror whose decision would likely be affected by prior knowledge of the facts, a relationship with one of the parties, or some other circumstance creating a danger of partiality. Each party may exercise an unlimited number of challenges for cause. Challenges for cause may be granted or denied in the judge's discretion.

Peremptory Challenge. Lawyers may also use a limited number of peremptory challenges to eliminate jurors who are technically qualified to serve, but who are—in the lawyer's opinion—not suitable or desirable as jurors in the case.

The number of peremptory challenges available to each party is governed by statute or rules of procedure. Typically, each party to a civil or misdemeanor case is allowed three peremptory challenges.[4] In some states, where there are multiple

---

2. *See* Taylor v. Louisiana, 419 U.S. 522 (1975). If there has been some irregularity in the process of assembling the venire, you may have grounds to challenge the array. A challenge to the array should be made before any voir dire has taken place.

3. *See, e.g.,* 28 U.S.C. § 1866(c): ". . . no person or class of persons shall be disqualified, excluded, excused, or exempt from service as jurors: Provided, That any person summoned for jury service may be (1) excused by the court, or by the clerk under supervision of the court if the court's jury selection plan so authorizes, upon a showing of undue hardship or extreme inconvenience . . . or (2) excluded by the court on the ground that such person may be unable to render impartial jury service or that his service as a juror would be likely to disrupt the proceedings, or (3) excluded upon peremptory challenge as provided by law, or (4) excluded pursuant to the procedure specified by law upon a challenge by any party for good cause shown, or (5) excluded upon determination by the court that his service as a juror would be likely to threaten the secrecy of the proceedings, or otherwise adversely affect the integrity of jury deliberations."

4. *See* 28 U.S.C. § 1870.

　　　　　　　　　　　　　　　　　　　　　National Institute for Trial Advocacy

plaintiffs or defendants, the peremptory challenges must be exercised jointly.[5] Federal judges have power to grant additional peremptory challenges.[6] More peremptory challenges are typically allowed in felony and capital cases, the defendant often being granted more than the prosecution.[7] Unlike challenges for cause, peremptory challenges may not be denied by the court. Traditionally, lawyers could exercise peremptory challenges for any reason or no reason at all and were not forced to justify the basis for their challenges. However, the traditional rule is limited by the Fourteenth Amendment's Equal Protection Clause and a party may not base its peremptory challenges solely on race or gender.[8]

In a typical courthouse on a typical trial day, people summoned to jury duty arrive at the courthouse at 8:30 a.m. and report to a jury assembly room, where they are shown an antiquated video about jury service, served bad coffee, and told to wait. When a judge sends word that a case is ready for trial, a court official leads a group of potential jurors (a venire panel) up to the courtroom where the trial will take place. Depending on the kind of voir dire examination the court uses in the particular case, members of the venire may be then questioned individually, in small groups (usually four), or as a larger panel of eighteen or more. In jurisdictions that use juries composed of fewer than the traditional twelve members, the number of venire persons selected for questioning is smaller.

The usual manner of conducting voir dire is to examine the prospective jurors as a group. However, if a venire person's revelations about prior knowledge of the case are likely to poison the minds of the entire panel if they hear them, individual voir dire may be necessary. The decision whether to grant a request for sequestered voir dire is left to the discretion of the trial judge.[9] In death penalty cases, jurors often are questioned individually.

The American Bar Association has attempted to offer some guidance when the problem of jury panel contamination arises. Its Project on Standards for Criminal

---

5. *See, e.g.*, Ark. Code Ann. § 16-33-203(a); Utley v. Heckinger, 362 S.W.2d 13 (Ark. 1962) (holding that each side has three peremptory challenges regardless of the number of parties). Where the parties' interests diverge, the court may allow each to have three peremptory challenges. *See, e.g.*, O'Loughlin v. Mercy Hosp. Fairfield, 152 Ohio App. 1 (2015); Nichols v. Hazelip, 374 S.W.3d 333 (2012).

6. *See* In re Cir Crash Disaster, 86 F.3d 498 (8th Cir. 1996) (holding that where there is more than one plaintiff or defendant, 28 U.S.C. § 1870 gives the trial judge discretion to allocate the number of peremptory challenges among the parties).

7. In federal criminal cases punishable by death, each side gets twenty peremptory challenges; in other felony cases, the government gets six peremptory challenges and the defendant(s) jointly get ten; in misdemeanor cases, each side gets three peremptory challenges. Fed. R. Crim. P. 24(b).

8. Batson v. Kentucky, 476 U.S. 79 (1986) (holding that a prosecutor may not exercise peremptory challenges solely on the basis of race); Georgia v. McCollum, 505 U.S. 42 (1992) (holding that defendant in a criminal case may not use race as a basis for a peremptory challenge); J.E.B. v. Alabama ex rel. T.B., 511 U.S. 127 (1994) (litigants may not use gender as a basis for a peremptory challenge). Edmonson v. Leesville Concrete Co., 500 U.S. 614 (1991) (holding that Batson rule also applies in civil cases).

9. *See, e.g.*, Com. v. Reavis, 992 N.E.2d 304 (Mass. 2013); Burnett v. State, 697 S.W.2d 95 (Ark. 1985).

Justice has promulgated Standards Relating to Fair Trial and Free Press. The Standards do not have the force of law, but may offer guidance to judges when exercising their discretion whether to grant requests for individual, sequestered voir dire. Standard 3.4(a) states:

> Whenever there is believed to be a significant possibility that individual talesmen will be ineligible to serve because of exposure to potentially prejudicial material, the examination of each juror with respect to his exposure shall take place outside the presence of other chosen and prospective jurors.

In most cases, there is no request for sequestered voir dire. The most common style of voir dire is known as "drawn and struck jury selection." Where this method is used, a court official randomly draws from the venire a number of prospective jurors sufficient to fill the jury, together with a handful of alternate jurors, after each party exercises all of its peremptory challenges. If the jury is to be composed of twelve persons, eighteen names are typically drawn. The prospective jurors' names are called out in the order drawn and they line up at the bar in that order. Then, all prospective jurors are examined as a group. Challenges for cause are made during voir dire as soon as prejudicial information is uncovered. When a prospective juror is stricken for cause, another member of the venire replaces the one stricken. Voir dire examination ends when a sufficient number of qualified jurors have been identified.

At the conclusion of voir dire examination, each party is allowed to exercise peremptory challenges. Peremptory challenges are usually exercised secretly, so that the jury does not know which party struck whom. The court declares a short recess and the court reporter hands each lawyer a list containing the eighteen qualified juror names in the order they were drawn. The lawyers then huddle with their clients and decide which persons to strike. The parties typically take turns exercising their peremptory challenges by drawing a line through the name of one juror they want to strike and then handing the list of names to the lawyer for the other side. Then the other party draws a line through one name and gives the sheet back again. The paper is passed back and forth until all of the peremptory strikes have been exercised. When the panel returns from recess, a courtroom deputy calls the names of the twelve panel members and the desired number of alternate jurors on the list whose names were not stricken and those persons take seats in the jury box.[10] Each will remain in the same seat throughout the trial. The jury is then impaneled and sworn in to hear the case.

---

10. A statute defining the procedure for a drawn and struck jury is found at 22 UNIFORM RULES FOR THE NEW YORK STATE TRIAL COURTS 202.33(f).

4.2 Preparation before Trial

Before starting voir dire, you will need information about the process that is specific to your case. You will need to know the details of the issues that will be heard. You will also need to know your judge and your location. Getting ready may require research, conversations with colleagues, practice, and deep thought.

4.2.1 Get Courtroom-Specific Information

The first step in preparing for voir dire is to find out how the process will be handled in the court where your case will be heard. Read the local rules of court. During your pretrial conference, ask the judge specifically how she prefers to conduct voir dire. Then find a lawyer who has tried cases before the judge assigned to your case and ask as many questions as you can think of. For example, ask:

- Will I have pretrial access to information about the jurors?

- What information will be included?

- Will I be permitted to submit a pretrial juror questionnaire of my own design?

- How many jurors will be questioned at a time?

- Who will conduct the voir dire?

- Are there standard questions that the judge asks?

- How long will I be allowed to question each juror?

- If a juror raises a sensitive issue, will the judge allow follow-up questions to be conducted in private?

- Will the jurors have heard a "juror orientation" lecture? What will they be told?

- What kind of introduction to the case will the judge provide? If you do not know a lawyer with experience before the judge, visit the courtroom during the jury selection phase of another case. Find out everything you can about jury selection in that specific courtroom.

It is difficult to overstate the diversity of approaches to voir dire taken by various judges. In fact, some judges believe that lawyers should not be allowed to question the panel at all. In federal court, in both criminal and civil cases, the court may allow the attorneys to conduct voir dire or may conduct the voir dire itself.[11] If the court conducts voir dire, it must either allow the lawyers to ask supplementary questions

---

11. FED. R. CRIM. P. 24(a); FED. R. CIV. P. 47(a). Voir dire is a procedural matter governed by the Federal Rules of Civil Procedure in diversity cases. *See* Smith v. Vicorp, Inc., 107 F.3d 816 (10th Cir. 1997).

or submit supplementary questions in writing for the judge to ask.[12] Many federal judges conduct all questioning of the jury panel themselves and do not allow the lawyers to address the jury panel. In most state courts, lawyers have the right to conduct some voir dire, although the scope is left almost entirely to the discretion of the court.[13]

> *If you don't know where you are going,*
> *you will wind up somewhere else.*
>
> —Yogi Berra

Even where extensive attorney voir dire questioning is allowed, the judge normally will give the jurors an introduction to the case and conduct some preliminary questioning so that the lawyers can devote their time to ferreting out less obvious sources of prejudice. The court should read the indictment or information in a criminal case or give a short synopsis of the issues raised by the pleadings in a civil case, determine whether any panel member has knowledge of the facts of the case being tried, and introduce the lawyers and parties in order to learn whether any juror knows any of them. Some judges may read the jury a summary of your contentions and may allow you to prepare that summary. In a few courts, judges allow the attorneys to present a mini-opening statement before voir dire questioning begins. Knowledge of the specific practices of the judge who will hear your case will help you prepare ahead of time to take advantage of these early opportunities to persuade the jury.

4.2.2 Decide What Kind of People You Most Want and Do Not Want as Jurors

From the trial lawyer's point of view, voir dire is really a process of juror elimination, not juror selection. You cannot control who is chosen, but by utilizing challenges for cause and peremptory challenges you can exert limited control over who is eliminated. Therefore, you must decide what kind of people will be most unfavorably disposed toward your client or your factual theory of the case. You must also decide what characteristics people who are favorably disposed toward

---

12. *Id.* When the court is conducting voir dire, it does not have to ask questions in the exact form suggested by counsel. Darbin v. Nourse, 664 F.2d 1109 (9th Cir. 1981). If the trial court refuses a particular question counsel deems essential and the refusal could be reversible error, counsel must preserve the issue for appeal by advising the trial court of the proposed question and the reason why it is essential before the trial court has completed voir dire. Failure to raise it at that time does not give the trial judge a fair chance to avoid error. King v. Jones, 824 F.2d 324 (4th Cir. 1987).
13. The extent of voir dire rests within the trial court's discretion, and absent a showing of abuse, the trial court's decision on the extent of voir dire will be upheld. *See, e.g.*, Nat'l Bank of Commerce v. Beavers, 802 S.W.2d 132 (Ark. 1990).

your client or story are likely to possess so that you can avoid challenging them and attempt to prevent their being stricken for cause.

Creating profiles of favorable and unfavorable jurors is one of the most difficult and intuitive tasks of a trial lawyer. There is no substitute for experience and knowledge of human nature gained in the school of life. Make a list of factors likely to cause jurors to be prejudiced against your client. Those factors will be different in each case. Some lawyers unwisely rely blindly on stereotypes based on race, sex, age, national origin, or other group identification. This blind reliance on broad stereotypes is not only unconstitutional; it can lead to incorrect assumptions about individuals. For example, any lawyer who assumes that a potential juror who is a woman may automatically sympathize with a woman who made a sexual assault complaint may make a tragic mistake. You must not let your own prejudices, whatever they may be, cloud your objective judgment. Every human being is a complex crazy quilt of unconscious predilections and prejudices. You must strive to discover the essence of each individual on the jury panel.

Psychologists can provide "juror profiles" identifying characteristics that are likely to cause jurors to favor one party or the other. In fact, a satellite industry of "jury consultants" has emerged. There is no certifying or licensing mechanism for these consultants, and they range from highly qualified professionals to charlatans.

Whatever criteria you select for your "good juror" and "bad juror" profiles and whether you engage the services of a consultant, the overriding principle, verified both by experience and behavioral science, is that people tend to identify with others who are most like themselves. Therefore, you should usually try to strike the prospective jurors who are most like the opposing party.

4.2.3 Learn as Much as You Can About the Members of the Jury Panel

Trial lawyers in some jurisdictions are afforded the luxury of obtaining a jury information sheet before the day of trial. These jury information sheets contain basic information concerning each member of the panel, such as occupation, age, marital status, employment, and jury experience. They are valuable tools. If jury information sheets are available in the jurisdiction where your trial is set, you should get one and study it. In other jurisdictions, you may be able to look at jury information cards in the clerk's office on the morning of trial.

Some court reporters mail trial summaries to subscribing lawyers in which they report jury verdicts, which members of the venire were struck by each lawyer, who was the foreperson, and, in jurisdictions where a less-than-unanimous verdict is allowed in civil cases, which jurors signed a less-than-unanimous verdict. These summaries offer valuable insights, both into jurors' track records and into other lawyers' evaluations of panel members. If a case is important enough to justify the expense and if you know in advance the identity of the venire members, you can have their backgrounds investigated.

When trying a case in an unfamiliar jurisdiction or venue, you should associate a local lawyer to aide in jury selection. A lawyer who practices in that community and who regularly tries cases in that courthouse can provide valuable assistance to you. Imagine, for example, that you are given a jury information sheet that includes each juror's name, address, and occupation. If you are unfamiliar with the community, the information "Albert Tuttle, 47 West Palm Drive, unemployed" may not mean very much to you. On the other hand, a local lawyer could look at that same information and tell you:

> The Tuttle family is a prominent and well-liked family in this area; the address on West Palm is one of the most exclusive neighborhoods in town; and Albert Tuttle is likely "unemployed" only because he spends his time managing his own money and engaging in philanthropy.

Working with a local lawyer can also help you avoid being seen as an outsider. In fact, where you are cast in the role of the "city slicker" lawyer and perceive the danger of being the victim of "home cooking" by a local jury and local lawyer, you should consider asking local counsel to conduct the voir dire examination. Whether you are perceived as a city slicker or a simple country lawyer depends on the population of the county where the case is tried and has nothing to do with your intelligence or ability. In Evening Shade, Arkansas, lawyers from Little Rock are city slickers. In Little Rock, lawyers from Memphis, Dallas, or St. Louis are city slickers. Of course, a lawyer from New York or Los Angeles is a city slicker everywhere. But this is not to suggest that you only need local counsel if you going from a city to a smaller town. Even in the biggest cities, a local lawyer will have special, irreplaceable information about neighborhoods, schools, large employers, past political battles, and what matters have been in the local paper lately.

Using whatever juror information is available to you before trial, you should decide tentatively who to strike before you go to the courthouse to try the case. Make a preliminary list of peremptory challenges you would make if there were no voir dire examination. After voir dire, you may change your choices. However, you will find that in many instances your pretrial list will have been correct.

4.3   Techniques for Conducting Voir Dire

Voir dire, when the lawyers are allowed to conduct it, can be the most important part of the trial. It affords lawyers the opportunity to uncover prejudice, challenge unfit jurors for cause, and exercise peremptory challenges to strike those whom they suspect may be unfavorably disposed toward their side of the case. Those objectives are, of course, extremely important and are, in fact, the legal justification for conducting voir dire.[14] To accomplish these objectives, you need to begin to get to know

---

14. Nutt v. State, 848 S.W.2d 427 (Ark. 1993) (voir dire is allowed to determine whether there is any basis for challenge for cause and to gain knowledge for the informed exercise of peremptory challenges).

the people on the jury as individuals. Your voir dire will be designed to get the jurors talking about themselves. You can learn a great deal about the jurors in a fairly short time by listening carefully and observing what they say, what they do not say, the words they use, their gestures and body language.

While you are getting to know the jurors, however, they are also getting to know you and your case. Making a favorable first impression on the jurors (and avoiding offending and alienating them) is as important as uncovering unsuitable jurors. It is quite likely that you will not be able to strike every juror you do not like. After all, in civil cases, challenges for cause are not readily granted. Further, the venire member who is really out to get your client may deny prejudice in order to stay on the jury. With only three peremptory challenges, you are rarely going to get an ideal jury. Therefore, it is imperative that you attempt to make the jurors trust you and like you. You must build rapport with the jurors and establish your personal credibility. Be unfailingly courteous to each member of the jury panel, even though a member exhibits sarcasm or rudeness toward you.

No two lawyers agree on the best way to conduct voir dire. Conducting an effective voir dire requires the observational and deductive skills of a detective, the social and conversational knack of a talk show host, the sensitivity of a psychotherapist, and the communication ability of an accomplished teacher. Voir dire is an art. Every experienced trial lawyer develops a personal style and approach. Nevertheless, there are some techniques that are commonly used and that will be helpful to you as you develop your own voir dire style.

4.3.1 Basic Jury Questioning Techniques

Use jurors' names. Any politician will tell you that the ability to remember names is one of the most valuable personal communication skills one can develop. The sweetest sound in the world to most of us is the sound of our own name. Therefore, you should impress and flatter the jurors by calling them by name. As the prospective jurors names are being selected from the venire, you should make a list of the panel members' names in the order drawn. Unless you have a photographic memory, you will need this list to keep their names and faces straight. The prospective jurors line up in the order called and it is a simple matter to refer to your list and identify by name any juror you wish to question. Voir dire is the only time during a trial when lawyers are allowed to call jurors by name. Seize the opportunity.

Ask broad, open-ended, non-leading questions to start a conversation with the jurors. Ask the panel general, non-leading questions that call for responses. Invite the panel to express their feelings on key issues. When a panel member responds, act interested and draw out the prospective juror's thoughts. Try to get the jurors talking and expressing themselves freely. Borrowing a technique from our psychotherapist friends, we should ask "How do you feel about that?" questions.

Use this opportunity to start a conversation with the jurors. Voir dire is the only time during a trial when you are allowed to find out what the jurors are thinking. You may address them in opening statement and closing argument, but only on voir dire are you given the opportunity to invite them to converse with you. Whenever you engage in pleasant conversation with another person, you have usually made a friend. Therefore, you should encourage the prospective jurors to speak up during voir dire. Listen respectfully to what they say and try to make them feel comfortable conversing with you. Resist the temptation to take the easy route by allowing your voir dire to become nothing more than a speech, punctuated by periodic leading questions to which no informational answer is invited.

Getting to know you / Getting to know all about you.
Getting to like you / Getting to hope you like me.

—Oscar Hammerstein

Never allow yourself to become adversarial, and try never to embarrass a prospective juror. Avoid asking any panel member whether she is prejudiced. Use some other word or phrase in your question. For instance, if you represent an injured plaintiff and a venire-man reveals that he is claims manager of an insurance company, you might phrase your question, "Mr. Eisenberg, do you think your position as claims manager of State Industrial Liability Insurance Company might cause you to lean a little bit in favor of the defendant in this suit?" rather than, "Mr. Eisenberg, would your position cause you to be prejudiced against the plaintiff today?" Prejudice is a hard word to swallow. To admit prejudice is difficult; to deny it is easy.

Use general and follow-up questions. Your basic technique in group voir dire should be to ask the group general questions calling for a show of hands, then to ask follow-up questions of those who respond to the general question. When you ask the general question, tell the panel specifically what behavior you want in response: If you want the panel members to raise their hands, ask them to do so. They will appreciate your guidance and, by responding to your request, will begin to become accustomed to doing as you ask. For example, if you need to know if any persons on the venire are affiliated with liability insurance companies, you may ask, "Do any of you own stock in a liability insurance company? If so, please raise your hand."

Some trial lawyers consider early subliminal conditioning of the jury to do as they ask so important that they ask questions calling for a show of hands by the entire panel. For example,

> The court is going to instruct you that you are to presume that my client, Mr. Fenton, is an innocent man until and unless the state proves beyond a reasonable doubt that he is guilty. Will you do that? Everyone who will do that, please raise your hand?

People are generally hesitant to raise their hands in a way that singles them out for attention. The jurors will be more comfortable raising their hands in response to the difficult questions if the first few questions are easy ones that require everyone to raise their hands. For example, you might start with:

> It will be important for the jury to be able to hear and see all of the evidence that is presented in this trial. Raise your hand if you can hear me clearly.

When you ask a general question that elicits a response from only a few jurors, you should usually follow up, asking those who raised their hands more specific questions on the subject. Do not ignore anyone. A juror who has raised her hand but then is asked nothing while others are asked follow-up questions will probably resent the snub.

A danger in the general question and follow-up technique is that the general question may be so broad that all or most of the panel members raise their hands. When this happens, you may be forced into asking further questions of each venire member who responded. This process could be long and if the judge has limited your time, as many do, you may have time for nothing else. In this situation, consider singling out one panel member for a follow-up question and then asking if everyone else who raised a hand agrees.

For example, the general question concerning prior jury experience is an effective entrance to a discussion of the burden of proof. Assume that you represent the plaintiff in a civil suit. When Mr. Allen raises his hand in response to your question about prior jury experience, your individual questioning could take the following form:

Q: Mr. Allen, did you serve on a criminal or civil case?

A: Civil.

Q: Do you remember that the judge instructed you that the plaintiff had to prove he was entitled to recover by a preponderance of the evidence?

A: Yes, Ma'am.

Q: Do you remember what a preponderance of evidence is?

A: Yes. It's just proof that something happened a certain way more likely than not.

Q: That's right. More likely than not, because it was a civil case like this one. Does anyone know what burden of proof the prosecution has in a criminal case?

Someone will volunteer the answer and you can proceed to emphasize the lower burden of proof in your civil case.

Prior jury service can sometimes yield valuable information about a panel member's general attitude toward the justice system and about his potential to be a leader in the jury room. If asked, "Do you feel that the jury reached a good result in that case?" he may say, "Yeah, but it took me a while to get some of the others to come around to my point of view."

Some lawyers ask questions of individual prospective jurors without a preceding question to the group asking for volunteers. Rather than ask, "Can anyone explain what the term 'preponderance of the evidence' means?" they may ask, "Ms. Adams, can you tell us what preponderance of the evidence means?" We never use this technique unless we have some excuse to single out the individual for questioning. We feel that if either of us were a juror, we would be offended that the lawyer had placed a spotlight on us as if one of us were a student being questioned by a teacher. Some judges prohibit individual questioning of panel members on voir dire except as follow-up to general questions. Even where unrestricted individual questioning is allowed, we recommend that you do it only when you can state some basis for questioning that individual.

If you have advance knowledge about panel members, you can usually question them individually without asking prefatory general questions. You can also use these questions to individuals to inform the panel about important aspects of the case. If this is handled courteously, you will appear to be well prepared and the panel members of whom you ask questions will be flattered to be considered so important. To avoid arousing their ire, you should disclose the source of your knowledge. For instance, you might say:

Q: You remember those jury information cards you filled out in the clerk's office? They are for the benefit of us lawyers, so we'll have a little bit of information about you before the trial. I've looked at the cards and I've got a few questions I need to ask some of you about information you put on your cards. Ms. Atkinson, I notice that you are a physical therapist. Do you work with physicians?

A: Yes, ma'am.

Q: This case is one against a physician for medical negligence. How do you feel about injured patients suing physicians for medical negligence?

Be non-judgmental. All of us recoil from judgmental people. We dislike talking with them and hesitate to express our views to them to avoid their criticism. Because you must encourage the prospective jurors to respond openly to your questions, be careful not to appear to be sitting in judgment of them—even though you are. Ask the panel members how they feel about issues, but do not be critical of a prospective juror's views when he expresses them. Show him respect. If the opinion he expresses is outlandish, other jurors will take issue with him if you give them the opportunity. For instance, assume you have said:

Q: The judge will instruct you that my client sits here an innocent man unless the prosecution proves to you beyond a reasonable doubt that he is guilty of every element of the offense he's charged with. Does everyone accept that? Does anyone on the panel, right now, think my client is probably guilty? [*One juror raises his hand.*]

A: Yeah, I think he probably wouldn't have been charged if he wasn't guilty.

Q: Does anyone else feel the way Mr. Alford does?

A: [*No one responds.*]

Q: I take it from your lack of response that no one else shares Mr. Alford's feelings. Why not? Anybody willing to tell us why you don't feel as he does?

Mr. Alford will probably be excused for cause. If not, you may be able to use a peremptory challenge to strike him. If you do not have enough peremptory challenges and are stuck with him, your courtesy may have neutralized his prejudice enough to avoid his hanging the jury. In any event, his view has been repudiated by the rest of the panel and he will be ignored if he expresses it during deliberations.

Shield favorable jurors from a challenge for cause. Although your questions seek to identify potentially harmful jurors, a panel member will often respond to one of your questions in a way that reveals bias in favor of your client's position or prejudice against the opponent. Obviously, you want this person on your jury and should do whatever you can to shield him from a challenge for cause. You should try to force your opponent to pay the price of using a peremptory challenge to get the person off the jury.

When the favorable information comes out, you must shift into a leading mode, asking questions designed to immunize the panel member from a challenge for cause. You must seek to obtain a commitment from the prospective juror that he will set aside his personal feelings and base his decision solely on the law and evidence. As an example, assume that you are representing a client accused of drug possession and you ask whether anyone feels that the drug laws should be harsher. Mr. Cranford responds that, on the contrary, he feels that the laws are ill-conceived and that drug possession should be decriminalized. You should then ask something like:

Mr. Cranford, if you are selected to serve in this case, will you set your personal feelings aside and apply the existing law, as the judge will instruct you, to the evidence presented and base your verdict solely on the law and evidence?"

If Mr. Cranford says no, you have lost a potentially favorable juror. However, if he says yes he is probably insulated from a challenge for cause.

Include indirect questions from which you can infer prejudice. Birds of a feather flock together. A person's attitudes and opinions are reflected in the activities with which he fills his leisure time and the people with whom he associates. Therefore, we can draw accurate inferences about a person's likes and dislikes if we know what he does with his spare time. For example, the names of organizations to which he belongs and magazines he reads tell us much about his outlook on certain issues. If those issues are pertinent to the lawsuit you are trying, identify potentially prejudiced jurors by asking questions about membership in organizations espousing certain points of view. You can also infer much about a person's predilections if you know what he reads. For instance, in a case arising out of a hunting accident, familiarity with guns could be an important juror characteristic. Questions like, "Are any of you members of the National Rifle Association?" or "How many of you are hunters?" and "How many of you read *Field & Stream* magazine?" can yield important information about individual jurors' interests.

4.3.2 Using Voir Dire to Teach Jurors about Your Case

In addition to learning all that you can about each juror, you should take advantage of the opportunity during voir dire to inform the jury of the key elements of your theory of the case. There are several things you can do to use voir dire to teach the jury about the case and to begin to persuade them that your cause is just.

Be sure the jury understands and accepts the premises of your cause of action or defense. You are not allowed to attempt to obtain a commitment from the jury to find in your client's favor. However, you may inform the panel of the essential elements of your cause of action or defense and make sure they understand them. You may discuss important issues. Most judges will allow you to seek a commitment that the jurors will follow the law and return a lawful verdict in your client's favor if the evidence justifies it.[15]

By the time the trial begins, you should know how the judge will instruct the jury on most major issues. Those anticipated instructions provide a rich source of topics to explore during jury selection. The panel members who remain on the jury will recall an issue you discussed in voir dire when it arises during the trial, and your credibility will be enhanced when the court's instruction to the jury echoes what you told them earlier. For example, if the damages in the case will depend heavily on whether the jury is willing to assign contributory fault to the plaintiff, alert them to the issue during voir dire. Discuss the concept of legal responsibility and

---

15. "[P]rospective jurors may not be questioned with respect to a hypothetical set of facts expected to be proved at trial and thus commit the jury to a decision in advance, but . . . they may be questioned . . . about their mental attitude toward certain types of evidence." Nutt v. State, 848 S.W.2d 427, 428 (Ark. 1993).

get the jury to agree that they will discount the plaintiff's damages by the amount that he contributed to his own injury. Be aware, however, that if there will be a jury instruction on an issue you discuss, you must be absolutely sure that whatever you say accurately anticipates the instruction. If the jury instructions do not echo whatever you say about the law during voir dire—if you say one thing and the judge says another—your client is doomed.

Try to get jurors to volunteer to explain key concepts and terms, rather than merely explaining them yourself and asking if the jurors understand. Jurors tend to ignore what lawyers tell them during voir dire, but will often remember and accept what other jurors say. You probably cannot educate the jurors, but the panel members can educate one another. Consequently, ask open-ended, non-leading questions to encourage juror participation.

Discuss key terms of art. Be sure the jury understands terms of art that are essential to your case, such as "constructive possession" or "the presumption of innocence." For example, assume that you represent the plaintiff in a medical negligence case against a well-liked local physician. You should begin to distinguish the concept of negligence from that of criminal liability with statements and questions such as:

> Q: This suit is one for medical negligence. It is not a criminal case and it is not a case saying that the defendant is a bad doctor. It is simply a suit saying that Ms. Dean's injuries were caused by the defendant's failing to exercise the ordinary care expected of a physician. Does everybody understand that?
>
> A: [*Eighteen nods.*]
>
> Q: Who knows what level of care is expected of a physician?

Someone will likely venture a guess, others may offer their insights. You should act as a moderator, letting them know when someone gets it right or contributing the information yourself if no one does.

Make contracts concerning key issues. Try to get the jury to agree with you on sensitive issues. Get a contract. Tell them honestly what you are required to prove and extract a promise that if you do prove those things, they will follow the law and return a verdict in your favor. During this stage of your voir dire examination, it is difficult to get jurors talking. Your questions should generally call for agreement or a physical response such as raising a hand if a juror does not agree. For instance, you may ask:

> Q: The offense of assault requires us to prove three elements: that the defendant made a threat to use force on Mr. Barger; that he had the apparent ability to carry out that threat; and that the threat caused Mr. Barger to be afraid he was about to suffer bodily harm. If we do prove those three elements beyond a reasonable

doubt, is there any of you who would be unable conscientiously to find the defendant guilty? If so, please raise your hand. [*Pause.*] I take it from your lack of response that we are agreed. If I prove to you beyond a reasonable doubt each of the elements of the offense of assault, you will find the defendant guilty. If that is not the case, please raise your hand.

When you represent the defendant in a civil case, you should discuss the order of proof and extract a promise from the panel to wait until all the evidence is in before making a decision. You might say:

Q: The plaintiff gets to present all her proof first, before we are able to present any proof. It's important that you keep an open mind and not make any decision in the case until you've heard all the evidence from both sides. Will you promise me that you'll keep an open mind and not make any decision until you've heard our evidence? If you don't think you can do that, please raise your hand. [*Scan them with your eyes.*] Since I don't see any hands, I take it you all agree to wait until you've heard all the evidence, ours as well as the plaintiff's, before you make up your mind.

Another issue frequently discussed is sympathy. Many civil plaintiffs are under-dogs suing defendants who are part of the power structure. They have often been mangled or maimed. Jurors are certain to feel pangs of sympathy as they hear of the dreadful injuries these poor souls have suffered. The natural sympathy the jurors feel will arouse in them a desire to help the plaintiff ease his plight. However, sympathy is not a proper basis for recovery in a lawsuit, and the court must attempt to counteract it by instructing the jury that the verdict must be based on the evidence, not sympathy.[16] Nevertheless, sympathy remains a powerful factor in most suits and when it runs against your client you must reinforce the court's instruction at every opportunity. The first and most important opportunity comes during voir dire. Say something like:

Q: The plaintiff has suffered serious injuries and it is only natural that all of us, if we are caring human beings, should feel sympathy for her. However, the court is going to instruct you that you have a duty, under the oath you will take if you are selected for this jury, to set aside those feelings of natural sympathy and base your verdict solely on the evidence and the law. That will be hard to do, but I need to know if you can do it, if selected. Can you do

---

16. The language contained in the Federal Civil Jury Instructions of the Seventh Circuit (2015) 1.01 is typical: "Perform these duties fairly and impartially. [Do not allow [sympathy/prejudice/fear/public opinion] to influence you.] [You should not be influenced by any person's race, color, religion, national ancestry, or sex.]"

that? Can you set aside your sympathy and base your verdict just on the law and the evidence? If you don't think you'd be able to do that, please raise your hand.

A: [*No hands go up.*]

Q: The court will also instruct you that unless the plaintiff proves by a preponderance of the evidence that the accident was Ms. Casey's fault, you should find in favor of Ms. Casey and against the plaintiff. If the plaintiff fails to meet her burden of proving that Ms. Casey was at fault, will you be able to ignore your natural sympathy for the plaintiff and find for Ms. Casey? If you don't think you can, please let me know now by raising your hand.

On the other hand, if you represent a plaintiff, you should go through each of the elements of damage, explaining that the jury will be instructed, once liability is established, to award an appropriate amount for each element. Ask if any panel member thinks an element of damages should not be allowed. If a panel member responds, you can either push him far enough out on a limb to justify a challenge for cause or obtain a contract that he will follow the instructions and award damages for that element if the evidence so justifies.

Lawyers for plaintiffs in civil cases usually discuss preponderance of the evidence, burden, and comparative negligence if the jurisdiction has such a statute. Issues commonly discussed on voir dire by criminal defense lawyers include the state's burden of proof, the defendant's right to remain silent, and the presumption of innocence.

Discuss the weakest points of your case. Most cases you try will have at least one weak point on which the jury's verdict may turn. It is impossible to hide this weakness; jurors will discuss it sooner or later. If you bring the issue up for discussion during voir dire, you can participate in the discussion and may be able to influence the way the jury deals with it. Jurors will also respect you for facing the issue confidently. If you ignore the point during voir dire, you yield control of the issue to your opponent. Jurors will rightfully wonder why you shied away from the issue and will likely conclude that you did so because you and your client were afraid and tried to hide it. The jurors will inevitably discuss the issue during deliberations and will punish you if you did not bring it to their attention at the beginning of trial. Therefore, you must confront your weakest points during voir dire and give the members of the venire an opportunity to express their views on them. After all, if you thought the point was so devastating that you could not win in spite of it, you would not be trying the case. Therefore, expose your Achilles' heel and obtain an agreement that it should not, alone, cause you to lose.

One useful technique is to prepare a "fear list" containing the most troubling aspects of your case. Then talk to the jury panel about them. Do not run from an unpleasant answer. Instead, continue to question an objecting panel member and find out why he feels that way.

You may accomplish three objectives by discussing your weakest points on voir dire. First, some jurors may admit enough prejudice to justify a challenge for cause. Second, the knowledge you gain during the discussion will enable you to exercise your peremptory challenges more intelligently. Third, an open discussion of your weak points provides an opportunity to neutralize the prejudice of jurors you cannot strike. If the panel members acknowledge during voir dire that a particular fact should not control their verdict and promise not to let that fact unduly influence them, they will probably try to keep their promise in the jury room.

As an example, assume that your key eyewitness to an auto accident has a prior felony conviction that your opponent will use to impeach him. You need to get the panel members to promise that the conviction will not, of itself, keep them from believing the witness's testimony. You may say something like:

> Q: How many of you feel that someone who has been convicted of
>   a crime is less worthy of belief than someone who hasn't?

At least one person is likely to raise a hand. Then you can follow up by asking her why she feels that way. You must be ready to allow the conversation to lead down whatever path it takes. Invite others to share their views by asking:

> Q: Who agrees with Ms. Garner?

The discussion among the prospective jurors will probably lead to a consensus that a convicted felon's credibility depends on the crime for which she was convicted and the subject matter of the witness's testimony. Then you can say:

> Q: One of our important witnesses is Jesse Burnett, who was an
>   eyewitness to the accident. Mr. Burnett was convicted of armed
>   robbery four years ago, but has now paid his debt to society.
>   Are there any of you who feel that you could not believe what
>   Mr. Burnett says under oath today just because he has been con-
>   victed of this felony in the past?

4.3.3 Exercising Challenges for Cause

Exercise as many challenges for cause as possible. While you are allowed to exercise only a limited number of peremptory challenges, you may exercise as many challenges for cause as you can justify. Therefore, you should try to eliminate unfavorable jurors for cause, saving your peremptory strikes to remove those you feel are most likely to go against you although they have admitted no prejudice.

Use leading questions to guide an unfavorable juror to admit prejudice. When a prospective juror openly admits that he could not be fair to your client, grounds for a cause challenge clearly exist. However, because most panel members are not so forthright about their predispositions, you will most likely need to develop grounds for a cause challenge by careful questioning. The form of your questions must change when your purpose shifts from seeking information to establishing grounds for a cause challenge. While seeking information, you should ask broad, open-ended, non-leading, and non-judgmental questions to encourage the panel to discuss unfavorable points. When a prospective juror reveals potential prejudice against your client, you should switch to leading questions in your follow-up examination. Do not argue or ask the potential juror to justify feeling as he does. Rather, try to lead him tactfully into admitting that he should be struck for cause. For instance, assume that you represent a plaintiff and ask the following:

Q: Do any of you feel that the testimony of a preacher [the defendant] should be given more weight just because he's a preacher?

A: Preachers are good and truthful men. I'd be inclined to believe whatever the preacher told me.

Q: Mr. Brown, since you feel that way and since it's important that the defendant's testimony be judged just like the testimony of every other witness, do you think that it would be better if the court excused you in this trial and chose someone else to serve on this particular jury?

If Mr. Brown says yes, the court is practically forced to exclude him for cause. If he says no, you should get a promise from him that he will disregard his bias and follow the judge's instruction to consider the preacher's testimony like that of any other witness. If he refuses to make that promise, you probably have established grounds to challenge him for cause against his will.

Approach the bench when you challenge for cause. Challenging a panel member for cause against his will is a delicate task. In our example, Mr. Brown obstinately refuses to admit he should not serve and refuses to agree to disregard his bias, which leaves you no alternative but to move the court to strike him for cause, even though he wants to serve. If you challenge him unsuccessfully in his presence, you will have incurred his enmity and be forced to use one of your peremptory challenges to strike him. Even if your challenge for cause is granted, the incident may have embarrassed him in front of his fellow panel members. Members of jury panels tend to become friends, and the remaining jurors may unconsciously resent your having challenged their fellow for cause. Therefore, you should always approach the bench before moving to strike a venire member for cause. Make the challenge at side-bar, out of the hearing of the jury.

4.3.4 Exercising Peremptory Challenges

If anyone could develop a foolproof method of identifying the most unfavorable jurors, that person would become an instant billionaire. Many subtle factors are involved in each human being's decision-making processes. Every legal issue will produce a psychological reaction in each juror. This reaction will differ, depending upon a myriad of factors. Jurors decide cases on perceptions and emotions rather than empirical analysis of evidence. All jurors filter the facts through their psychological screen to make them fit their perceptions. After all, to each of us, reality is nothing more than the confirmation of our expectations. Included here are some criteria for juror elimination that are used successfully by many lawyers.

Use your intuition. Some lawyers feel that intuition is the best guide to exercising peremptory challenges. To be sure, you should not ignore what your intuition tells you. Some people simply will not be on your wavelength. We all sometimes immediately feel a vague sense of discomfort in the presence of another person. We cannot put a finger on it, but somehow we just do not receive good vibrations from the person. Do not ignore those feelings; follow your gut.

Consult your client. Before exercising your peremptory challenges, discuss the strikes with your client. You must make the final decision yourself, but your client may have made valuable observations of potential jurors' body language or facial expressions or may have vague feelings of apprehension with regard to some panel members.

Observe body language. Body language can also provide valuable clues. The panel member who glares at you, leans back with his arms folded, or refuses to make eye contact may be revealing prejudice against you, your case, or your client. If that panelist exhibits positive body language toward your opponent, such as leaning forward, smiling, or nodding, you may infer that he is likely to favor the opposing side of the case. Likewise, a panel member who exhibits negative physical reactions to your opponent, but not to you, may be unwittingly revealing his bias in your favor. Consistently negative body language, no matter which lawyer is questioning, may indicate disgust with lawyers or the legal system in general. People with such attitudes can be as dangerous as one-eyed water moccasins. Consistent smiling and nodding to both lawyers may indicate an excessive desire to please—an indication that the panel member will probably follow, not lead.

Notice jurors' apparel. Do not ignore obvious clues, such as clothing, jewelry, and the like. Remembering that all persons tend to identify more readily with others who are most like themselves, we can reasonably suspect that a polyester cowboy, resplendent in his turquoise adornments and ostrich-hide boots, might feel little rapport with our dapper-grey, spit-and-polish banker client. Likewise, a Sunday school attendance medal or "Jesus Saves" lapel pin speaks volumes about its wearer. Such a pin may assume great significance if the evidence is going to show your client to be a hard-drinking, philandering rounder.

Look for leaders. Always look for the leaders. On a typical twelve-person jury, four or five jurors will effectively decide the case. The rest will be followers who will go along with what the leaders suggest. Even one leader can make a tremendous difference in the course of the jury deliberations. As President Andrew Jackson once said, "One man with courage makes a majority." You will often want to strike more panel members than you have peremptory challenges. In that situation, you must decide which of the unfavorable panelists will be likely to hurt you most. Obviously, you should strike the unfavorable panel member who exhibits the characteristics of a leader before striking one who appears to be a follower. There is also another reason to identify leaders. If you have identified the leaders who seem favorably disposed toward your case, you can concentrate your case presentation on them.

Listen for the telltale use of "I." People who speak frequently in the first person tend to be authoritarian and critical. They will assert themselves in a jury room. When you ask questions seeking opinions, note which prospective jurors are eager to tell what they think.

The single most useful piece of information in identifying leaders is occupation. When you know a person's occupation, you have a fairly good idea of the person's educational level, socio-economic level, social status, and ego capability. The term "ego capability" describes a person's ability to assert himself and influence the behavior of others. One's occupation often tells us whether he is a person capable of and accustomed to giving or following orders.

Try to identify the foreperson. The average American jury foreperson is forty-seven years old, completed one-and-a-half years of college, and makes $35,000 a year. Seventy percent of jury forepersons are male and ninety percent are white. Another key factor is prior jury experience. Unless no juror has served before, the jury is likely to select one who has previously sat on a jury as foreperson.

Watch the hallways. Watch the hallways to see which prospective jurors congregate together. Try to observe those whose personalities seem to mesh. They will probably agree in the jury room. Look for loners. They are usually followers. Also look for the "over-identification" juror—the one who seems overly anxious for everyone on the jury to like him. He will usually follow.

Try to identify "experts." As a general rule, neither party wants a juror who is or claims to be an expert in a subject crucial to the outcome of the lawsuit. That juror will inevitably become an unsworn expert witness in the jury room and is likely to sway the jury with his opinions. In effect, he may become a one-person jury. When opposing expert opinions will be presented in evidence, the last person you want in the jury room is one who will presume to tell his fellow jurors that he knows who is right because of his expertise. Only in the unlikely event that your position is unquestionably sound, your opponent's clearly unsupportable, and the juror truly qualified as an expert in the field would you want this person on the jury (and then your opponent would surely strike him).

4.4   Final Thoughts and the Final Question

Voir dire examination, as all other segments of trial, should end strong. It makes sense to finish with one or more catch-all questions that will give the jurors a final opportunity to let you know if they do not want to serve on the case. A juror who is feeling sick or uncomfortable, who is unhappy, feeling pressured by family problems, anxious to get out of town to start a vacation, or worried about children at home is not likely to be a good juror for your case. You would like to eliminate those jurors if you can. Your ideal juror will serve willingly and give the trial her full attention.

Most lawyers have a final question that they ask in virtually every case. Some ask if there is any physical reason a panel member would not be comfortable serving. Others ask if anyone would be greatly inconvenienced by serving. We have even heard a lawyer offer to use a peremptory challenge to excuse anyone for whom service would be inconvenient (a dangerous technique if four people raise their hands). Some lawyers ask jurors to contact a courtroom deputy after voir dire if they feel they have a reason why they should not serve—a reason that they did not feel comfortable disclosing in front of the group.

One of the authors throws out a "dragnet" question to invite the panel members to volunteer any information he may have neglected to seek. On this question, he assumes an aspect of deadly serious earnestness and pauses after the question long enough to look each member of the panel squarely in the eye. Here is the question:

> Finally, ladies and gentlemen, I don't know if I've covered everything. Only you know in your hearts whether you can be absolutely fair in this case. I ask you now to take a moment and look into your heart. Ask yourself, 'If I were one of the parties in this trial, would I be comfortable with me as a juror?' If there is any reason you think you might not be able to be absolutely fair to both parties in this trial, please, please tell me now by raising your hand. [*Long pause.*] Thank you very much. Nothing further, Your Honor.

CHAPTER FIVE

OPENING STATEMENT

"Is that really the best you can do?" he asked. "You know my client has already refused that offer."

For a long moment, he listened to the silence of the telephone line. He could hear his watch ticking out the seconds. Finally, he heard the voice on the other end say, "Yes that is our best offer."

He paused and tried to force all emotion out of his voice. "I'll see you in court then," he said in a serious tone. But as he hung up the phone, he could feel his excitement growing. He wanted to try this case. It had a compelling story. Since he began working on it, he had understood its theme. Now he was ready to communicate and persuade. He was ready to tell the story to jurors in an opening statement. A quick telephone call to the clerk of court confirmed that the trial was set "first out" tomorrow morning. Good. All he had to do was to review the opening statement he had begun writing months ago.

5.1 The Goals of Opening Statement

Opening statement provides an opportunity to tell the story that brought you to the courtroom. It is an opportunity to make that story compelling and memorable. This is a good time to reach the jurors and be sure they will hear the case as you will present it. You should have had this opportunity in mind since you began working on the case.

5.1.1 The Purpose of the Opening under the Law

From the law's perspective, the opening statement plays a negligible role at trial. In the eyes of the law, the lone purpose of the opening is to provide the jury a preview of the evidence you will present. During the trial, jurors will hear testimony from a variety of witnesses and will see numerous exhibits. No matter how well you have organized the presentation of testimony, the information will come out in a way that is somewhat disjointed. It would be difficult, if not impossible, for the jurors to put the evidence together into a coherent narrative. Therefore, the law affords each party the opportunity to give an overview of his case that will help the jury understand the evidence as it is offered during witness examinations. Much like the cover to the box of a jigsaw puzzle, the opening gives jurors the complete picture to enable them to understand and assemble the individual pieces of testimony and exhibits offered at trial.

While allowing counsel to tell jurors what he believes the evidence will show, the law makes clear that the opening statement does not constitute evidence. The jurors should not rely on anything said during the opening statement in reaching their decision. The jury certainly is not supposed to be persuaded by the opening. To the contrary, most judges will admonish the jurors to keep an open mind throughout the trial and to refrain from discussing the case among themselves until they have heard closing arguments and received instructions on the governing law.

5.1.2 The Effect of the Opening in Reality

The law's view of the opening statement ignores the reality of how jurors will respond to the opening. The jury has just been empaneled and sworn in. The jurors are fresh, open minded, and listening. They may be more interested and attentive now than at any other point in the trial. System 1 of their brain is primed to sub-consciously and intuitively decide what happened, fitting the facts into the pattern of how people ordinarily behave given their character and motive.[1]

Notwithstanding the judge's instructions, it will be impossible for the jurors to withhold judgment until the end of the case. Your goal in the opening statement, then, is to capture the jurors' interest and imagination and to teach them your story of the case in a way that is both persuasive and memorable. If the jury buys in to your story during opening statement, all of the evidence that follows will seem to fall into place, simply confirming what they already have concluded about the case.

But opening statement is not only important for instructing the mind of the jury. It is an opportunity to capture the heart of the jurors as well. It is imperative to per-suade them of the virtue of your cause. Your opening statement should be morally and emotionally compelling. It should make jurors want your client to win because of what is at stake.

5.2 How to Prepare Your Opening Statement

To properly prepare your opening statement, you must take two separate steps. First, you determine the substance of the opening—what specific facts and law will you tell the jury? Second, you create the organizational structure—or chapters—of the opening. You have to undertake these two tasks separately. If you try to craft the order of your closing at the same time you are deciding what facts and law to include, you will compromise both the content of your opening and the jurors' abil-ity to follow and understand what you are saying.

---

1. *See* chapter two at 2.3.

5.2.1 *The Substance of the Opening Statement*

The first step in preparing the opening is to list, without regard to order, each of the facts and rules of law that you want to include in the statement. While the specifics of course will vary from case to case, every opening should convey the following to jurors.

The Story of the Case. As more fully explained in chapter two,[2] you must choose one person's story to tell. That story must convey the character → motive → plot continuum that will cause the jury's System 1 brain instinctively to find your version of the disputed facts to be predictable, if not inevitable.

Stories constitute the single most powerful weapon in a leader's arsenal.

— *Dr. Howard Gardner*

The Theme of the Case. By the time you prepare your opening statement, the theme of your case should be clear. Your theme distills your case to a memorable word or phrase that you will repeat throughout the trial.[3] You should establish the theme during voir dire, reinforce it during opening statement, hammer it home during the presentation of evidence, and recall it during closing argument. It is the thread of continuity running through your case.

The Stakes. While the story of the case helps convince the jury that your version of the disputed facts logically must be what occurred, persuasion requires that you also satisfy the emotional needs of the jurors. They need to want your story to be the truth. As more fully discussed in chapter two,[4] you can cause jurors to root for a verdict in favor of your client by properly identifying the real world, non-material, relatable effect of the verdict, above and beyond the legal consequences. You must share those stakes with jurors in your opening statement.

The Law. The lawyer is not supposed to instruct jurors about the applicable law in the opening. The law of the case is not part of what the evidence will show. Furthermore, it is the province of the judge, not the lawyers, to instruct jurors on the law that governs the case. While some judges will give a mini-charge on the law at the outset of the trial, the judge will not deliver the full instruction to the jury until just before or after closing argument.[5]

On the other hand, there may be a risk that without understanding certain legal concepts, the jury will wrongfully conclude you should lose the case even if it accepts your story. If so, you must gently tiptoe into the judge's domain and explain that

---

2. *See id.* at 2.3.1–2.3.4.
3. *See id.* at 2.3.5(b).
4. *See id.* at 2.3.5(a).
5. *See* Fed. R. Civ. P. 51(a).

law in your opening. For example, if you are representing the accused in a murder case who freely admits she shot her husband but did so in self-defense, you have to tell jurors in the opening statement that a person is entitled to kill if necessary to save her own life. Without a lay understanding of the law of self-defense, at the end of your opening jurors could accept your entire story but nonetheless conclude that your client is guilty because you admitted that she pulled the trigger. Even in a garden-variety negligence case, as the plaintiff's attorney you need to educate jurors that the defendant is liable even if he did not intend to harm your client. You must tell the jurors that negligence does not mean that the defendant is a bad person, or that he generally is a bad driver. Rather, the defendant is negligent if, on this solitary occasion, he made a mistake by failing to do what a reasonable driver would have done under the circumstances.

It is not permissible, necessary, nor advisable to discuss every element of the cause of action, crime, or defense in the opening. Doing so runs the risk of confusing jurors and triggering an objection from the judge. However, there is some authority for the proposition that if the party with the burden of proof on an issue does not include in the opening statement facts sufficient to establish each element, the court may enter full or partial judgment as a matter of law after the opening.[6] Without discussing each legal element with the jury, the substance of your opening should include facts sufficient to establish each element for which you bear the burden of proof.

5.2.2 *The Organizational Structure of the Opening Statement*

Only after you have finished listing the facts, theme, stakes and law that you will include in your opening should you decide the order in which you will present this information to jurors. As in a written brief, you should organize the opening statement to have the most persuasive impact on jurors. There is an extra reason to be attentive to the ordering of topics in the opening. Voir dire made it likely that most of the people sitting in the jury box know nothing about the case. Save for exhibits the judge will permit you to use during the opening,[7] the jurors will have to absorb the information you are conveying through their ears rather than their eyes—decidedly the least effective means by which humans comprehend information. Consequently, it is critical that you organize your opening into chapters that are designed to help the jurors to follow and understand what you are telling them. This section will address the content and structure of three separate segments

---

6. The trial court has power to "direct a verdict for the defendant upon the opening statement of plaintiff's counsel where that statement establishes that the plaintiff has no right to recover." Best v. District of Columbia, 291 U.S. 411, 4215 (1934). *See also* Phillip E. Hassman, "Power of Trial Court to Dismiss Prosecution or Direct Acquittal on Basis of Prosecutor's Opening Statement," 75 A.L.R. 3d 649.
7. *See* chapter five at 5.3.4

you must prepare for every opening statement: the introduction, the body of the opening, and the conclusion.

The Introduction to the Opening Statement

Law libraries are replete with books on trial advocacy that instruct lawyers to begin their opening with some variation on the following boilerplate:

> Good morning, ladies and gentlemen of the jury. While we met during the jury selection process, let me reintroduce myself. My name is Sawyer Bennett, and it is my privilege and deep responsibility to represent the plaintiff in this case, Ellery Ruben.

> Both Ms. Ruben and I want to thank you for taking time from your families and jobs to sit as jurors on this case. Jury service is one of the highest civic duties a citizen can perform. One of the great features of the American system of justice, the finest in the world, is that that we resolve disputes by a jury of one's peers.

> This is the portion of the trial known as the opening statement. Each party has the opportunity to tell you what it believes the evidence we will present in this case will show. The opening statement is like the cover to a box containing a jigsaw puzzle. While the opening statement is not evidence in this case, it will show you a picture of what we believe the evidence will show so you can better understand the individual pieces of testimony you will hear from the witnesses when they are called to the witness stand.[8]

This stock opening had several laudable objectives. The lawyer demonstrated basic courtesy, motivated the jurors to approach the trial with requisite seriousness, and established credibility by accurately educating the jurors about the limited purpose of the opening in the eyes of the law.

One of the joys of being a trial lawyer is that we must always be willing to adapt our advocacy skills to changes in society, technological advances, and discoveries from the hard and social sciences as to how people learn and make decisions. We have long known of the psychological principle of primacy—that people tend

---

8. Some commentators urged defense counsel to admonish the jury to withhold judgment until the defense has presented evidence:
> The plaintiff gets to present all of her evidence first before we are allowed to present any evidence on behalf of Mr. Shrackle and the Shrackle Construction Company. It is important that you hear both sides before you make up your mind. Please wait until you have heard all the evidence.

to understand, accept, and remember what they hear first.[9] We now live in a world where, due to technology and other forces, our need to be constantly entertained has increased while our attention spans have diminished. If we do not like what we are watching on television, a simple press of a button on the remote will deliver a new option. We can fast-forward through commercials. Rather than waiting a week for the next episode, we can binge-watch an entire season of a series at a single prolonged sitting. We walk around in possession of smartphones that give us access to information and amusement at any time and any place.

The traditional introduction to the opening—designed to ring the "ethos" bell of persuasion—now undermines our credibility with jurors. There is nothing interesting, entertaining, or novel about that introduction that is likely to cause the jurors to pay attention to, or care about, what you are saying. Instead, the jurors are likely to change stations on their mental remote control, hoping that opposing counsel will be worth watching.

A man's mind, stretched by a new idea,
can never go back to its original dimension.

—*Oliver Wendell Holmes*

Those in the media charged with informing and educating viewers have adapted their methods to attract and retain an audience with mosquito-like attention spans. One of the pioneers was the twenty-four-hour sports network ESPN. Every installment of its mainstay news hour, SportsCenter, begins with a series of short video clips, each of which contains a dramatic vignette from the stories that will be addressed more fully over the arc of the show. These vignettes whet the viewers' appetite, motivating them to put down the remote and hunker down for the full broadcast. Only at the conclusion of the video teasers does the camera turn to the studio broadcasters, who then introduce themselves and proceed to the first story.

The most staid deliverers of "hard news" have mimicked ESPN's technique of recruiting and maintaining viewership. It was not that long ago that national television networks relied upon the credibility of their news anchor for ratings. Generations depended upon the face and voice of Walter Cronkite, Chet Huntley and David Brinkley, John Chancellor, Tom Brokaw, or Peter Jennings for accurate information about national and world events of significance. While not wholly shedding the notion that the attractiveness and credibility of the anchor is a necessary condition to viewership, national television networks now commence their

---

9. The pioneering study, which coined the term "primacy," is reported in Lund, "The Psychology of Belief," 20 *J. Abnormal & Soc. Psych.* 174, 183–91 (1925). *See also* Lawson, "Order of Presentation as a Factor in Jury Persuasion," 56 *Ky. L. J.* 523 (1968); Linz & Penrod, "Increasing Attorney Persuasiveness in the Courtroom," 8 *Law & Psychology Rev.* 1, 8 (1984).

news broadcasts in the same manner as ESPN. Short dramatic video clips with voiceovers offer the bait designed to lure the viewer to watch the full half-hour show. Only once the hook is set does the camera turn to the anchor, who introduces himself to the viewer.

The modern trial lawyer must adopt the wisdom of ESPN and national nightly news programming. Our disciplines are engaged in precisely the same business—informing our respective audiences about what we believe to be the truth of events that have occurred in the past. As trial lawyers, we must execute a modern ingredient of our credibility/ethos as persuaders—inducing the audience to be interested and engaged in what we want them to understand and accept. The introduction to our opening, then, must 1) capture the jurors' interest, 2) deliver a verbal video clip of the essence of our story, and 3) convey the theme of our case.[10]

One of the earliest and most iconic case files published by the National Institute of Trial Advocacy is *Potter v. Shrackle and the Shrackle Construction Company*. Law students and young lawyers across the country learned the art of trial advocacy by litigating the negligence claim of the Estate of Katherine Potter. The Potter family claims that Katherine Potter was walking in the crosswalk on Mattis Avenue with the green light. Shrackle, the owner of a construction company, was behind the wheel of his truck hurrying to be on time for an appointment with his largest client at a problematic job site. Shrackle turned left from Kirby Avenue on to Mattis when he struck Ms. Potter with his truck, causing her death.

Abandoning the traditional introduction, plaintiff's counsel could begin his opening as follows:

> On the morning of July 11, Professor Jeffrey Potter kissed his wife Katherine goodbye as she left their home to go to work. As he watched her walk down the stairs, go down the block, look back and wave to him just before she turned the corner, Jeffrey never would have imagined that the next time he would see Katherine was in a bed at Nita Hospital where she lay dying.
>
> What neither Jeffrey Potter nor Katherine Potter could have anticipated is that on the afternoon of the same day, Charles Shrackle would ignore the lesson all of us learned from our parents from our earliest days—Walk, Don't Run. Whether we were dashing about the house, sprinting along the sidewalk, or flying up or down stairs, our parents' constant warning was to walk, not run. In the earliest days of school, tempted by the marvelously long and wide hallway, and with our minds on recess, our legs began to churn. And we were met by the same refrain from our teachers—walk, don't run. What both our parents and teachers understood

---

10. *See* Peter Perlman, "The First Two Minutes of the Opening Statement," *Practical Litigator* (Sept. 2005), at 23; James McElhaney, "No Time to Waste," *ABA J.* (Apr. 2004), at 32.

and taught us is that if we were in a hurry, if we rushed, we might hurt ourselves. And if we were in a hurry, if we rushed, we could hurt other people as well.

As Charles Shrackle turned the wheel of his truck to make a left-hand turn onto Kirby Avenue, he certainly had heard the same words from his parents and teachers. But on the afternoon of July 11, Charles Shrackle had a more urgent concern on his mind. He had quit his secure job as a construction worker to start his own construction company. Two days earlier, Shrackle had received an email from his largest client, Clarke Poe, telling him there were serious problems at the Greenbrier job site that Mr. Shrackle's excavation company was to prepare for construction. The entire Greenbrier contract, and perhaps Mr. Shrackle's entire business, was at stake. Mr. Poe's email told Mr. Shrackle in no uncertain terms to meet him at the job site promptly at 3:30 and "be there and be on time." Mr. Shrackle immediately sent a return email promising that "unlike some times in the past, I assure you I won't be late." But as Charles Shrackle approached the green light on Kirby Avenue to make a left turn onto Mattis, he was in serious jeopardy of breaking that promise. At that very moment, Katherine Potter with the green light and walk sign in her favor, slowly stepped into the crosswalk and began walking across Mattis Avenue.

Good morning, ladies and gentlemen, again my name is Sandra Walker, and it is my privilege and serious responsibility to represent the family of the late Katherine Potter.

Like the video vignettes that open the broadcasts of SportsCenter and national news, this introduction immediately piques the jury's curiosity as to what is to follow, making clear that something will occur that will tragically kill Katherine Potter. Having captured the jury's interest, the opening proceeds to establish the theme—the universal principle of human behavior, hopefully expressed in a familiar phrase, that persons in a hurry are likely to be less careful and make mistakes.[11] Finally, the opening gives the essence of the story—in this instance, Charles Shrackle's motivation—that will cause the jurors' System 1 brain to predict that Shrackle will abandon ordinary caution when driving to the Greenbrier worksite.

Only after giving the jury a reason to want to hear the fuller story does the lawyer introduce herself. At that point, you also may wish to introduce your client to the jurors. If you want to send a subliminal message that your client is an accept-

---

11. The impact of the theme is so great that many lawyers state the theme with the first words they utter on opening. These lawyers consider the very first sentence they speak, while they have the jurors' rapt attention, to be of overriding importance. This technique has proven effective. For example, in a case alleging breach of contract, the theme might be "broken promise," and you could say, "We are here today because the defendant broke a promise to deliver one thousand wheelbarrows to Joe Zenith."

able person of whom you are not afraid, you may draw physically near the client. Because we all instinctively move closer to those we like and withdraw from those we find repugnant, jurors will unconsciously conclude that you like your client. Physical intimacy is something we reserve for those for whom we feel affection. If you want jurors to know that you feel fondness for your client, touch him. Place a hand on his shoulder as you introduce him to the jury. But before touching the client, you should consider a couple of things. First, for this technique to be effective, your client must actually be a somewhat likeable person. If you appear too chummy with a despicable client, the jury is likely to conclude that you must be a sleazy lawyer. Secondly, be wary of this technique if your client is a member of the opposite sex. Human nature loves to assume the worst and the jury could easily get the wrong idea about your relationship with the client.

The Body of the Opening Statement

Properly executed, the introduction of the opening will motivate jurors to want to hear the more in-depth report about the case. The jurors' System 1 brain has already predicted how Charles Shrackle will drive, and they are primed to view the facts through the prism of the theme. The body of the opening is the time to get across your chosen story of the case. You have selected the one person's story to tell. Now tell the story—not only the plot, but the character and motive that will lead jurors instinctively to accept your version of the disputed facts.[12]

Organizational Structure of the Story

There are several ways you could organize your telling of the story. You will be sorely tempted to preview for jurors each witness who will testify and what he or she will say. But your goal is not to tell them the fragmented story of the forthcoming trial, but rather to present a cogent story of what occurred at a much earlier time outside the courtroom. With rare exceptions, then, you should reject the convenience of a witness-by-witness accounting of the evidence.

A second structure that invariably will pop into your mind is to organize the body of the opening under the elements of the cause of action, crime, or defense. You have been using the elements throughout the pretrial proceedings—in drafting pleadings, in formal and informal discovery, and in filing and defending motions. You took pains to verify that the witnesses you plan to call, and the testimony you will elicit will establish each and every legal element. You have drafted jury instructions that explain the legal elements. You will be naturally inclined to continue to use the elements in the opening as the template to tell the jurors about the case.

---

12. For an excellent discussion of how to tell the story in the opening, see Gerald Reading Powell, "Opening Statements: The Art of Storytelling," XXXI *Stetson L. Rev.* 89 (2001).

You must remember that you continually resorted to the legal elements as the beacon to ensure that your case was legally sufficient. As more fully explained in chapter two, the legal elements will not help you succeed in the separate task of persuading jurors that your version of the disputed facts is the true account of what occurred. Hence, you should not use the elements of the law as the organizing principle for your story of your case.

The easiest way to organize your story is the pure chronology. Start with the events that portray character; proceed to the facts that gave rise to motive; and finish with the plot, told in the precise sequence in which the events occurred. Even when using a strict chronology as your structure, you must choose the person through whose eyes the jurors will see the events unfold. You could tell the story from the vantage point of your client, from the point of view of the opposing party, or as experienced by a neutral witness, such as a bystander. The television series *CSI* has created a franchise out of the conceit of slowly and dramatically teasing out the investigation of a crime. As prosecutor, you similarly could choose to tell your story by tracking the actions of the detective charged with solving the crime.

The pure chronology will mirror the order in which the events unfolded in the real world. This does not mean that this is necessarily the most persuasive or interesting way to tell the story. You should feel free to warp the chronology. You could choose to begin at or just before the moment of the crime to build interest and tension, flash back to reveal character and motive, and then return to the scene to finish the plot of the story. Or you may unfold the story using a parallel structure. In the *Potter* case file, you could take the jurors through Katherine Potter's day until the moment she takes her first step into the crosswalk on Mattis Avenue. You then could go back in time to tell the story of Charles Shrackle, his character, motive, and the progression of the plot through Shrackle moving his truck into the left turn lane on Kirby Avenue. You finish by bringing the two stories together at the tragic moment when Shrackle predictably runs over and kills Katherine Potter as she is walking in the crosswalk.

You could choose common sense elements, as opposed to legal elements, to structure your story. People who commit crimes typically have both a motive and opportunity to do so. As prosecutor, then, the first chapter of the body of the opening would be the story of the defendant's motive to commit the crime. Chapter two would be defendant's opportunity to commit the crime, in his view without being detected. Chapter three would walk the jurors through the discovery of the evidence the investigation found that confirmed that the defendant acted upon that motive and opportunity.

All of the suggested structures have a **common goal**: to compellingly and persuasively tell the jury the character → motive → plot continuum of our chosen factual story of the case.

Theme

Whichever structure you use to tell the story of your case, you should explicitly invoke the theme one time in the body of the opening. Reference the theme at the precise moment where the theme is manifested in the story.

> Charles Shrackle was relieved that the light was green in his favor as he moved his truck into the left-hand turn lane of Kirby Avenue at the Mattis Avenue intersection. Perhaps he could satisfactorily explain to Mr. Poe that there was a good excuse for the delay in excavating the site at the Greenbrier project so that Mr. Poe would not cancel the contract. Maybe Mr. Shrackle could keep alive his dream of owning his own business by keeping his largest client happy. Hopefully, Mr. Shrackle could prove to his wife that her support of the decision to quit his job and start his own business was not misplaced.

> But Mr. Poe had told Charles Shrackle to meet him at 3:30 p.m.—at the project—to "be there and be on time." Mr. Shrackle had promised "unlike some times in the past, I assure you I won't be late." If he could get to the Greenbrier site by 3:30, Charles Shrackle would have a much better chance of persuading Mr. Poe that the delay in excavating the Greenbrier site was not due to any failing on Mr. Shrackle's part. On the other hand, if Mr. Shrackle could not keep a simple promise to be on time for a meeting, how could he expect Mr. Poe to believe that Mr. Shrackle was not at fault for failing to timely perform the excavation work needed to prepare the job site for construction?

> Tragically, consumed by his thoughts about getting to the Greenbrier project by 3:30, one phrase did not cross Mr. Shrackle's mind. It was a phrase he most certainly had heard many times from his parents. It was a phrase his teachers repeated from the first day of kindergarten. It was a phrase Mr. Shrackle no doubt said to his own children. "Walk, don't run." A simple phrase that captured the universal truth that when you are in a hurry you may hurt yourself. You might hurt somebody else.

> Charles Shrackle kept his eyes on the oncoming traffic, so he could make the left hand turn as soon as possible and continue with his urgent quest to get to the Greenbrier project on time. But in his rush to make the turn before he would be further delayed by the oncoming traffic, Mr. Shrackle did not see Katherine Potter as she walked in the crosswalk of Mattis Avenue.

While you should weave the theme into the body of the opening, it is equally important not to overuse the device. Rather than helping the jury understand the essence of your story of the case, constantly reiterating the theme will relegate it to a cliché. You unveiled the theme in the introduction to the opening. Refer to the theme once in the body of the statement. You will invoke the theme for the third and final time in the conclusion to the opening statement.

Address the Law

In addition to telling the story and referencing the theme of the case, you should address the governing law in the body of the opening.

One school of thought advocates that after telling the story, you should proceed to fit the facts into the full legal framework that governs liability or guilt. The party with the burden of proof would break each issue into its legal elements and tell the jurors how the evidence will support each element. The opposing party would go through the elements of the offense or cause of action and discuss the places where the prosecution's or plaintiff's proof will fall short. The virtue of this approach is that it prepares jurors for both of the tasks it will perform at the close of the evidence—deciding which version of the disputed facts occurred and then applying those facts to the law as given in the judge's instructions.

There are two drawbacks to discussing and applying the legal elements in the opening. First, some judges may interrupt your opening and admonish you to stick to telling the jurors what your evidence will show. Whether or not the judge is correct in her assessment that you have invaded her province, you can ill afford the loss of credibility at the very onset of the trial by the jury hearing the judge declare that you have not played by the rules.

Even if the judge permits you to address the legal elements, jurors will certainly find the discussion boring and quite likely find your presentation to be confusing. You invested a great deal of time before trial finding the factual story of the case that will most likely cause the jurors' System 1 to accept your version of what occurred. You have just told that story through the most compelling and persuasive structure, aided by a relatable theme that similarly appeals to System 1 intuition. Once you start to discuss and apply legal elements, you propel the jurors into System 2 analysis, inviting them to apply rules not anchored in their life experience. By inducing the jurors to engage in "slow" thinking, you jeopardize their acceptance of your story that they had arrived at by their "fast" and intuitive thinking.

While it may be prudent to avoid a full-throated discussion of the legal elements, you need not and should not entirely abandon the law in your opening. You must consider whether there is a legal concept that, if not addressed, might lead the jurors to mistakenly conclude that you should lose the case even if your story of the case is true. If so, you must explain that law to the jury—in common sense terms—in the body of your opening statement. For example, plaintiff's counsel may rightfully worry that the jurors will find Mr. Shrackle, a husband who is working hard to pursue the American dream of owning his own business, to be an honorable man. Mr. Shrackle would never intend to harm another person, and certainly did not want to or mean to hurt Katherine Potter. The jurors must understand that their assumptions about Mr. Shrackle's character are wholly compatible with finding Mr. Shrackle negligent in the case. After telling the jurors the story and theme, plaintiff's counsel could address the concept of negligence in the body of the opening as follows.

> Ladies and gentlemen, the Potter family has brought this lawsuit because Katherine Potter's untimely death was caused by Mr. Shrackle's negligence. First, let me make clear that this is not a criminal case. No one is claiming for a moment that Mr. Shrackle wanted or intended to hurt Mrs. Potter. We are not here to punish Mr. Shrackle. But under the law, Mr. Shrackle and the Shrackle Construction Company are responsible to compensate the Potter family for all the losses caused if Mr. Shrackle was negligent when he made the left turn from Kirby Avenue.

> Negligence does not mean that Mr. Shrackle is a bad person—he most certainly is a good husband and father and provider. Negligence does not mean that Mr. Shrackle generally is an unsafe driver. Negligence simply means that under all the circumstances, as he made the left-hand turn onto Mattis Avenue, Mr. Shrackle did not use the care that we would expect and demand of a reasonable driver at that moment.

The Conclusion to the Opening Statement

Once you have finished the body of the opening statement, you frankly will have no more substance to convey to jurors. They will have heard the theme (twice); the character, motive, and plot of your story; and clarification of any legal concept that, if left unexplained, risked the jurors deciding against you even if they accepted your version of the disputed facts. Unless you plan for how to conclude your opening, you will stand awkwardly before jurors in search of some graceful way to excuse yourself. Your last words will be something akin to "thank you for your time" or "have a nice trial."

The psychological principal of recency teaches that the jurors will most remember what they hear last. Just as you carefully crafted the introduction of the opening to capitalize on primacy, you must separately plan the conclusion to your statement to leave a powerful final impression on the jury.

You deliberately structured the body of the opening to tell the story of the case in the most compelling way. Little is to be gained, and much is to be lost, by attempting to cram an abridged version of that story into the conclusion of your opening. On the other hand, it may be useful to invoke the theme for the third and final time to remind the jurors that your story of what occurred squares with universal understanding of how and why people behave.

Following the theme, you may conclude by addressing the stakes to appeal (legitimately) to the jurors' emotion. As more fully discussed in chapter two,[13] the purpose of identifying the stakes is to motivate the jurors to root for your client to win given the real-world effect of the verdict. The legal consequence of finding in favor of the Potter family is requiring Mr. Shrackle and his construction company (or more likely, their insurance companies) to pay damages to Jeffrey Potter. The jury will most likely understand that while making Mr. Potter a wealthy man, damages will not bring Katherine Potter back to life. The jurors will be more likely to want to return a verdict in favor of the Potter family if they believe, in a non-material and relatable way, that someone's life could be changed for the better. Plaintiff's counsel in *Potter v. Shrackle* could conclude the opening as follows.

> We understand why Mr. Shrackle has difficulty believing or accepting that his worries over breaking his promise to be on time for the meeting at the Greenbrier project—with the prospect of losing that contract and jeopardizing his entire business—caused him to drive less carefully, with tragic consequences for Katherine Potter and the entire Potter family. But as we know, when our parents and teachers told us to walk, not run, they were not only concerned that we would hurt someone else—as happened in this case—but were fearful that we would hurt ourselves as well. Charles Shrackle continues to own and operate the Shrackle Construction Company. There will be good moments for that business. But the construction business is challenging and volatile. As with the Greenbrier project, there will be hard times as well. You have a precious opportunity to remind Mr. Shrackle that, however important his work may seem at any given moment, he must always put safety first, not only to protect the public, but to protect himself and his loved ones.

Some commentators recommend concluding the opening statement by telling jurors exactly what you will ask them to do at the end of the case.

> At the end of the trial, I'll have another chance to talk with you. At that time, after you've heard all the evidence, apply the law as the court will instruct you and return a verdict awarding the Potter family full and fair compensation for all the losses caused by Mr. Shrackle's negligence.

The purpose of the explicit specific request for relief is to be sure the jurors understand exactly what you want them to do. On the other hand, jurors will not be called upon to render a verdict until the end of the trial—hours, days, weeks, or months after the opening. You will be explaining the verdict form and the desired verdict fully during your closing argument. While the specific request for relief reflects the legal stakes, it does not embody the drama and emotion of the human stakes. Therefore you may prefer to end your opening by confronting the jurors

---

13. *See* chapter two at 2.3.5(a).

with the real-world consequences that should motivate them to root for a verdict in your client's favor.

5.3   How to Deliver Your Opening Statement

When you make an opening statement, even if you are experienced and confident, you will feel nervous. That is good. You can use your nervous energy as a motor behind the message. You won't appear nervous to the jury. You will appear to be energetic and on top of the issues.

5.3.1 Follow the Cardinal Principles of Sincerity, Honesty, and Simplicity

Be sincere. In delivering your opening statement, be sincere. An indispensable part of sincerity is to be yourself. Some people are inherently flamboyant in their public speaking. Others are more even-tempered and deliberate by nature. It is critical that you not imitate or try on a new style in your opening. As discussed in chapter one, as is true outside the courtroom, the jury will find you relatable and credible if you allow your unique lovable essence to show.

Because the jurors are likely to reach a tentative conclusion about who should prevail by the end of the opening statements, give your opening statement as if the jury were going to retire and deliberate immediately after you finish. While being yourself, you must make evident that you are utterly convinced about what you are saying. At the same time, you should not be overbearing. No one likes to be forced into making a decision. Do not lecture the jurors. While always maintaining the jurors' interest, do not adopt the state of mind that you are delivering a sermon or a speech for posterity. Rather, view the opening as conversing with the jurors about the case, leading them to the edge of the cliff, with the jurors making their own decision to take the leap.

Part of sincerity is concern for the feelings of others, so be considerate of the jurors' feelings. Warn jurors if you are going to introduce evidence that will shock or upset them.

Safeguard your integrity and the jury's confidence in you by being scrupulously honest during opening statement. During opening statement, you make promises to the jury. *Never* promise anything you cannot support with evidence. If the admissibility of an item of evidence is questionable, do not mention it.[14] If you tell the jurors they will hear something and they do not hear it, you will have lost your credibility.

---

14. While motions in limine are more frequently used to get a ruling in advance of trial excluding evidence, you may file a motion in advance of trial seeking a ruling that evidence you wish to offer is admissible. Motions in limine are more fully discussed in chapter thirteen.

The primary purpose of the opening is to tell your story of the case. On the other hand, no case ever goes to trial if one side has the perfect, undisputed story. You will know the most problematic facts in your case. Without turning your opening into a defensive exercise, you must acknowledge those facts. When you decided on your factual theory of the case, you should have figured out how to embrace the most significant bad facts or how to diminish their impact. Confession is good not only for the soul, but for your lawsuit. For instance, if one of your witnesses is subject to impeachment for bias, acknowledge the relationship that raises an inference of bias. The fact that the words come from your mouth while looking the jurors straight in the eye alone blunts the sting of the relationship.

Leadership is a matter of having people look at you and gain confidence, seeing how you react. If you're in control, they're in control.

—Tom Landry

Keep it simple. The acid test of an effective opening statement is whether the jurors understands your story of the case when you have finished. Without being condescending or underestimating their collective wisdom, use words the jurors can understand. When preparing your opening statement, pretend that a twelve-year-old child has come to you and said, "Tell me about that case you're gonna try tomorrow." An effective reply to that child's question will be an effective opening statement.

Do not overwhelm the jury with details. Lawyers are famous for their ability to account for and explain the relevance of every fact in the case. However, the jurors will not have the mental capacity to absorb and understand all the details of the case when listening to your opening statement. Cases are usually decided on broad, general impressions, rather than a careful analysis of evidentiary data. Briefly cover the important facts and leave out the minor ones. Do not allow yourself to get bogged down in the process of giving blow-by-blow accounts of conversations or events. Do not burden the jurors with names, dates, and directions that are not essential to a basic understanding of your story. Leave some of the work for the witnesses.

As we mentioned earlier, you will destroy your credibility if you promise evidence that is not later introduced. However, the reverse is not true. When you say what you expect to prove and then prove more, the jurors will be impressed. Think of your case as a hot fudge sundae. If you promise to produce a sundae composed of ice cream and hot fudge topping, you had better produce both. If you do not, the jury has every right to hold you responsible for breaking your promise. If you do produce both, they will probably pay you for the sundae. If you surprise them by serving up a sundae with whipped cream, chopped nuts, and a maraschino cherry on top, they are likely to reward you with a nice tip.

5.3.2 Do Not Memorize Your Opening

The opening statement is the only part of the trial you can prepare completely in advance. During voir dire and witness examinations you must remain flexible enough to react to unexpected answers. You cannot completely prepare your summation until the close of the evidence. However, except for responding to objections, you could deliver your opening statement exactly as you plan it before trial. Therefore, you should rehearse it. Rehearse the opening statement aloud—do not just think about it. Say it to yourself without notes in the shower. Deliver it to the birds and squirrels during your morning jog. Try it out on your spouse. Stand in front of a mirror as you give it. Rehearse, rehearse, rehearse, so that when you finally stand before the jurors you will be familiar with the structure of the opening and the transition between the chapters.

Your goal, however, is not to deliver at trial a verbatim version of the opening that you rehearsed. As with every aspect of the trial, you must accept that perfection in the opening statement comes at a heavy price: your loss of credibility. If you attempt to memorize your opening, the jurors will see you "reading" the statement from the inside of your mind. For the same reason, you should bring to the lectern an outline, but not a script, of your opening. A verbatim text of the opening is counterproductive in two ways. First, the more words that are written on the paper, the stronger your lawyerly preference for perfection will pull your eyes away from the jury and towards the script. Second, if you do get lost in the course of delivering your opening, it will be much more difficult to find your place in a full script than in a skeletal outline.

But an outline must not be the full text of your opening, formatted using the outline function of your word processing program. To be a true outline, no entry should be more than four words. The purposes of the outline are 1) to relieve you of the self-fulfilling fear of what would happen if you were to forget all or part of your opening and had nothing in writing to jog your memory, and 2) to provide a prompt reminding you of the chapters of your opening and the key points to get across in each chapter.

At all times during the opening, your focus must be on the message, not how the messenger is doing. While the jurors will reject your speech if they believe it is delivered from memory, they will not punish your client if on occasion you have the need to glance over at your outline before continuing to tell your story.

5.3.3 Stick to Your Own Agenda

As a general rule, you should prepare and deliver your opening statement as if your opponent were not in the courtroom. Establish your own agenda and stick with it. If you are on the defense, do not react to your opponent's opening statement. In large measure, a trial is a struggle between lawyers for control of the courtroom—or at least the appearance of control. Do not inadvertently create the impression that your opponent is in control by dwelling too much on the reasons the opposing party should not win. Instead, emphasize why your client *should* win. The advice contained in the old song is as applicable to trial practice as to life: "Accentuate the positive, eliminate the negative, and latch on to the affirmative, don't mess with Mister In-between."

On the other hand, as defense counsel you should pay close attention to the opening delivered by the plaintiff or prosecutor. Without deviating from your game plan, you should feel free to weave into your opening concessions or omissions in the plaintiff or prosecutor's statement that are consistent with your story of the case.

5.3.4 Use Visual Aids

Visual aids can help get your points across to jurors on opening statement, as well as at other times during the trial. Jurors tend to remember and understand what they have seen. A visual aid may be a key exhibit whose admission is certain, such as the policy in an insurance case. For example, if your defense relies on a policy exclusion, you should exhibit the policy and emphasize the exclusionary language during opening. Computer slides, charts, and diagrams can also be useful during opening statement. Since nothing has been accepted into evidence at the time you give your opening statement, you should advise the court of each visual aid you intend to use and obtain the court's permission.

5.3.5 Stand at a Comfortable Distance in Front of the Jurors

If the court has a rule or custom governing the place from which you are to deliver the opening, you must abide by the court's mandate. If the court gives you latitude as to positioning, however, place yourself about six feet away from the first row of jurors. If you stand too far away, you seem frightened. If you approach too near, you risk invading the jury's space. Jurors, like all of us, are repelled by a person who tries the hard sell. They are likewise offended by a person who comes on too strong too soon. Put yourself in the place of a typical juror. When you meet someone, how do you feel if that person gets right up in your face?

If you are using an outline, move the lectern so it is at your side rather than between you and the jury. If the lectern is not in a position you prefer, do not be shy about asking the court's permission to move the lectern to your desired location.

Your physical stature may affect your decision about where to stand. No lawyer should want to appear intimidating or threatening. The larger you are, the more space the jury needs. Some physically imposing lawyers deliver their opening statements behind a lectern for the specific reason that they feel that the presence of an obstacle between them and the jury makes the jurors feel more comfortable during the early stages of the trial. After the jury has gotten to know you, and if the trial seems to be going well, you may approach the jury box more closely. However, to do so during opening statement is too early.

5.3.6 Purge Your Pockets

Before you stand to open, empty your pockets of their contents. Like papers on the lectern, items in your pocket seem to exert a magnetic force. Your hands will search for whatever is in your pockets as a security blanket to hold. The adrenaline coursing through your body will cause you unknowingly to begin jingling keys or change, distracting the jurors from the words flowing from your mouth.

Do not take a pen with you when you stand to open. You certainly will not and should not have a sudden urge to write a note during your opening. If a pen is within reach, it somehow will find its way into your hand. Once there, you will either distract jurors by fidgeting or alienate them by pointing the pen at them in the excitement of your remarks.

5.3.7 Maintain Eye Contact

Maintain eye contact with the jurors. When our parents were testing the veracity of an excuse we were fobbing off, they asked us to tell the story while looking them in the eye. Our parents recognized that our willingness and ability to maintain eye contact was a reliable test of our sincerity and truthfulness. If we fail to maintain eye contact with our jurors, they may conclude that we do not believe what we are saying.

At some point in your opening, establish one-on-one eye contact with each juror as if that juror were the only other person in the universe. The eyes are the windows of the soul and you can share some of your soul's passion for your case by giving each juror your undivided attention for at least a few seconds. Needless to say, you cannot maintain eye contact if you read your statement.

5.3.8 Move with Purpose

Assuming the judge does not require you to remain behind a lectern, you should move about during your opening. However, do not surrender to the rush of adrenaline that will cause you to consistently pace back and forth across the jury box. The jurors should not have to consistently swivel their heads as if watching a tennis match. Rather, your movements should enhance the jury's interest in and understanding of the discussion by synching with the chapters of your opening. Begin by standing in the center of the jury box for your introduction and the first chapter of your opening. Move to the left half of the jury box, and then to the right half, as the story unfolds. Return to the center for your conclusion.

5.4 Objections to Improper Opening Statement

Lawyers usually try to avoid objecting during opening statement because they fear that interrupting the opponent with objections will give jurors an early impression that they are rude or obstreperous. They also fear that, worse still, jurors may conclude that they have something to hide. Another factor that minimizes objections during opening statements is the fact that many judges discourage them. Most judges prefer to give each attorney some latitude in opening statement and frown on objections that disrupt the flow. In some courts, the judge will direct counsel to hold all objections until the end of the opening statement, when objections may be raised and addressed at sidebar. Moreover, even if the judge agrees that an objectionable argument was made, the remedy for the breach of propriety is usually no more than a cautionary instruction. Following an improper argument, the judge may "cure" the impropriety by merely instructing the jury that the statements of counsel are not evidence in the case.

Nevertheless, there are times when you must object if your opponent breaches the bounds of proper opening statement. Further, if the impropriety of an opening statement is so egregious as to sully the entire trial, you should move for a mistrial. Failure to make a timely objection may be deemed a waiver.

The first legal limit on opening statement flows from the federal and state constitutions. In a criminal case, the prosecution cannot make any statement that invades the defendant's presumption of innocence or privilege against self-incrimination. The presentation must scrupulously avoid reference to anything it expects the defense will argue. Instead, for purposes of the opening, the prosecution must assume the defendant will rest without calling any witnesses in the case and restrict her statement to the story that will be supported by the prosecution's own witnesses.

The second legal limit on opening statements is the rules of evidence. If a fact is not admissible at trial under the law of evidence, obviously the lawyer should not include that fact in the opening statement. Judges are inclined to sustain objections to a fact that is plainly precluded by the law of evidence. On the other hand, if admissibility will depend on the context in which the evidence is offered at trial, the judge may be less willing to make a definitive ruling in the opening.

As we discussed earlier, you should never discuss evidence in your opening statement unless you are absolutely sure that it will be admitted. But how should you react if your opponent commits this cardinal sin? Should you object or sit tight? It is generally not objectionable to refer to matters that may be inadmissible, but about which no pretrial ruling has been made.[15] If you are fairly certain that your opponent is raising matters that will not be capable of proof in the trial, you may raise

---

15. As will be more fully discussed in chapter thirteen, you should file a motion in limine in advance of trial, seeking to exclude evidence that is both inadmissible and highly damaging.

an objection. But this is a judgment call. If the matter is insignificant, it is usually better to withhold objection. Then if evidence of the matter does not come in, you can utilize closing argument to recall the unfulfilled promise your opponent made during opening statement.

The most common objection during opening statement is to improper argument. Improper argument includes discussing why the adversary's theory of the case is flawed, making extensive comments on the credibility of witnesses,[16] giving a personal opinion on the merits of the case, asking jurors to put themselves in the shoes of the injured plaintiff or the victim of the crime, or overtly appealing to emotion.

Another appropriate objection is to your opponent's giving the jury detailed instructions on the applicable law—a matter that is the court's proper function. The extent to which lawyers are allowed to discuss law varies from judge to judge. Most judges will allow lawyers to discuss the burden of proof and other general concepts of the trial process. However, nearly all judges have an arbitrary point beyond which they will not let lawyers go. Before making this objection, you need to know the judge's policy.

The fuzziest, but broadest, category of improper argument is the judge's perception that your opening has gone beyond a statement of what the evidence will show. Each judge has an individual concept of where to draw the line between a properly persuasive statement of what the evidence will show and improper argument, and the power to use her discretion to draw that limit. The distinction between statement and argument is not a bright line, but a matter of degree, tone and tradition.

The opening statement must persuade the heart and mind of the jurors. The prohibition against argument in opening statement does not mean that you should be boring, bland, or tentative. It has nothing to do with your manner of delivery. You may show emotion. You can choose language calculated to arouse the jury's sympathy for your client. You should project total belief in your client's position. Notwithstanding the prohibition on argument, you must deliver your opening statement with conviction and intensity.

---

16. If done selectively, opposing counsel will not object to your asking the jurors to listen for particularly crucial evidence so that they will recognize its importance when they see or hear it. For example, if liability may turn on the testimony of your expert witness, you could tell the jurors that the expert will testify and what the expert's opinion will be, and ask the jurors to listen carefully when the expert testifies. Conversely, when you know you will be able to impeach the credibility of one of your opponent's witnesses successfully, you could ask the jurors to listen carefully to the witness's testimony, and particularly your cross-examination, so they will be able to decide accurately how much weight to give to the witness's testimony.

While such observations will not draw an objection, they could undermine the persuasive effect of the opening by reminding the jurors that they will need to suspend any judgment about the case until they see and hear the witnesses testify.

Further, the prohibition against argument does not mean that you should preface everything you say with "The evidence will show. . . ." Qualifying words are weak and usually unnecessary. Say "The traffic light was red," rather than "It is our contention that . . ." or "Our side of the story is that . . . ." Choose words that bear the connotation you seek to convey to jurors. For example, describing an automobile accident, a plaintiff's lawyer may say that the defendant "slammed" or "crashed" into the plaintiff's car, while the defense lawyer says an accident occurred when the plaintiff's and defendant's cars "bumped."

Neither are you prohibited from telling the jurors your story of the case in a way that makes the evidence add up to the inferences you want the jury to draw at the conclusion of the case. Instead, the rule against argument prohibits you from commenting extensively on the credibility of the evidence and from discussing explicitly why jurors should reject your opponent's evidence and draw the inferences you suggest. For example, in a burglary prosecution in which the defendant's alibi defense is based on his wife's statement that he was at home and asleep at the time of the crime, the prosecutor may say in opening statement:

> On that cold night in February, John Smith was restless. Just before midnight, he got up out of his bed, put on his size twelve boots, and walked out into the night, leaving his sleeping wife behind.

The prosecutor may go on to say:

> The only two people in the world who know where John Smith was at midnight are John Smith himself and Amy Blake, who will never forget the shattering crash of glass and the sight of his size twelve boots kicking through the window of her basement bedroom.

On the other hand, the prosecutor should not argue in opening statement:

> Mrs. Smith may come in here and testify that John Smith was at home asleep at midnight, but that is a load of hogwash. Mrs. Smith is just a woman who is willing to lie to keep her husband out of jail.

If the judge sustains an objection to your opening on the ground that you are arguing, do not abandon your planned statement. Rather, calmly and unemotionally utter the magic words "the evidence will show," and proceed with the story you intended to tell. Tactically, opposing counsel should be reluctant to object a second time, particularly when you now have situated your remarks squarely within the law's concept of the purpose of the opening statement.

Although most judges give attorneys a great deal of latitude in making opening statements and verdicts are rarely overturned on the basis of improper argument during opening statement, it makes sense to tell the story of your case without characterizing the evidence and without overtly selling it. The rule against argument in opening statement forces you to be a better advocate. Instead of relying on easy characterizations of the evidence and the witnesses, you must use details and images that make a lasting impression. You must find the drama in the facts. You must pull the threads of evidence together in a way that makes them compelling. Your opening statement will not include the phrase, "My theory is true and credible and my opponent's is not." Nevertheless, every word of your opening statement should demonstrate the truth and justice of your cause.

CHAPTER SIX

DIRECT EXAMINATION

John was brooding over the direct examination of his client in his upcoming trial. "You know," he told his old friend and advisor, "if I were creating the trial system from scratch, I'd do away with direct examination. I would just let the witness tell her story without the conventions of the witness box and the questions from counsel."

"Why, John?"

"It just seems ridiculous. The whole thing is planned anyway. Why not just let the witness read a prepared statement?"

"Why, indeed?" the seasoned trial lawyer smiled. "Why does every talk show on television put the guest in a chair and ask questions? Couldn't the guests simply tell their own stories or read prepared statements?"

"That's different," complained John. "When you watch a talk show, you want to be entertained. You want to see the interaction of the guest and the host. The questions and answers make the guest seem more interesting, more accessible, more human. And even though you know the interview may be planned, when you watch a television talk show you get the feeling that you are having a conversation with the guest. It feels spontaneous. When it is over, you feel like you have had a good visit."

"Ahh, you have just described a perfect direct examination. Give the jurors a good, informative visit with your witness and you will have done your job."

6.1 Introduction

Movies, television dramas, and books about trials rarely feature great direct examinations. A devastating cross-examination or closing argument is almost always the focus of every dramatic representation of a trial. You can buy books containing the powerful closing arguments made by legendary trial lawyers, but you will search the shelves in vain to find a book of great direct examinations.

Courtroom dramas often portray unexpected reversals of fortune or emotionally charged confrontation between the witness and the lawyer. In these scenes, an intense dramatic moment unfolds in the courtroom among the players assembled there. Such moments rarely occur in any trial, and almost never during direct examination. During a real-life direct examination, the drama, in a sense, is off-screen. The drama is in the story of past events being told by the witness. Meanwhile, the scene in the courtroom is a person sitting in a witness chair answering questions. The challenge of direct examination is to make this real-life courtroom scene an effective vehicle for telling about the off-scene events.

A trial lawyer's most essential skill is the ability to conduct effective direct examinations. No matter how mesmerizing and persuasive your opening statement, cross-examinations, and summation are, your case cannot succeed unless your witnesses tell your client's side of the story clearly.[1] The reality is that you will seldom have the opportunity to demolish a witness on cross-examination, and by the time you get to closing argument the case has probably been either won or lost long before.

Conducting a competent direct examination is far more difficult and complex than simply asking your witnesses to tell what they know. However, many inexperienced lawyers think it is easy and consequently they prepare and perform it poorly. Your task on direct examination is to control the flow of information from the witness to the jury in a way that ensures the jurors' understanding and enhances the witness's credibility. Every witness's testimony must be logical, understandable, and believable. And all of this must be achieved in an interview format.

When direct examination is performed effectively, it has the lively, conversational feel of a television talk show. The lawyer is not at center stage. Like the television talk show host who makes his guest look good, a good direct examiner makes the witness appear interesting, credible, and memorable. The spotlight is always focused on the witness. If a direct examination is conducted well, no one will remember the lawyer's role in it; they will only remember the witness and what the witness said. The lawyer is the host who makes sure that the witness's performance is a success and makes sure that the audience (the jury) feels that they have had a conversation with the star.

6.2 Organizing Direct Examination

As was true of the opening statement, preparing for a direct examination is a two-step process. You first must identify the substance of the direct, the facts you need to elicit from the witness. You separately must determine the organization of the exam that will best allow jurors to understand and be persuaded by the testimony of the witness.

---

1. In criminal cases where the defendant presents no evidence, this statement is, of course, inapplicable. In those cases, the defense lawyer must rely solely on her skills in cross-examination and persuasion.

To determine the substance of the direct, you should consider the following categories:

1) Facts the witness knows that can establish the legal elements of your cause of action, case or defense;

2) Facts the witness knows that support your factual story of this case—character, motive, plot, stakes, or theme;

3) Facts the witness knows that can rebut the legal elements on which your adversary bears the burden of proof;

4) Facts the witness knows that refute your adversary's factual story of the case; and

5) Facts the witness knows that significantly harm your case and are better disclosed and explained during direct examination than unveiled for the first time on cross.

Once you have listed the facts to be included in the direct, arrange the sequence of each witness's testimony carefully so that the jury will understand his story and how it fits into your theory of the case. Emphasize the most important facts. While chronological order usually is the most logical way to present facts, your witnesses are not bound to describe events in the order in which they occurred. If some other order of presentation will be more effective, organize your examination that way.

You should organize the sequence of the direct examination of each witness so that it begins and ends on a positive note. Remember the principles of primacy and recency[2] that apply to the sequence of each witness's testimony, as well as to the sequence of your opening statement, closing argument, and entire case. Questions accrediting your witness and a question foreshadowing the main purpose of the witness's testimony can serve to set the tone for the rest of the witness's story. When you reach the end of a direct examination, try to conclude with a climactic question and answer. If you must bring out unfavorable facts on direct examination, bury them somewhere in the middle. Have the witness frankly acknowledge the unfavorable facts, but do not emphasize them.

Each direct examination should be organized into the four segments that follow. You may emphasize different segments with different witnesses and embellish the basic outline with details that add interest and credibility to a witness's testimony, but the essential four segments should be present in each direct examination.

6.2.1 Introduce and Humanize the Witness

After asking the witness his name, elicit other special data about the witness that will cause jurors to like, respect, or identify with him. Do not allow witnesses to

---

2. *See* chapter five at 5.2.2.

launch into their stories immediately. Take time to ask each witness some questions calculated to put the jurors in a receptive frame of mind.

The jurors need to know why they should believe this witness. Before asking a witness to tell what he knows about the case, allow him to offer the jurors some personal information that will serve to enhance his credibility. For example, you should usually ask a police officer to describe her experience and training. A witness who is a solid, upright citizen should be given the opportunity to share some of his attributes with the jurors. Of course, you must establish the qualifications of any witness who will offer an expert opinion.[3]

But what if the witness is a despicable human being—one whose personal characteristics are thoroughly repulsive—a common thug with a criminal record as long as your arm? Can you personalize him? Of course not. You should still accredit this witness by asking any questions that support an inference that his testimony on this occasion should be believed. For example, if your witness is a habitual felon who happened to be in a particularly good place to observe the events of your case, bring out his proximity to the events and his ability to observe. Avoid eliciting personal information about him unless you know the opponent will bring it out on cross-examination. If there is something negative that will almost certainly come out on cross, bury it in the middle of your direct examination.

6.2.2 *Have the Witness Establish His Connection to the Case*

Once the jury has become acquainted with the witness, have the witness describe his connection to the case. Have him insert himself into your story. For instance, if he was an eyewitness to an accident, place him at the scene by asking, "Where were you at 3:00 p.m. on Thursday, August 18, 2014?"

6.2.3 *Have the Witness Describe the Scene*

A stage play has a set—an arrangement of objects on the stage and usually a painted backdrop. Why? To help the audience form visual images of the story being enacted. The impact of seeing the scene brings the oral drama to life. The scenery transforms the play from a mere reading into a true drama.

You have only limited ability to decorate a courtroom as you could a stage. Of course, you may use charts, photographs, diagrams, and other visual aids, and you should do so. But the fact remains that a trial is primarily an oral and aural experience. In other words, it is primarily based on what is said and heard. Therefore, you must use the testimony of your witnesses to create the visual images of what occurred by having them set the scene and paint a backdrop with their answers to your questions.

---

3. Fed. R. Evid. 702.

This segment of direct examination serves another purpose as well. It enhances the witness's credibility by demonstrating the specificity of his recollection. Do not simply ask, "Please describe the scene." You must ask narrowly focused questions about particular things. Specific questions such as "Were there traffic lights on the corner?" "How many?" and "Where were they?" give the witness the opportunity to show just how intricate his memory of the incident is. By describing the location precisely, the witness establishes the accuracy of his perception and recollection.

Charts, diagrams, enlarged photographs, or other visual aids can serve to reinforce the witness's testimony during this stage of direct examination. Looking at a picture or diagram of what the witness is describing will help the jurors form their mental pictures and understand the testimony.

6.2.4 Let the Witness Tell His Story

After you have provided a backdrop to the action, it is time to let the witness describe what took place. Your questions should encourage the witness to relate what he perceived simply, logically, and clearly. At this stage of direct examination, it is a good idea to think of yourself as the representative of the jury. The jurors' awesome task is to sort through the mass of evidentiary information with which they are bombarded. In some courtrooms and in one state, they are not allowed to ask questions and their role prior to deliberations is almost entirely passive. In other states—e.g., Arizona, Florida, Indiana, Iowa, Kentucky, Nevada, North Carolina—jurors are invited to ask witnesses questions.[4]

The practice of jurors asking questions remains controversial, but you should welcome it as an opportunity to gain insight into the jurors' thinking about the trial issues. You don't have to imagine what the jury wants to know. You still have to ask yourself what the jurors are curious about, but their questions will give you some big hints.

Appoint yourself the representative of the jury and ask the questions they would ask, before they request the judge to do so. Make yourself the person who gives them the information they need in order to make an informed and just decision in the case.

6.3 Performing Direct Examination

Evidence comes from witnesses, not lawyers. Direct examination is the witness's show. You are only an instrument whose function is to direct the jurors'

---

4. The procedure for jurors to ask questions may involve jurors submitting written questions to the judge or, in Indiana and Kentucky, asking questions themselves. In Pennsylvania and Michigan, the trial judge has discretion to allow jurors to ask questions. In Texas, jurors are not permitted to question witnesses in criminal trials. Jurors are prohibited from asking questions only in Mississippi.

attention toward the witness. Therefore, your demeanor and questions during direct examination must always focus the spotlight on your witness.

6.3.1 *Your Demeanor*

Make yourself inconspicuous. Get out of the way. Position yourself as near the far end of the jury box as you can, so the jurors will be between you and witness. From your position near the far end of the jury box, both you and your witness will have to speak loudly enough to hear each other. Because the jurors are between you, if you can hear each other the jurors will also be able to hear. Stand still. Do not pace; do not fidget; do not fiddle with a pen; do not jingle the change in your pocket. Project your voice so the jurors can hear your questions. Remind the witness to speak up when she speaks too softly to be heard clearly.

Give each witness your undivided attention. Fix your eyes on the witness so that when a juror's attention strays to you (as it inevitably will), your attentive attitude will direct that juror's mind back to the witness. Listen to the witness's answers and do not ask your next question while the witness is answering. If you watch and listen, the witness will lead you through the testimony, and each of your questions can be framed to follow logically from the witness's previous answer.

Act interested, as though you were hearing the witness's story for the first time. Your demeanor sets an example for the jurors. When you seem interested, you telegraph a subliminal message to them that your witness's testimony is important.

A word about notes is in order. You must use them in trial. No lawyer can try a case competently without them. You should prepare a set of notes pertaining to each witness. Many top lawyers write out all their questions; all have at least a checklist. However, no effective lawyer reads questions. To the listener, an effective direct examination seems to be an informal, spontaneous conversation between the witness and the lawyer. A conversation cannot appear spontaneous when one party reads his or her part.

Your demeanor on direct examination includes your state of mind. Before trial, you painstakingly organized the topics to be covered within each of the four segments of the direct examination. You shared your game plan with the witness and may have practiced this direct examination as part of your witness preparation. You must accept, however, that it is unlikely that you will be able to exert full control over the direct examination at trial. At any instant, your planned direct may be derailed by the answer of the witness, objection lodged by opposing counsel, or ruling of the judge. When the inevitable hiccup occurs, your focus must be entirely on creating a Plan B to get into evidence the testimony you need from the witness. At no time should you mentally bemoan how the witness, opposing counsel, or the judge has spoiled the perfection of the intended direct examination. If the jurors understood and were persuaded by the witness's testimony, you have done your job.

While you must always appear confident and in control, there are no additional "style points" awarded for how seamlessly you and the witness performed during this direct examination. You will be a more effective advocate and live a longer life if you accept the fact that direct examination is a messy business, the least controllable part of the trial, which will require you to remain calm, think, and adapt.

6.3.2 Your Questions

A trial lawyer must be able to formulate clear, concise questions that leave no doubt in anyone's mind exactly what information is sought. If you incorporate the following techniques, your questions will enable your witnesses to tell their stories in a way that will be compelling to the trier of fact.

Do not lead. Do not ask leading questions unless it is absolutely necessary. Federal Rule of Evidence 611(c) states, "Leading questions should not be used on the direct examination of a witness except as may be necessary to develop the witness' testimony." As is often the case, the law of evidence discourages what good judgment proscribes anyway. Leading on direct examination is usually ineffective as well as improper; witnesses are more believable when they tell their stories in their own words without prompting from a lawyer.

What is a leading question? Simply one that unduly suggests the answer desired. There is no bright line distinguishing leading from non-leading questions. The spectrum ranging from clearly leading to clearly non-leading questions contains many subtle shades. The court has wide discretion to decide how much leading to allow. Questions that are really statements in interrogatory form, merely seeking agreement from the witness, are clearly leading. Example: "You saw the shooting, didn't you?" Questions beginning with the words "did" or "was" may be leading if their content conveys to the witness the answer desired. Examples: "Was the man wearing a green shirt?" "Did the yellow car have the green light?" Questions beginning with the words "who," "what," "when," "where," "why," "how," "tell," "describe," and "explain" can almost never be made leading. You should strive to begin all of your direct examination questions with those words.

Ask short, specific questions. Evidence is more easily digested if it is taken in small bites. Therefore, ask precise, tightly crafted questions designed to elicit specific facts, and instruct your witnesses to answer them succinctly. Short, specific questions help to avoid ambiguity and confusion. They control the pace and flow of the examination.

Craft your questions so that they are neither too broad nor too narrow. Questions that are too narrow will unnecessarily prolong an examination. Questions that are too broad may draw an objection that a witness is testifying in an uninterrupted, narrative style.[5] These objections are often sustained. Aside from the fact that it may draw an objection, a witness's uninterrupted narrative is usually an ineffective way to present his testimony. Most witnesses simply are not articulate enough to testify coherently unless the examining lawyer draws out the testimony in digestible, bite-sized pieces.

The task of devising questions that are neither too broad nor too narrow requires you to do some strategic thinking about the pacing and emphasis of the examination. Generally, broad questions may be appropriate to move the testimony quickly through a topic. Narrow questions will slow the pace of the examination and put emphasis on the facts being discussed. Your decision about how narrowly to craft your questions will depend on what is important in the particular case. For example, if you are examining a police officer who responded to the scene of an accident, you may want to ask a few questions about the officer's training and experience to establish credibility. You might pose a broadly constructed question: "Officer, tell us about your background as a police officer." This question allows that officer to talk about a few of the highlights of her training. Next, you may need a series of questions that are somewhat more narrowly crafted to allow the officer to paint the scene of the accident for the jurors: "What was the weather like on that day?" "Who was already on the scene when you arrived?" The officer's answers to these questions may include some summary of events and some description. When you reach the most important and contested points, however, you do not want a summary. You want the most precise answers you can get. You will ask a series of very narrowly constructed questions: "When you arrived at the scene of the accident, where was the blue car?" "Which direction was it facing?" "Where was the driver of the blue car?" "What was the first thing the driver said to you?" These questions are designed to elicit specific information, one fact at a time.

The pattern of broad and narrow questions will vary from witness to witness. If, for example, your next witness is an expert in accident reconstruction, you will not breeze through the expert's background with one or two broadly constructed questions. Instead, you will emphasize the witness's expertise by asking narrowly crafted questions about the expert's credentials: "When did you become interested in accident reconstruction?" "Where did you attend school to study it?" "What kinds of courses did you have to take to learn accident reconstruction?" These narrow questions slow the pace of the examination and emphasize the credentials of the witness.

Before examining any witness, you should make sure you know exactly what information you need from him. Be sure to ask at least one question about each

---

5. It is difficult to prevent a witness testifying in the form of an uninterrupted narrative from blurting out inadmissible evidence. The court's authority to limit narrative testimony is found in its general power to control the mode and order of interrogation and presentation. *See* FED. R. EVID. 611(a).

point that you need to cover. If the information is very important, break it down into smaller pieces and ask about it using the most narrow questions.

Be conversational. A direct examination should not seem like an interrogation. It should be an informal conversation between the witness and the lawyer. Relax. Ask your questions as if the witness were a friend who recently returned from climbing Mount Everest. Imagine that you have just run into the friend at a cocktail party and are dying to hear all the details about the trip. Ask your questions of the witness as you would your questions of your peripatetic friend. Use ordinary words. For example—

Q: How was the weather up there?

A: It was really cold.

Q: How did you keep warm?

A: We wore these really heavy parkas and insulated snow boots . . . .

—is more effective than:

Q: Please describe the weather in that location.

A: It was really cold.

Q: What equipment did you employ to protect yourself from the cold?

A: We wore these really heavy parkas and insulated snow boots . . . .

Emphasize important facts. Every important fact is worth at least one question, and you can emphasize a fact's importance by asking several questions about it. Every question accentuates the fact's significance and affords the witness an additional opportunity to add rich detail to his testimony. For example, rather than asking, "Tell us what you saw when you arrived at the scene," you can ask, "When you opened the door, what did you see first?" If the witness answers, "I saw Joe standing over Jim holding a smoking gun," you can emphasize that fact by asking a number of follow-up questions. "How was Joe standing?" "What kind of expression did he have on his face?" "Which hand was he holding the gun in?" "Tell us about the gun."

Use uninterrupted narrative—sometimes. Despite what we said earlier about the general ineffectiveness of the uninterrupted narrative, an occasional witness, usually an experienced expert, has the ability to spellbind her listeners. Such a witness is able to tell the tale more effectively when uninterrupted by questions. When you are fortunate enough to have such a witness, you can allow her to deliver a lecture on her subject of expertise with powerful effect. For example, an orthopedic surgeon who is also an experienced expert witness might stand before the jurors, preferably with a demonstrative aid such as a plastic skeleton, and explain exactly how a plaintiff was injured and how those injuries have affected him. When you are able to use this technique, you simply give the witness the opportunity to speak, get out of the way, and look interested.

Use repetition. Repetition is a powerful tool. The more we hear something, the more likely that it will sear its way into our minds. That is why we are bombarded with the same television advertisements over and over again, ad nauseum. That is why politicians endlessly repeat the same tired slogans.

Because repetition of the same evidence may sway the jury, your opponent may object to repetitive testimony. A common way of phrasing the objection is, "Objection. Asked and answered." Federal Rule of Evidence 403 and state evidence rules authorize the court to sustain the objection if the evidence is "unnecessarily cumulative."[6] Note the important word "unnecessarily." The rule does not say that evidence may be mentioned only once. It vests discretion in the court to determine when repetition has become unnecessary.

On the other hand, excessive repetition by one witness may weaken that witness's credibility. By overemphasizing a fact, the witness may telegraph a message to the jurors that he is unsure of its veracity. Repetition is more effective if the evidence is repeated by different witnesses. Nevertheless, it is often effective to ask a witness to repeat a key answer at the conclusion of direct examination in case some jurors may have missed it the first time. Example: "Finally, Ms. Davis, would you please tell us again which hand the defendant was holding the gun in?" This question may draw an "asked and answered" objection, but so what? If you have conducted a clean direct examination and have avoided wearing the judge and jury out with needless reiteration, the objection will probably only make the objector appear cantankerous and may even serve to underscore the importance of the answer.[7]

Another way to repeat important information without drawing an "asked and answered" objection is to pick up and loop important information into your next question. For example, if your witness says, "He was holding a gun in his left hand," your next question might be, "Did you notice anything about the gun in his left hand?" Or you might also ask, "Why did you notice that the gun was in the left hand as opposed to the right?" During the questioning of this witness, you can probably think of five or six ways to repeat the information that the witness saw the gun in the left hand without asking a question that has already been answered. If you do not overuse this technique, it will not be obvious or tiresome to jurors and will not draw an objection.

---

6. Fed. R. Evid. 403.
7. You should be judicious in using the "asked and answered" objection. Many judges are loath to sustain it unless the accumulation has clearly become needless. Even if the judge keeps a tight rein on repetition, the objection often sounds rude—merely an annoying interruption of a witness's attempt to tell her story.

National Institute for Trial Advocacy

Responding to objections. In the early years of your trial practice, you probably come to the courtroom with the vague feeling that everyone there knows more than you. When some question you ask draws an objection your immediate reaction is to think, "Oh, my God! I got an objection. I must have screwed up." The natural reaction is to either withdraw the question or offer to rephrase. Meanwhile the judge sits there, having never been given the opportunity to rule on the objection, and thinks, "What a groundless objection! I would have overruled it if I'd only been given the chance."

The point is, of course, not to assume that your opponent is right. When you draw an objection, do not just give in. Stand there and give the judge an opportunity to rule. Remember that the law of evidence invests the trial judge with enormous discretion. Whenever you draw an objection, you stand a fifty-fifty chance of its being overruled.

If the judge looks to you for a response, make one. Be sure to respond to the ground upon which the objection was based. Too often have we heard, "Objection, Your Honor, that's irrelevant," followed by the response, "Your Honor, that statement was an excited utterance." The objection was based on relevance; the response was based on an exception to the hearsay rule.

Many times judges rule on objections immediately without giving you an opportunity to respond. When this happens to you, if the evidence you are eliciting is important and you feel that you have a good argument for its admissibility, you should say to the judge, "Your Honor, may I be heard on that point?" That statement will alert the judge that you have an important issue. You are entitled to be heard. Every judge will allow you to present your argument. After all, judges do not like to commit error and hearing your argument may prevent a reversal.

When your opponent's objection is sustained, do not react. Do not sigh, frown, or look disappointed. Most importantly, do not apologize for having asked the question. Just go on to another question as if nothing had happened. After all, some jurors will not be paying attention during the boring exchange of objection and response and others probably do not know the difference between "sustained" and "overruled."

If the judge sustained an objection on the ground that the form of your question was leading, do not move on to the next topic of your planned examination. Unless you have been abusing the rule against leading questions, opposing counsel will not have objected unless the answer to the question is important and harmful to her case. By sustaining the objection, the judge did not rule that the information you are seeking is inadmissible, merely that you must rephrase this question. That is exactly what you should do. Re-ask the same question, beginning with "who," "what," "when," "where," "why," "how," "tell," describe," or "explain."

If the court sustained the objection on the ground that the question called for inadmissible evidence and the evidence was so important to your case that exclusion could constitute reversible error, you must take an additional step to preserve that error for appeal. To reverse a judgment due to an evidentiary ruling, the court of appeals must find not only that the trial court's evidence ruling was wrong, but also that exclusion of the evidence was prejudicial error.[8] To determine whether the error was prejudicial, the court of appeals needs to know what the witness's answer would have been if the court had not sustained the objection.

When the objection is sustained, the direct examiner must make an offer of proof, informing the court—and equally importantly the court reporter—of the substance of the witness's excluded answer.[9] This is typically done by asking to approach sidebar and, outside the hearing of the jurors, indicating you are making an offer of proof—not re-arguing the court's ruling—and stating the substance of the evidence the court has just excluded.[10]

6.3.3 *Handling a Witness's Problems on the Stand*

Despite all of your meticulous pretrial preparation, some witnesses will present problems during their direct examinations. Others will be unable to remember things they said before trial. Some, though their memories are perfectly sound, will be unable to recount precise details about the things they observed. Some will change their stories, either through honest mistake or treachery. Finally, there will be witnesses who are antagonistic toward you or your client. Each of these witnesses poses unique problems to the lawyer conducting direct examination. Fortunately, the law provides us with specifically sanctioned methods of dealing with these problems.

The Witness Who Forgets. Have you ever seen an old friend at a reunion but were unable to recall her name? You agonize over it, knowing that you should remember, but for some reason your memory is simply blank. Then you look at the list of names in the program and see one that immediately causes the floodgates of memory to reopen. It all comes back to you in a flash. The friend's name is again as fresh in your memory as it ever was. Seeing her name in the program served to recharge the battery of your memory. The law has long recognized that witnesses sometimes need something to jog their memories. Consequently, the law allows you to show a witness anything that will serve that purpose.[11] The document or object you show the witness does not become evidence; it serves merely as the jumper cable to recharge the witness's run-down memory.

The predicate for refreshing recollection is the witness's testimony that she cannot remember. Once she has said she cannot remember, you simply show the witness

---

8. *See* FED. R. EVID. 103(a) ("A party may claim error in a ruling to admit or exclude evidence only if the error affects a substantial right of the party . . .").
9. FED. R. EVID. 103(a)(2).
10. In rare instances, the court may dismiss the jury and require you to present the offer of proof by questioning the witness in the manner of an ordinary direct examination. *See* FED. R. EVID. 103(c).
11. *See* United States v. Rappy, 157 F.2d 964, 967 (2d Cir. 1946).

the document or thing, allow her to examine it, take it back, and have the witness continue testifying based on her now-refreshed memory.

Here is a brief example:

Q: Who did you see at the reunion?

A: I saw the guy who was president of our class.

Q: What is his name?

A: Hmm . . . I just can't remember.

Q: Might it help you remember if you looked at a list of the people who were at the reunion?

A: I'm sure it would.

[*At this point, you should show opposing counsel the document you are about to use to refresh.*[12]]

Q: Your Honor, may I approach the witness?[13]

[*Permission is granted and the lawyer approaches.*]

Q: Take a look at this document and then tell me if you can remember the class president's name.

[*Witness examines list.*]

A: Okay, I remember now. [*Lawyer takes the list back.*]

Q: What is his name?

A: His name is Allen Alford.

The Witness Whose Memory Cannot Be Refreshed. Assume for a moment that your witness suffers from amnesia and can no longer remember an event she observed. Or assume that your witness is a CPA testifying about specific figures contained in a set of financial statements. Each of these cases presents a similar problem: No matter what you show the witness, she will remain unable to answer your questions fully

---

12. FED. R. EVID. 612 provides that when you use a document to refresh memory while the witness is testifying, the "adverse party is entitled to have the writing produced at the hearing, to inspect it, to cross-examine the witness about it, and to introduce into evidence any portion that relates to the witness' testimony."

13. Note that in this example we have not marked the exhibit for identification. Many people believe that every document produced at trial, whether introduced or not, must be marked for identification. Others believe that items that are not to be introduced should not be marked. Those who do not mark non-evidentiary documents feel that the absence of an exhibit number is insurance against an inadmissible document's being inadvertently introduced. In a complex trial, documents floating around the courtroom with identification numbers on them sometimes have a way of finding their way into the evidence pile and may end up in the jury room. On this topic we can only advise you to use your best judgment, and most importantly, learn what the judge requires and do it.

and completely based upon her present recollection. The amnesia victim's memory is erased. The CPA, although her memory is fine, simply cannot testify from memory about so many specific numbers contained in the financial statements. Likewise, an inventory-taker will not be able to remember the item number of each product on the shelves; a physician may not be able to remember the details of a regimen of treatment; a police officer will not be able to remember the vehicle identification number of the stolen car.

Using documents to refresh the memory of witnesses such as these rarely works. To refresh the CPA's memory by presenting each line of the financial statement to her, and having her testify to it from her temporarily refreshed recollection, would take forever. It would be completely unrealistic to expect the police officer to memorize vehicle identification numbers.

Fortunately, the law provides a tool that enables us to present this testimony to the jurors despite the witness's inability to remember. If the witness accurately wrote a memorandum containing the information while it was still fresh in her memory, we are allowed to use that memorandum as substitute evidence for the witness's present recollection.[14] However, we are allowed only to have the witness read from the document; we may not introduce the document into evidence. This limitation arises from the realization that the document, if introduced, might carry more weight than the witness's testimony would have carried if she had been able to remember.

The elements of the foundation that must be laid before reading from the document that records recollection are:

1) The witness once had personal knowledge of the matter;

2) The witness cannot testify fully and accurately to the matter from present recollection;

3) The witness made or adopted a memorandum or other record of the matter when the matter was still fresh in the witness's memory; and

4) The writing correctly reflected the witness's knowledge.

---

14. Such a memorandum, because it was made out of court and is offered for its truth, is hearsay. Therefore, the rule that allows us to use it is an exception to the hearsay rule. Federal Rule of Evidence 803(5) provides:

> The following are not excluded by the rule against hearsay, regardless of whether the declarant is available as a witness: . . .
> (5) **Recorded Recollection.** A record that:
> > (A) is on a matter the witness once knew about but now cannot recall well enough to testify fully and accurately;
> > (B) was made or adopted by the witness when the matter was fresh in the witness's memory; and
> > (C) accurately reflects the witness's knowledge.
> If admitted, the record may be read into evidence but may be received as an exhibit only if offered by an adverse party.

National Institute for Trial Advocacy

The scenario will unfold something like this:

Q: Officer Lawrence, what was the vehicle identification number of the car the defendant was driving?

A: I can't remember.

Q: Did you write it down?

A: Yes, I did.

Q: When?

A: Right there at the scene. Right after I placed the defendant in the squad car.

Q: Did you prepare an official report of this investigation?

A: Yes, sir.

Q: Do you have that report with you?

A: Yes. This is it, right here.

Q: Did you record that vehicle identification number in that report?

A: Yes, sir.

Q: Is the number you wrote down and later included in your report accurate?

A: Yes.

Q: Officer, if you looked at your report, could you then tell us the number from memory?

A: No. It's too long.

Q: Officer Lawrence, please read the vehicle identification number from your report.

A: 597824GWF2042CG11-43.

It should be obvious that the technique of refreshing recollection, where the witness testifies from memory after having her memory refreshed, is quite similar to the technique of reading from a recorded recollection when the witness's memory cannot be refreshed. In practice, the two techniques are often used interchangeably and no formal distinction is drawn. Doctors, police officers, accountants, and other professional witnesses routinely bring their records to the witness stand with them. Everyone in the courtroom knows that they cannot testify fully and accurately without referring to those records. Usually, no one objects and the witnesses look at their notes without formal foundation. Nevertheless, when an objection is made you will need to know the difference between the two techniques and the subtle differences in the foundation questions each requires.

The Witness Who Changes Her Story. What if your witness, rather than testifying that she cannot remember, testifies differently than she did when she gave an earlier statement? When asked if she remembers, she confidently answers yes. But you know that she has it wrong—or at least that she said something different when she gave a previous statement. This different story may be an innocent mistake or you may have a turncoat witness on your hands.

You cannot refresh recollection or read past recollection recorded because there is no evidence that the witness cannot remember. In this situation, you are permitted to impeach the witness with her prior inconsistent statement.[15] Before you impeach your own witness, however, consider the possibility that you or your witness may be confused. Are you on the same page? Are you both thinking about the same time, date, or event? Think through your last few questions. Did you misstate something? Make sure that the context and content of your question were understood. You may need to clarify your question or go back to an earlier question and revise it. Sometimes you can put a witness back on track by asking a leading question or two. Even if the questions draw an objection, they will have served their purpose if they correct a witness's honest mistake. Most of the time, what appears as a "new" story or a loss of memory about an important event is really just an honest mistake. Jurors can easily forgive the witness who says, "Oh, I'm sorry. Were you asking about the second meeting between me and Mr. Jones? That changes my answer."

If the witness does, indeed, have a new story, this is where the rule that allows you to impeach your own witness may come in handy.[16] To be sure, when the witness has made an innocent mistake, you should impeach her gently and in a friendly manner. Unlike hostile impeachment conducted during cross-examination, where you should never give the witness an opportunity to explain the inconsistency, when dealing with a friendly, but mistaken witness, you should generally give him an opportunity to explain the difference between his testimony and his previous statement.

When dealing with a friendly witness, the major distinction between refreshing recollection and impeachment is whether the witness testifies to a loss of memory. If so, the technique is refreshing; if not, it is impeachment.

Adverse and Hostile Witnesses. The general rule that requires you to ask non-leading questions on direct examination is premised on the assumption that the

---

15. Other forms of impeachment are also permissible under Rule 607. The form most often used is impeachment for bias. Obviously, you would use bias to impeach only the turncoat witness, not the innocently mistaken one. Impeachment with a prior inconsistent statement is by far the most common tool utilized pursuant to Rule 607.

16. Fed. R. Evid. 607.

witnesses you call to the stand will be friendly to you, or at least neutral. When a witness demonstrates hostility toward you, the rule is reversed—you may then examine the witness with leading questions.[17] If you choose to call the opposing party and witnesses "identified with an adverse party"[18] during your portion of the case, they are presumed to be hostile and you may examine them with leading questions even if they do not exhibit hostility on the stand.

When should you call the defendant as an adverse witness in a civil case? The answer is that you usually should not. However, there is no more powerful piece of evidence than a devastating admission elicited from the defendant. Such an admission will have greater impact if presented as part of your case, rather than on cross-examination later in the trial. Therefore, you might decide to call the defendant when—and only when—you are absolutely certain that you can elicit that dynamite piece of evidence. That means that you must have the admission in a prior statement of the witness so that you can impeach him if he does not acknowledge it.

Calling an adverse witness is dangerous for another reason: you may open the door to a full-scale examination of the witness on "cross-examination" by his own lawyer, thus allowing him to tell his entire story during your case presentation. Whether the lawyer gets to do this is up to the judge. The court has authority to allow interrogation of a witness beyond the scope of direct examination in the interests of time or efficiency.[19] To avoid this dreadful result, you must tailor your questions carefully, only examining the witness to the extent necessary to bring out the admission. It is a good idea to let the judge know your plan and seek assurance that the court will limit the cross-examination to the scope of direct.

6.3.4 Some Specific Techniques

Headline your witness's testimony.[20] A newspaper headline enables readers to discern at a glance what the article that follows will be about. It also serves to mold opinion by emphasizing one ingredient of the story over others. You can "headline" each witness's testimony by asking a question early in the examination that allows the witness to state the essential fact you want the jurors to remember. When a witness prefaces her testimony with a headline, the jurors learn immediately why you called the witness and they are more likely to understand the significance of the facts the witness relates. For example, immediately after an eyewitness identifies himself and before you accredit him and place him at the scene of an accident, you can ask, "Did you see an accident at Fifth and Main last July 8?" His affirmative answer lets the jurors know why you called this witness to the stand and what his testimony will

---

17. FED. R. EVID. 611 (c).
18. *Id.* People who are "identified with an adverse party" might include the opposing party, his family, business partners, employees, and close associates.
19. *See* FED. R. EVID. 611(a).
20. This technique is sometimes referred to as "foreshadowing."

concern. After presenting the headline, you can backtrack, accredit the witness, and elicit the details of the facts he observed.

Be sure to prepare your witness to expect a headline question and to respond with only a one-sentence, general answer. An unprepared witness may launch into a rambling narrative in response to your general question that will lessen the impact of her testimony.

Put up direction signs. Imagine yourself driving in a strange city looking for an address. What if there were no direction signs or street markers? To locate your destination would be well-nigh impossible. So it is with direct examination. The jurors are like drivers trying to negotiate the unfamiliar streets of each witness's testimony. Even a simple story is difficult to follow on a single hearing. Without direction signs, the jurors are likely to become hopelessly lost.

To help jurors find their way, you should make directional statements when you come to intersections in the testimony. Whenever the witness's story changes from topic to topic or moves from place to place, let the jurors know where you are going. Although you generally may not lead witnesses, you may certainly direct their attention to the next topic or location. These simple statements are helpful to the jury, the witness, and the court. For example, when you have completed accrediting a witness, you can say, "Now let me direct your attention to the evening of July 6, 2014. Where were you at 8:00 that evening?" Or, you can lay out the direction of the examination even more explicitly for the jurors by adding a brief introductory sentence before you begin a line of questioning. For example, after your witness has testified that his brakes malfunctioned and he collided with the blue car, you can say, "I am going to ask you about the collision in detail in a moment. But first, I want to ask you some questions about the brakes."

Focus your and the witness's attention to the jury. Throughout the trial, your focus must be on the jurors. Consider them your friends. Your every action should be calculated to help them receive the information they need to resolve the case in your client's favor. In a jury trial, the jury—not the court—is your audience.

Your choice of words can help to create the impression that you and the jurors are all in this thing together and that you are trying to help them find their way through the thicket. By merely using the first person plural, you can delicately and indirectly suggest that you and the jurors are one. "Tell us . . ." places you in the jury box as a "thirteenth juror," seeking the same information as the rest.

Direct examinations can easily turn into private conversations between the witness and the lawyer. You must avoid this by constantly reminding yourself that you and the witness are on stage, relating the story for an audience—the jurors. Occasionally preface a question with "Tell the jurors . . ." or "Could you explain to the jurors . . . ." Such introductory phrases serve two purposes: They remind the witness that she is talking to the jurors and they reinforce the impression that you, the examiner, are endeavoring to provide the jurors with needed data. Note that we suggested that you use the phrase "Tell the jurors . . . ," not "Tell the court . . . ."

Anticipate cross-examination. If your witness is subject to being impeached with something like a prior conviction, a prior inconsistent statement, or bias and you are sure the cross-examiner will raise it, you should bring that matter out during direct examination. This technique is often referred to as "drawing the sting." Such negative information will probably be less damaging if the witness admits it forthrightly during direct examination. It will still damage the witness's credibility; it will just hurt less. If you do not bring it out but your opponent does, it will appear that the witness tried to hide the matter. Even worse, the jurors may think that you tried to keep the information from them. The opposing lawyer then seems to be a hero when she brings out the evidence on cross-examination.

You should not use this technique indiscriminately. A cross-examiner's questions on a subject not closely relevant to the present case, even though they are evidentially proper and embarrassing to the witness, may have the net effect of arousing sympathy for the witness. Therefore, do not anticipate the cross-examiner's questions unless you are reasonably certain that the matter will be raised and that, when raised, it will significantly diminish the witness's believability. If you conclude that the cross-examination will be perceived as a cheap shot, do not raise the subject on direct.

When you decide to reveal negative information during direct examination, mention it off-handedly; do not dwell on it. Because of the principle of primacy (that people tend to believe what they hear first[21]), you should elicit all of the witness's favorable testimony before bringing out the harmful information. Because of the principle of recency (that people tend to remember that which they hear last[22]), you should not end with the harmful information. Bring it up near the end of the witness's direct testimony, but do not make it the last question and answer.

Use illustrative aids.[23] People receive impressions through the five senses: sight, hearing, touch, smell, and taste. Despite the fact that a trial by its very nature is an essentially oral and aural experience, you should incorporate exhibits and techniques that appeal to the other four senses at every opportunity. The more senses you can touch in telling your story, the greater the likelihood that you will get your point across effectively. Any time you can employ a photograph, diagram, sound or video recording, or physical object to help your witness describe persons, places, or events, you should do so. Never forget the old adage that a picture is worth a thousand words.

––––––––––––––

21. *See* chapter five at n. 9.
22. *Id.*
23. *See* chapter ten, *infra*.

Get the witness out of the witness chair. A trial can get awfully boring. It is difficult to remain alert throughout hours, days, or even weeks of listening to people talk. One after another, witnesses sit in the witness box and relate their stories. You should seize every opportunity to relieve the boredom by getting your witnesses out of that box and moving them around the courtroom as they testify.[24] Physical demonstrations can sometimes be effective means of moving witnesses around. You can also have a witness stand in front of the jury box while pointing out things on an exhibit.

The point here is to "show and tell." Be sure to position the witness and the exhibit where the jurors can see them well. Most judges do not care whether they can see the exhibit from the bench and, if curious, will move to a place where they can see. However, some judges are sticklers for making lawyers place everything where their view from the bench is unobstructed.[25] Be sure you know the judge's preference before you begin moving witnesses and objects around.

Once you have your witness in place, hopefully directly in front of the jury box, position yourself where you can question the witness, but not between the jurors and the witness. Then just stand still, ask your questions, and let the witness teach the jury. Finally, do not forget to have the witness return to the witness box. Finish the examination with the witness comfortably seated and ready for cross-examination.

---

24. Of course, you must use some discretion. You obviously cannot do this with every minor witness, and some witnesses are so inarticulate that they are best confined to the box. And as a general rule, you should never get a witness out of the box during cross-examination. You do not need any loose cannons rolling around on your deck.

25. Whether opposing counsel can see is not your concern. But when you are opposing counsel and your opponent sets up an illustrative aid in a place where you cannot see, you should ask the court's permission to move to a place where you can see what is going on. Remember that you have an absolute right to see and hear everything that goes on in the courtroom. Do not be shy about asserting that right.

CHAPTER SEVEN

CROSS-EXAMINATION

Today she was tired and struggled to listen to the testimony of the defense expert. She wanted to go home. She took notes anyway. After the jurors left, she sighed and started putting her notes into her briefcase. As she did so, her partner asked, "So, what are you going to do in your cross-examination tomorrow?"

"I'm going to ask him if he really expects us to believe all he said today. Then I'm going to cite some authorities that make him look like a fool."

"Are you sure that's the best course?"

"I think it is. What would you do?"

"I noticed that he said some things that agree with our version of the case. He also cited some of the same authorities our expert uses. And he worked from facts provided by the defendant—which were incomplete. I don't think the jury thought this guy was a fool. They liked him. Why not use his cross-examination to build our case?"

7.1 Introduction

Cross-examination is a dangerous and difficult part of the trial lawyer's repertoire. Done poorly it can lose your case. Rarely will a single cross-examination win your case. But rarely will you be able to win a case without a single cross-examination. Cross-examination is a necessary skill, and, done effectively, it can affirmatively advance your factual story of the case.

While rife with the potential for disaster with every question, cross-examination of the lay witness arguably is the easiest of all the trial skills. This is particularly true if the cross-examiner resists the natural temptation to explore uncharted waters and instead restricts questioning to answers unambiguously documented through informal and formal pretrial discovery. The properly prepared and executed cross-examination guarantees that each question results in either 1) the witness admitting fact sought by the question or, equally valuably, 2) impeaching the witness who dares to deny that fact.

Before conducting each cross-examination, the advocate first must determine the purpose(s) (section 7.2) and demeanor (section 7.3) of the particular cross-examination as well as craft the organizational structure of the cross (section 7.4). All the techniques utilized while conducting the cross-examination (sections 7.5-7.9) are animated by a single aim: to control the witness, who will exploit every opportunity to repeat and reinforce his direct examination testimony.

7.2 Identify the Purpose(s) of the Cross-Examination

Effective cross-examination is not done on the spur of the moment. Before trial, you must decide which points to cover and the order in which you intend to cover them. You must thoroughly familiarize yourself with each witness's deposition and/ or other pretrial statements. As you review the statements, identify important points you might want to bring out at trial.

The first task of the advocate is to identify the purpose(s) of the particular cross-examination. Every question in the examination must be consistent with and contribute to the legal and factual theory you selected for the case. You should not question the adverse witness to elicit facts that would support an alternative factual story of the case or to display your mastery of the art of cross-examination by gratuitously attacking the witnesses.

Thoroughness characterizes all successful men.
Genius is the art of taking infinite pains.
All great achievement has been characterized by extreme care,
infinite painstaking, even to the minutest detail.

—Elbert Hubbard

All the legendary cross-examiners of television and of movies had a common purpose. Perry Mason never delivered a closing argument; every trial ended by a confession extracted during one of Mason's cross-examinations. His cross-examinations were so powerful that the confessor was not the witness, but an observer of the trial overcome at a distance by the sheer force of Mason's questioning. Tom Cruise's cross-examination of Jack Nicholson in *A Few Good Men* ended in Nicholson being led from the witness stand in handcuffs. After shouting at Cruise that he "could not handle the truth," Nicholson confessed to issuing the "Code Red" on Private Santiago that led to Santiago's death. Even Reese Witherspoon's fumbling cross-examination in *Legally Blonde* caused Chutney Windham to confess to shooting her father and induced the court to *sua sponte* order dismissal of murder charges against Brooke Taylor Windham.

Although each of these media cross-examinations sought to attack the credibility of the witness (or others), destroying credibility is but one of four possible purposes of any chapter of a cross-examination.

7.2.1 Purpose One: Constructive Cross-Examination

Novice trial lawyers often approach cross-examination as if they were wielding chain saws. They assume that every witness must be impeached and they attack every witness's credibility with a vengeance. Though there is certainly a place for destructive cross-examination, many witnesses should not be impeached. Most witnesses are honest people who happen to know something relevant to a case and who have been subpoenaed to relate that information to the jury. They do not lie and their veracity cannot be successfully challenged. However, you can often accomplish goals other than impeachment during cross-examination.

You should first consider whether the witness you are crossing will admit any facts that are favorable to your client's theory of the case. Cross-examination may be used constructively to bring out facts that support a legal element, facts that support portions of your factual story of the case: character, motive, plot, or stakes, and/or facts that support the theme of the case.[1] You should review pleadings, discovery responses, and other pretrial statements of the witness for the following three categories of facts:

1) Facts the witness knows and admits *did occur* that are helpful to the character, motive, plot, or stakes of your story of the case.

2) Facts the witness knows and admits *did not occur*, whose non-occurrence is consistent with the plot of your story of the case.

3) Facts as to which the witness does not know whether or not they occurred. The adverse witness's inability to repudiate facts favorable to your story may cause the jurors to find that those helpful facts are true. Likewise, the adverse witness's inability to affirm facts harmful to your story may lead jurors to conclude those facts are not true. You should be mindful that judges have varying tolerance of these lines of cross-examination.

Cross-examination also can help persuade the jury to accept your theory of the case by extracting admissions that undermine the adversary's legal elements, factual theory, and/or theme. You may be able to use cross-examination constructively to establish a foundation for testimony or documents that you will present through another witness. Or you may be able to gather information from this witness that discredits another of your opponent's witnesses or that reflects favorably on one of your witnesses. In sum, before you set out to destroy a witness's credibility through cross-examination, think carefully about ways in which this witness might help your case.

---

1. As discussed in chapter two, plaintiff's counsel or the prosecution cannot rely solely on cross-examination of defense witnesses to establish an element of the prima facie case. *See* Fed. R. Civ. P. 50(a); Fed. R. Crim. P. 29(a); Pa. R. Civ. P. 224 and 230.1; Pa. R. Crim. P. 1124. The ability to bring out favorable facts on cross-examination may be somewhat limited by the requirement that cross-examination be within the scope of direct examination. *See* Fed. R. Evid. 611(b); Pa. R. Evid. 611(b).

7.2.2 Purpose 2: "Thank You for Your Honest, Albeit Mistaken" Cross-Examination

Most witnesses called by your opponent will present some evidence that is potentially damaging to your case. If you contend that the witness is wrong about that evidence, you should have a theory in mind that explains why the witness is wrong. Before resorting to a destructive cross, consider why the witness may be mistaken rather than lying. Perhaps the witness lacks sufficient knowledge or information to have properly understood the facts or events in their true context. A witness may be perfectly honest and observant, but may still be mistaken in what he believes because of limited contextual knowledge. Perhaps the witness had insufficient opportunity to observe the events. Think about the factors that may have affected the witness's ability to perceive. Was the witness upset or in a rush when the events took place? The witness also may harbor a mistaken recollection. Were the events or details so unimportant to the witness that the witness is unlikely to remember them accurately, especially if he never gave a formal statement at the time? Or, did the witness have some bias or prejudice that caused him to reach an honest but inaccurate conclusion about what he observed? Jurors know that perfectly honest people make mistakes. Jurors are willing to acknowledge that a witness's perception, interpretation, or memory of an event may be flawed in some respects, even if the witness is testifying honestly.

7.2.3 Purpose 3: Destructive Cross-Examination

Like Perry Mason, Tom Cruise, and Reese Witherspoon, you may use cross-examination to give the jury a basis for concluding that the witness is lying due to bias, prior conviction, prior inconsistent statements, prior bad acts, or the witness's bad character for truthfulness.[2] While a mainstay of television and movie trials, you should consider the destructive cross-examination to be a last resort rather than your default move. Keep in mind that the destructive cross requires the jury to accept that the witness chose to commit a felony—perjury—under the plain gaze of the judge in the courtroom.

Jurors are aware that people sometimes lie. But, generally, people do not lie unless they have an emotional or financial investment in the issue. If you contend that the witness is lying, think about why the witness would lie. What is motivating the witness to give false testimony? Does he have something to gain or something to hide? Is the witness motivated by an emotional tie; by previous experiences; by pride, prejudice, bias, or corruption? If you do not have a clear picture in your own mind about why this witness is lying, you will not be able to convince the jurors on that point.

During cross-examination, you are unlikely to be able to get a witness to admit to a mistake or a lie. Sometimes it happens. It feels great when it does. But admission

---

2. *See* FED. R. EVID. 608, 609, and 613; PA. R. EVID. 608, 609, and 613.

and confession are not the bread and butter of cross-examination. Your job on cross-examination is not to convince the witness that he may be mistaken, or to squeeze out a confession to a lie. Instead, your job is to show the jurors the reasons why the witness is mistaken or lying. As more fully discussed in section 7.9, your task is to elicit evidence that creates the basis for an inference of mistake or lie. The jurors will conclude for themselves that the witness's testimony should not be believed.[3]

7.2.4 Purpose 4: The "Really?" Cross-Examination

Some cross-examiners try to discredit a witness by affecting an overtly skeptical tone, taking the witness back over the direct examination testimony and asking, in essence, "Really?"

Q: Mr. Robertson, you testified on direct examination that you were having breakfast with the defendant at Fay's Country Kitchen at 6:00 a.m. on July 20, the day and time the victim was killed.

A: That is correct.

Q: You would have the jury believe that you remember the exact date, time, and place of that breakfast?

A: Yes.

Q: Do you realize that you are under oath?

A: I do.

Q: Let me give you one more chance, then. Are you willing to state under oath that you were having breakfast with the defendant at Fay's on the day and time the victim was murdered?

A: I am and I do.

Q: I have no further use for this witness, Your Honor.

You never should use cross-examination to review the direct examination in the usually futile hope that the witness will change the story or that the jurors will disbelieve the testimony. As next discussed, the jurors' sympathy will lie with the witness, not the lawyer. The "Really?" cross-examination merely reminds the jurors of the direct examination testimony and diminishes your credibility in their eyes.

If you have nothing to establish by cross-examining a witness, you should ask no questions. Though it is difficult to make yourself do, the best cross-examination sometimes is to say, "No questions." If a witness has hurt your position badly and

---

3. It is important to remember that evidence supporting an inference that the witness is mistaken or lying (impeachment evidence) does not have to be introduced exclusively during cross-examination. It may be introduced through other witnesses and documents. *See* chapter eight.

you have nothing to impeach her with, the best strategy may be to get her off the stand and out of the courtroom as quickly as possible. If a witness has not hurt you, there is usually no need to cross-examine unless there is some favorable fact you need to bring out through the witness's testimony. To forego cross-examination communicates to the jurors that you consider the witness's testimony unimportant.

7.3   Do Not Be Inappropriately Cross on Cross-Examination

7.3.1 Be Firm but Courteous

The purpose of the particular cross-examination dictates your demeanor during that cross. Given the general ban on the use of leading questions, there is nothing inherently direct about direct examination. In the same vein, the term cross-examination (perhaps more accurately understood as the "second" examination) does not demand that you approach the adversary's witness with hostility. You always must adopt a sufficiently firm—which is not synonymous with antagonistic—demeanor to maintain control over the witness. However, if the purpose of the cross is constructive or "thank you for your honesty, albeit mistaken," displaying verbal or non-verbal behavior suggesting the witness is lying is inconsistent with your goal.

Lawyers should be professionals. Mind your manners and be courteous to the witness. You will score more points if you treat witnesses with respect during cross-examination than if you bludgeon them. As you begin to cross-examine, every juror will probably identify with the witness. You start in the position of a potential bully, with the helpless witness as your intended victim. The jury considers you to be a smart, wily interrogator, at home in the courtroom setting, armed with a formidable bag of tricks. No matter that you really are trembling in terror and at that moment would trade your law degree for a reprieve from the ordeal facing you. Laypersons think we have the advantage and that the witness is helpless in our hands—at least, they subconsciously feel that way when cross-examination begins. You must remain unfailingly courteous during cross-examination to command and retain the high ground of rapport with the jurors. If the witness gives sarcastic answers, becomes angry, avoids answering your questions, or otherwise fails to respond in kind to your civility, the jury's support will be likely to shift toward you. Never mistreat a witness.

You should, however, allow the manner and words of your questions to reflect your theory of that examination. Your tone with a witness you contend is a liar and a child molester will be different than your tone with a sweet, old grandmother who you contend could not see the events clearly. Occasionally, when you are quite certain that due to the substance of the answers and the attitude of the witness the jurors have nothing but contempt for the witness in the box, you can allow yourself a little controlled, righteous anger.

7.3.2 Where to Stand? Take Center Stage

Unlike your direct examination, during which you should strive to keep the jury's attention directed toward the witness, your cross-examination should focus the spotlight on yourself. One way of capturing the jurors' attention is to stand at center stage, at a point in front of the center of the jury box.

While we suggest that during direct examination you position yourself near the end of the jury box furthest from the witness, on cross-examination, you should move forward. Although the judge or court reporter may restrict you to the area near the lectern, you should utilize the courtroom stage to capture the spotlight as much as you are permitted. If the lectern is moveable, roll it forward to a spot in front of the center of the jury box. If you are allowed to leave the lectern, do so. However, you must be careful not to bully the witness or be overbearing. Assume center stage gently and cordially. Do not get in a witness's face. As with every other portion of the trial, you must ask the court's permission before approaching the witness.

7.3.3 Keep Up the Questioning Pace

Your questions should usually be asked at a rapid pace. Do not give the witness an opportunity to consider his answers while you are pondering your next question. Decide in advance the points you intend to make when you cross-examine and serve up your questions rapidly. A brisk pace of questioning also helps keep the jurors alert and interested. Avoid boring the jurors: One of the surest ways to bore them is to ask your questions too slowly and deliberately.

7.3.4 Maintain Eye Contact

During cross-examination, do not keep your eyes down on your legal pad. Most of the time, it is effective to maintain eye contact with the witness. Your steady eye contact can help exert control over the witness, causing him to think twice before he evades or challenges you. Your calm, steady gaze may cause the witness to fidget, look away, lean back with arms folded across his chest, or otherwise telegraph subtle messages of incredibility to the jury. Your piercing gaze may cause him to become defensive or snarl at you, and when he does that, the momentum shifts your way. The jurors will be instructed to take the witness's demeanor on the stand into account in judging credibility.

When a witness is answering evasively or adding long explanations where none are required, it may be very effective for you to direct the jurors' attention away from the witness by turning to face them. When you establish eye contact with the jurors, their attention will refocus on you. Your inattention to the witness will communicate to the jurors that the witness's answers are not responsive and do not contain information valuable to their task.

You should also make eye contact with the jurors when you are using a cross-examination question to make a particularly important point. Look at the jurors while you state the question: "You did not come to a complete stop, did you?" By maintaining eye contact with the jurors, you can make sure they are listening to you and hearing your points.

7.4 Determine the Sequence of the Chapters of the Cross-Examination

The third task of the advocate is to determine the sequence of the chapters of the cross-examination. Each cross-examination should be organized 1) to ensure that during the examination, the jurors understand the purpose(s) of the cross, and 2) to maximize the persuasive impact of the examination.

During cross-examination, you do not have to, and should not, deal with every event or damaging piece of information that this witness has presented on direct examination. Limit your cross-examination to those purposes that you are certain you can accomplish with this witness. Do not under any circumstances retrace the entire direct examination, allowing the witness to reiterate everything he has already said once. Pick those points that you can establish clearly and powerfully. Do it and sit down.

Just as in the direct examination, there should be a logical structure to the cross-examination. An old school of thought advocated bouncing around randomly from point to point during cross, facilitating the ability to extract admissions from the witness who does not know where the examination is heading. The problem with this approach is that the jurors will be similarly mystified. Waiting until closing argument to explain what you accomplished on cross will be far too late to influence the jurors' view of the case.

If the examiner utilizes proper control techniques, the witness will not be able to thwart the cross-examination even if, like the jurors, the witness knows precisely the aim of the lawyer's questioning. Rather than attempting to confuse the witness (and jurors), every cross-examination must proceed in a series of intentionally selected and ordered chapters, each of which builds slowly towards a single point. The gurus of organizing cross-examination are Larry Pozner and Roger Dodd, who codify "The Chapter Method of Cross-Examination" in their treatise, *Cross-Examination: Science and Techniques*.[4] While the substance of the cross-examination will vary from case to case and witness to witness, there are four discrete steps to assembling the chapters for every individual cross-examination:

1) Without regard to order, list all the facts that you might elicit during the cross (with a citation to where in the pretrial record each fact appears).

---

4. Larry S. Pozner & Roger J. Dodd, *Cross-Examination: Science and Techniques*, chapter 9 (1993).

2) Cluster related facts into discrete chapters. If there is a fact from your initial list that cannot be joined with other facts, you generally should omit that fact from your cross. Not only are the jurors unlikely to take note of a single fact that does not ripen into a chapter, eliciting that fact risks confusing the jurors and causing them to miss the point of both the preceding and following chapters.

3) Decide the order in which you will bring out the individual facts in each chapter.

4) Determine the order in which you will address the chapters.

Preparing a cross-examination requires the same investment of time, thought, writing, and rewriting as drafting a Supreme Court brief. You must continually revisit whether you have identified the chapters with sufficient clarity, whether the facts in a chapter can be reordered to more effectively establish the point of the chapter, and whether the cross would paint a better story if the chapters were presented in a different order.

In most cross-examinations, it makes sense to proceed from "soft" to "hard" questioning. Organize your cross-examination to move from supportive to challenging and finally, if necessary, to confrontational questioning. Save any zinger for the end of the examination.

7.4.1 First, Bring out Evidence Favorable to Your Client's Case

The constructive cross-examination exploits the fact that witnesses called by your opponent will have information helpful to your case—the kind of information you would elicit if you had called the witness. For example, a physician who treated the plaintiff in the emergency room may have noted that the plaintiff was intoxicated. When this physician is called by the plaintiff to establish damages, the fact of the plaintiff's drunkenness may be brought out on cross-examination. The drunkenness testimony does not diminish the doctor's credibility. Rather, it is helpful to the defendant's case on liability.

A witness often possesses information helpful or harmful to each of the parties in varying degrees. The question whether to call the witness is frequently a close one for both sides. If the opponent calls a witness whose overall testimony will be favorable to your position, treat him as if he were your witness. That is, bring out only helpful testimony on cross-examination and do not attack his credibility.

Even if you decide to attack other points covered by the direct examination, you should bring out the witness's favorable testimony at the beginning of your cross-examination. There are two good reasons for this. First, psychologists tell us that after a person's honesty has been impeached on any point we tend not to believe anything else that person says. Therefore, it makes sense to bring out information you want the jurors to accept before you attack the witness's credibility. Second, the witness will be more likely to open up and help you if you ask about the favorable information before you unsheathe your sword.

7.4.2 Next, Have the Witness Acknowledge the Weak Spots in His Testimony

After bringing out favorable information, you may force witnesses to acknowledge any weaknesses, soft spots, or missing links in their testimony. For example, an eyewitness may have been standing half a block away at the time she claims to have recognized your client. Make her acknowledge that fact. Ask, "At the time you say you saw my client, you were standing half a block away, weren't you?" As discussed more fully in section 7.9, do not pursue the point further by asking, "So, you couldn't really see what happened, could you?" Remember, you are not trying to convince the witness that she could not see the events. You are establishing facts that will permit the jurors to infer that she could not see.

Force witnesses to admit the things they do not know. These negative admissions may seem inconsequential, but it can be important to have a witness concede the limitations of his knowledge. For instance, an investigating police officer may be asked, "Officer, just to be sure there's no misunderstanding, you did not see this accident happen, did you?" As noted in section 7.2.1, establishing all the facts that the witness does not know may lead the jurors to find those facts in your favor. At the very least, they will see the limited role the witness can play in helping them determine what happened.

Lawyers characterize this type of cross-examination in various ways. Some refer to it as "sealing the story" because your goal is to plug up the holes in the direct testimony through which unwarranted inferences may leak. Others liken this stage of cross-examination to walking down a hallway lined with doors leading into numerous rooms of inferences. As you proceed down the hall, you close each of the doors.

Cross-examination is also useful to inform the jurors that the opinion of your opponent's expert is not cast in stone. Expert witnesses will usually acknowledge that other equally qualified experts may have different opinions. When an expert witness's opinion is based on assumed facts, you can change one of the assumptions and force the expert to admit that his opinion might be different if that assumed fact were different. In these ways, you prepare the jurors to accept your expert's opinion.

7.4.3 Finally, Challenge the Witness

There are at least three good reasons to leave the most hostile questioning for last. First, when you finish your cross-examination by eliciting highly destructive evidence, you improve the odds that you will leave the jurors with the general impression that the witness is not worthy of belief. Second, if you save the more confrontational matters for the end, you increase the chance that the witness will make some concessions during the early part of the cross-examination. Third, the witness may have struck out at you with rude or defensive answers by then. As long as you remain courteous, the witness loses rapport with the jurors each time he lashes out at you. Meanwhile, you gain sympathy as a hard-working person trying to do your job fairly in the face of an obstreperous, uncooperative witness. When the jurors' sympathy has begun shifting from the witness to you, they will welcome questions successfully attacking the witness personally.

7.5 Five Techniques to Control the Witness

Once you have determined the purpose(s) and demeanor of the cross and have organized the cross into its chapters, your remaining task is to control the witness during the questioning. There are five fundamental and universal control techniques. Departure from these techniques at any time cedes the keys to the car to the witness, allowing him to drive the cross.

7.5.1 Do Not Ask Any Question Unless . . .

The first technique of controlling the witness is exercised outside the courtroom. The only way to ensure the cross-examination will be 100 percent successful is to "know the answer" to every question that is asked. However, "knowing the answer" is not the same as believing by a preponderance of the evidence, by clear and convincing evidence, or even beyond a reasonable doubt what the response to the question will be. In the well of the courtroom, "knowing the answer" requires that should the witness deny the fact posed by the question, the examiner has the ability to confront the witness with a document, admission in a pleading, or discovery response in which the witness unambiguously admitted the very fact.[5] In this way, for every question the examiner is guaranteed 1) to obtain the desired response and/or 2) to impeach the witness.

There is nothing new—absolutely nothing—you need to learn from a witness during cross-examination. Acquisition of information is not one of your goals at this point in the trial. Cross-examination is not the time for seeking answers to questions you regret not having asked in discovery. Ask only questions to which there can be only one possible, plausible answer. Do not engage in wishful thinking here. If there is room for the witness to disagree with you or if you do not know exactly what he has to say to avoid appearing to be a fool or liar, do not ask the question.

---

5. In some instances, confrontation takes the form of a later witness testifying to the fact posed by the questions. The techniques of impeachment are addressed in chapter eight.

The leading obstacle to a fail-safe cross is succumbing to the temptation to obtain admission of new facts that, not codified in pretrial statements, logically follow from admissions that have been documented. To thwart the natural human tendency towards temptation, the outline of your cross-examination should contain a citation to the page and line of the document, admission in the pleading, or discovery response where each answer unambiguously appears. If you cannot provide a citation, do not ask the question. And to exert maximum control—and maximize the impact of impeachment should the witness deny the fact—your questions should use the precise words that the witness used in the document, pleading or discovery response.

The sole exception to the rule that you should know the answer to every question you ask on cross-examination is when you do not care what the answer will be. When any answer the witness gives will diminish his credibility, you can toss the open-ended question out and let the witness hang himself with his own rope. For example, the question, "Do you believe people should drive safely?" will benefit the examiner whether the witness answers "yes" or "no." There are also situations where you do not care what a witness's answer will be because you have ammunition to impeach him after any answer he gives. Until you become expert in the art of cross-examination, however, the wiser course is to ask only those questions to which you know the answer and have the means to unambiguously impeach the witness if he offers a different answer at trial.

7.5.2 Use Only Leading Questions on Cross-Examination

The second technique of controlling the witness is the form of the question. You should presume the witness will pounce upon every slender opportunity to offer harmful testimony. Even a neutral witness will subconsciously identify with the party who called him to testify, and will endeavor to reiterate the direct examination whenever possible on cross-examination.

An effective cross-examiner must maintain constant control of the examination. If the witness is ever allowed to gain control over what he says, the cross-examination becomes a debacle for the examiner. The rules of evidence recognize the motivation of the witness and permit leading questions on cross-examination.[6] You should ask only leading questions on cross-examination because leading questions enable the cross-examiner to maintain control over the witness.

No hard, fast line separates leading from non-leading questions. Consequently, there are degrees of leading. The questions you ask on cross should be grossly leading, not merely the kind of questions that would draw objections if asked on direct examination. These narrowly focused leading questions should really be statements that allow the witness to respond only with yes or no. As a general rule, that is all you want the witness to say during your cross-examination. Your goal should be

---

6. *See* Fed. R. Evid. 611(c).

to have the jurors hear your statements/questions punctuated only by the witness's monosyllabic responses.

You must utilize the means conferred by the law of evidence to control the witness by asking only leading questions on cross-examination. However, to avoid boring the jurors, you should vary the form of the leading questions.

- Isn't it true that the light was red?

- The light was red, wasn't it?

- And the light was red?

Example

The defendant was prosecuted for knowing receipt of a stolen boat and trailer. The investigating officer testified on direct examination as to the observations he made when he was called to the road where the boat had fallen off the trailer.

Cross-Examination without Leading Questions

Q: Officer, when you arrived at Highway 11, was Mr. Mills standing next to the boat and trailer?

A: Yes.

Q: Did you see anything suspicious?

A: It was quite odd that Mr. Mills was hauling a boat on a back road at around midnight. I also found it strange that Mills would not tell me the name of the person at whose house he claimed to have been storing the boat.

Cross-Examination with Leading Questions

Q: Between the time you received the dispatch and the time you arrived at the scene, Mr. Mills had the opportunity to drive away in his truck, isn't that correct?

A: Yes.

Q: But he hadn't left the scene, had he?

A: Apparently not, sir.

Q: After you arrived, Mr. Mills offered to go to a friend's house to see if he could get something to pull that boat back onto the trailer, isn't that right?

A: That's correct, sir.

Q: And he left the scene then?

A: That's correct, sir.

Q: You did not insist on going with Mr. Mills, did you?

A: No, sir.

Q: In fact, you stayed at the scene?

A: Yes.

Q: Mr. Mills then left in his truck?

A: He did.

Q: Mr. Mills did return to the scene, isn't that right?

A: That is correct.

Q: You had a chance to observe Mr. Mills that evening, right?

A: Yes, I did.

Q: And you were in uniform?

A: That's correct, sir.

Q: In a marked car?

A: That's correct.

Q: Mr. Mills gave you his correct name didn't he?

A: Yes, sir.

Q: He gave you his correct address?

A: Yes.

Q: When you looked at the boat, the ignition did not look like it had been broken as if it someone tried to start it without a key, did it?

A: No, sir.

Q: In fact, the ignition looked completely intact, isn't that right?

A: Yes, sir.

Q: There was a registration number on the side of the boat, wasn't there?

A: Yes.

Q: And that registration number is unique to that particular boat?

A: That's correct, sir.

Q: And that unique identifier was still on that boat, wasn't it?

A: Yes.

The conventional technique of asking only leading questions is tried and true. Lawyers should acquire the habit of leading on cross-examination. Nevertheless, non-leading questions can sometimes be used for greater impact. Testimony is more believable when it comes from the witness's lips. Therefore, when eliciting favorable testimony, it could be better to ask the witness non-leading questions. The keys to asking effective non-leading questions on cross-examination are to know what the witness's answer has to be and to have something to impeach him with if he gives the wrong answer. But until you have gained sufficient experience, you will be best served by asking only leading questions on cross-examination.

7.5.3 *Every Question Should Present Only One Fact to the Witness*

Asking leading questions is a necessary, but not sufficient, means of controlling the witness on cross-examination. In addition to asking every question in a form that is leading, you must present only one fact to the witness in each question. This technique serves several purposes:

First, asking one-fact questions curtails the witness's ability to escape the examiner's control. Where you pose only one fact in a question, the witness's lone choice is to admit the fact or be impeached by his earlier admission. Putting two facts in a question—even where the witness has admitted each fact in discovery—provides the witness with a new option. Rather than admit the facts, the witness may deny the inference created by the combination of facts.

Asking questions that elicit only one fact at a time permits to you to build inferences from individual, incontrovertible facts, inferences the witness would deny if given the opportunity. Imagine that your client is charged with breaking and entering Apartment 101 in the middle of the night. On the witness stand you have Aunt Willie, the elderly neighbor, who just testified that on the night in question she saw your client leaving Apartment 101 at 2 A.M. You contend that Aunt Willie is mistaken in her identification.

Q: You were asleep at 2:00 a.m., weren't you?

A: I'm generally asleep at that hour. Yes.

Q: You were in bed, asleep at 2:00 a.m. on October 29?

A: Yes.

Q: You were awakened by a sound outside your window?

A: That's right.

Q: And you looked out the window from your bed?

Q: Yes, I did.

Q: The window is across the room from your bed?

A: Yes.

Q: You wear glasses, don't you?

A: Yes.

Q: You are nearsighted?

A: That's right.

Q: So your glasses help you see in the distance?

A: Yes.

Q: And you don't wear your glasses to bed, do you?

A: No, of course not.

This examination takes one incontrovertible fact at a time. Each question, taken alone, is innocuous. Together they create a strong inference that Aunt Willie's identification of your client should not be relied on, while never putting two facts together in a question that would allow Aunt Willie to deny the inference.

Second, bringing out the facts one at a time may also provide emphasis that will reinforce your point with the jurors. For example, if you were cross-examining an expert on a study that the expert conducted, you could simply ask the witness, "Your study was not subject to peer review, was it?" The witness's negative response might not mean much to the jurors. On the other hand, if you ask a series of questions you can establish, explain, and reinforce this point with the jurors.

Q: You are familiar with peer review?

A: Yes.

Q: That is the process by which scientists review and comment on each other's work?

A: That's correct.

Q: It allows scientists to get valuable feedback from other scientists about their work, doesn't it?

A: Yes.

Q: Peer review can help point up problems in the research, can't it?

A: Yes.

Q: It can also confirm a study's conclusions?

A: Yes.

Q: Can this be very valuable in the scientific process?

A: It can.

Q: Scientists actively seek peer review, don't they?

A: Most of them do.

Q: They may seek it by presenting their work at conferences?

A: That's one way.

Q: And they may seek it by submitting their work to a journal that peer-reviews its articles?

A: Yes.

Q: Your study was conducted six years ago, wasn't it?

A: That's right.

Q: And it has not been subjected to any kind of peer review, has it?

A: No.

Now the witness's "no" will mean something to the jury. To make sure the jury understands and remembers your cross-examination points, take the cross-examination in small steps. Any important point is worth at least three questions. Little details can support large inferences.

7.5.4 Celebrate, Rather than Panic, if the Witness Does Not Answer Your Question

You should not be so naïve as to presume the witness will admit every fact posed on cross-examination simply because you 1) asked only questions to which you know the answer and have the means unambiguously to impeach the witness if a different answer is offered, 2) used only leading questions, and 3) asked questions that add only one fact to the previous question. When so cornered, the witness may rely upon the "fight or flight" instinct rather than admit the one-fact posed by the question. The fourth control technique allows you to successfully thwart the witness' attempt to escape your question.

Generally, you want the witness to answer your questions with a simple yes or no. Witnesses, however, do not always cooperate. Asked if he was standing on the corner of Main Street and Vine, the witness may respond, "I was standing close enough to see everything I testified to." Asked if he was a hundred yards from the defendant, the witness may respond, "I would recognize that no-good dog from a thousand paces, if only by his smell." You need to be prepared for the uncooperative witness.

Your first inclination will be to panic at your seeming loss of control of the witness. Instead, you must celebrate the attempted evasion, fully confident that you eventually will procure the desired answer. As a bonus, you will make the witness's attempt to avoid answering the question obvious to the jurors, a self-inflicted wound that will damage the witness's credibility.

You may resort to a variety of techniques when the witness does not answer your question but instead begins to narrate in an attempt to damage your case.[7] Two strategies, however, will never succeed: interrupting the witness, or attempting to force her to answer "yes or no." In both instances, opposing counsel will successfully object to your interfering with the witness's attempt to fully answer your question. A third technique—asking the judge to instruct the witness to answer—rests on the often unfounded assumption that the judge will find the witness is not being sufficiently responsive.[8]

Here are four easy methods to control the runaway witness:

1) Calmly and politely interrupt the witness, graciously accepting the blame for any misunderstanding about what you are asking. "Excuse me for interrupting, Mr. Cowan, perhaps I confused you by my question. Let me see if I can ask it in a better way. My question is . . . ." Neither opposing counsel nor the court will perceive your acceptance of responsibility as an unfair attempt to thwart the witness's testimony.

2) Let the witness complete the narrative and then repeat the same one-fact leading question. "Thank you for volunteering that information, Mr. Cowan, but my question was . . . ." The jurors should recognize that the witness was avoiding the single proposition, which will both enhance the significance of the fact and undermine the credibility of the witness.

3) Reverse the question, asking the witness to admit the truth of the converse of the question she is evading. If the witness delivers a long speech

---

7. *See* Larry S. Pozner & Roger J. Dodd, *Cross Examination: Science and Techniques*, chapter 15 (1993), listing at least nineteen ways to control the runaway witness.

8. If a witness repeatedly refuses to answer your question or, as happens frequently, begins giving a speech no matter what you ask, you may ask the court to instruct the witness to answer your questions or to restrict the witness's responses to answering the specific questions asked. If a witness's answer is particularly harmful, you may ask the court to strike it and admonish the jurors to disregard it. Remember, however, that the judge's direction to disregard a point may have the unwelcome effect of re-emphasizing it.

Even though you have the right to complain to the court when a witness is unresponsive, the right should be exercised judiciously. You must not appear to be a crybaby. Remember that the appearance of control is your constant objective. Control the witness without the court's assistance if you can.

After two or three attempts to obtain a simple, obvious answer, an appeal to the court for assistance will probably be appreciated by the jurors. Of course, a witness's repeated dodging and parrying to avoid answering a crystal clear question may so destroy the witness's credibility that you may decide to leave the point with a shrug and a sigh of resignation.

in response to the question, "Isn't it true the light was green?" your next question would be, "I take it from your answer that the light was red?"

4) Show the palm of your hand to the witness, triggering the Pavlovian reaction the witness developed in response to the same gesture offered by a disapproving parent or teacher, school crossing guard, or traffic cop. This technique is worth trying at least once, if only to amaze yourself that it works!

Your goal is to remain calm and in full control while pinning the witness to the question's obvious answer and not allowing him to wriggle free from it. Do not allow a witness to evade your questions with impunity. Here is an example of the kind of patient persistence that is required in dealing with an uncooperative witness:

Q: You were standing on the corner of Main Street and Vine?

A: I would recognize that son of a dog from a thousand paces, if only by his smell.

Q: You did not smell the defendant, did you?

A: I'm glad I didn't have to.

Q: But you did not smell him, did you?

A: No, of course I didn't smell him.

Q: And you were standing on the corner of Main Street and Vine?

A: I was close enough to recognize him.

Q: But you were standing on the corner of Main Street and Vine, isn't that right?

A: I guess so.

Q: By that, you mean yes?

A: Yeah, I guess so.

Q: By that, you mean yes?

A: Yes.

Stay with him on every question until he "cries uncle," the judge admonishes him, or you turn him loose as an apparent act of charity.

7.5.5 Resist Temptation to Force the Witness to Voice What the Jury Already Understands

The witness will be powerless to undermine the intended purposes of the cross-examination, presented in the sequence of chapters planned by the cross-examiner, if the cross-examiner 1) knows the answer to every question asked and possesses a document, pleading, or discovery response that the witness must admit unambiguously sets forth the desire answer should the witness offer a different response than expected; 2) uses only leading questions; 3) ensures that each question adds only one fact; 4) celebrates, rather than panics, should the witness attempt to evade answering the questions; and 5) is able to react to any different response than expected by the techniques of impeachment by prior inconsistent statement or by omission in a prior statement that is explained in chapter eight. Only one person can prevent the guaranteed success of the examination: the cross-examiner who is unable to resist the urge to extract from the witness's mouth the conclusion as to what the examination already has clearly shown to the trier of fact.

Immortalized by the legendary Irving Younger as avoiding the "one question too many," this technique requires you to curtail what may be the least controllable force: your ego. Cross-examination is, to use an expression coined by Professor James McElhaney, "the art of honest innuendo"[9]—you induce the witness to admit a sequence of facts that point to an obvious conclusion, but never ask the witness to voice the conclusion. Ego gratification of the advocate is postponed from the moment of the cross-examination to the time of the favorable verdict.

There are at least three ways in which you might lose control by attempting to force the witness to voice the conclusion that the jurors already fully understand was established by the cross. *First*, you must restrict each question to a purely objective fact rather than ask a question that is open to the witness' subjective interpretation. The difference may be almost imperceptible, as the following example demonstrates:

Example

Cross-Examination Using Modestly Subjective/Conclusory Fact

Q: Sir, isn't it true that you were speeding just before the accident?

A: I was driving with the flow of traffic. I think that is what most people would do—in fact, that is what everyone else on the road at that time was doing.

Cross-Examination Using Only Objective Facts

Q: The accident happened on Highway 94, didn't it?

A: Yes

Q: Sir, the speed limit on Highway 94 on the day of the accident was 45 miles per hour, isn't that correct?

---

9. James W. McElhaney, *McElhaney's Trial Notebook* 126 (ABA 3d ed. 1994).

A: Yes.

Q: Isn't it true that at the time of the accident, you were driving 55 miles per hour?

A: Yes.

Q: No further questions, Your Honor.

Second, you may cede control to the witness by your inability to resist preening after establishing the witness's testimony contradicts a prior statement or includes facts omitted in a prior statement.

Example

Q: As you just admitted, in your direct examination today, you testified you were driving 45 miles per hour and at your deposition you testified you were driving 55 miles per hour. Were you lying then or were you lying today?

A: Neither, counsel. You never gave me a chance to explain. I was driving 55 miles per hour until I got near the Route 15 turn-off. Everyone knows that there is a lot of traffic there so, as I always do, I reduced my speed just before that turn-off to 45 miles per hour.

Q: Well, you testified on direct examination that you saw the plaintiff's right-hand turn signal light on, but you never mentioned that fact in the statement you gave to the police officer at the scene. You certainly don't remember the facts better three years after the accident than you did at the scene, do you?

A: Of course not. When he took my statement, the officer never asked me if I saw the turn signal and never gave me a chance to discuss that fact because he received a dispatch that a robbery was in progress. The officer told me that I had given him all the information he needed to complete his accident report and left the scene.

Third, you might surrender control by trying to make your closing argument during cross-examination. The basic idea of cross-examination is to force the witness to concede all of the underlying facts that justify a conclusion that will be obvious to the jurors, but refrain from mentioning the conclusion that flows from those facts until closing argument.

Questions on cross-examination that attempt to get a witness to agree with an inference or conclusion that should properly be reserved for closing argument are objectionable as argumentative and should not be asked.[10] Not only are argumentative questions improper, they are usually counterproductive because, by their very nature, they give witnesses an opportunity to disagree with the interrogator and to explain their reasons for disagreeing. This is, of course, helpful to the opponent. To be sure, lawyers sometimes get lucky and obtain favorable responses to these questions, but the chance of a lucky answer does not justify the risk. As football coach Darryl Royal said when explaining why he did not like his teams to pass, "When you pass, one of three things can happen and two of them are bad." If you toss up one of these bricks, the witness is liable to intercept it and score a touchdown for the other side.

Many experienced trial lawyers express the admonition against asking argumentative questions in terms of simply knowing when to stop or not asking one question too many. This question often begins with "So," or "Therefore," or "That means." For example, if you have carefully drawn out facts that show that it has been ten months since the identifying witness has seen the defendant and that the witness only saw the defendant for one to three seconds, it will be evidence to the jurors that the witness's identification of the defendant is not reliable. But if you establish these facts and then ask the witness, "So, you can't be sure that this defendant is the person you saw that night, can you?" the witness is likely to say, "No, I am sure. That face is etched in my memory like a tattoo. When somebody does something as horrible as this defendant, you never forget his face."

Any time you feel a question coming on that starts with the word "so" or "why," stop yourself. You are about to ask the witness to agree with your conclusion. Remember that this witness probably does not agree with your conclusion and that you do not need this witness to agree with your conclusion. You only need the jurors to agree. Before you ask an argumentative question, ask yourself what may happen if you ask and the witness disagrees and explains. Better yet, as soon as you hear the word "so" or "why" rise to your lips, stop yourself, and sit down.

Example

Q: You never saw Mrs. Pierce when you began you left turn, did you?

A: No, I did not.

Q: You never saw Mrs. Pierce when you heard the thud coming from the front bumper of your truck, did you?

A: Correct.

Q: You never saw Mrs. Pierce before you brought your truck to a stop?

---

10. *See* Holland v. State, 706 S.W.2d 375 (Ark. 1986); Gitchel, Admissibility of Evidence: A Manual for Arkansas Trial Lawyers 6 (1990). The objection to argumentative questions should be distinguished from the objection to badgering or harassing a witness.

A: That's right.

Q: In fact, the first time you saw Mrs. Pierce was when you got out of your truck and saw her lying on the ground?

A: That is true.

Q: So, why do you claim that the accident was her fault?

A: Sir, all I know is that I was watching the crosswalk at all times from the moment I approached the intersection until I completed my turn. If someone was in or even entering the crosswalk, I would have seen her. Mrs. Pierce must have darted out into the intersection beyond the cross-walk. Otherwise, I certainly would have seen her.

CHAPTER EIGHT

IMPEACHMENT

"I feel sure this guy is lying," the young lawyer said. "When I get him on the witness stand, I'm going to make him squirm. I'm going to make him sweat. I'm going to make him crumble."

"Witnesses aren't cake," the Professor replied. "They don't usually crumble. And they aren't Pinocchio either. Their noses don't grow longer when they lie. Most of the witnesses you will encounter will be well prepared, and most won't consciously lie. And when witnesses do lie, you won't be able to make them squirm, sweat, or give the jurors physical signs that they are lying."

"If that's true, then how can I show the jurors that this guy is lying?"

"To reveal the lie, uncover the details. The truth," said the Professor, "is always in the details."

8.1   Types of Impeachment

Cross-examination and impeachment are not synonymous terms, though impeachment does frequently occur during cross-examination. The term "cross-examination" simply refers to that part of the trial when a lawyer who did not call the particular witness to the stand is permitted to ask the witness questions. Cross-examination may or may not include impeachment as an objective. The term "impeachment," on the other hand, refers to a particular purpose for introducing evidence—not to a particular phase of the trial. The purpose for offering impeachment evidence is to reduce the credibility of a witness or piece of evidence. Any evidence that undermines the believability of other evidence is impeaching evidence.

Impeachment evidence may also serve some other purpose. That is, it may support an additional inference as well as the inference that this witness should not be believed. An example of such dual-purpose evidence is testimony that contradicts what a previous witness said. Assume that your opponent's witness testified that the assailant's shirt was blue. You now call a witness who testifies that the assailant's shirt was red. Your witness's testimony supports both the argument that the testimony of the first witness is not worthy of belief and the argument that the shirt was red.

Impeachment evidence is often introduced by means of asking the witness questions on cross-examination. It also may be proved by other evidence, which may be offered through another witness, documents, or other exhibits at some other time during the trial. For example, if the first witness in the case testified that he talked to Fred on Thursday, the very last witness in the case may impeach that testimony by saying that Fred died on the previous Tuesday. This contradictory evidence impeaches the first witness's testimony. But introducing contradictory or conflicting testimony alone is not enough. You must give the jury some reason to believe your evidence and to disbelieve your opponent's. In other words, the jury needs some reason to believe your witness who says Fred died on Tuesday, rather than the first witness who says that he talked to Fred on Thursday. You need to do something to undermine the credibility of the first witness.

This chapter focuses on ways to attack a witness's credibility using impeachment during cross-examination. Although there are many different reasons why a jury should not believe a witness, these reasons generally fit within two basic categories:

1) The witness is mistaken; or

2) The witness is lying.

Occasionally, you will have a witness who is both mistaken and lying. But, in general, as you set out to impeach a witness you should be thinking in terms of establishing either a mistake or a lie.

If you are successful in showing a mistake or a lie, you then have a reason to ask the jury to believe that the specific information the witness has given is wrong, and that they should believe other evidence that contradicts those specifics. Or, you may use the mistake or lie to show that the witness is generally not credible. In other words, if the witness can be mistaken or can lie about X, the jury should infer that he is likely to be mistaken or lie about Y and Z, too.

The beginning point for establishing either a mistake or a lie is to develop your impeachment story. Why should this testimony not be believed? If it is because the witness is mistaken, why did the witness make that mistake? What factors contributed to the mistake? If it is because the witness is lying, why did the witness lie in this situation? What motivation did the witness have? What details in the case are inconsistent with this lie? Each piece of false or mistaken testimony is a subplot in the grander story of your case. Tell the story of that sub-plot convincingly, and you will have successfully impeached your opponent's evidence.

When you are trying to establish that a witness is uninformed or mistaken, remember that the witness does not believe his testimony is false, incorrect, or mistaken. A person who is perfectly honest and well-meaning may take the stand and give false testimony with a clear conscience. His belief in what he says is pure. If you try to make this witness appear to be a liar, you will fail. If you try to get this witness to admit his mistake, you may also fail. If you point out to the witness all of the circumstances that indicate that he is wrong, he may still persist in his mistaken belief. Your mission in impeaching a mistaken witness is to develop the details that demonstrate to the jurors—not to the witness—that the witness's testimony is either uninformed or mistaken and cannot be credited. Often these details will include circumstances surrounding the events in the case—for example, the time available to observe, the lighting, the other distractions, the length of time between the events and the trial. Other details may relate to the witness himself—for example, the witness's own faulty memory, the witness's inability to observe, the witness's failure to pursue or follow up on available information, reasons the witness was distracted, and so on.

You may use some of the same details to demonstrate weaknesses in the testimony of a witness who you contend is lying. There are, however, several additional techniques available to help you reveal a lie. First, you may reveal the lie itself. Sometimes you may catch a witness in a lie on the witness stand. You may be able to impeach this witness with her own prior inconsistent statement. Often, however, you will ask the jurors to conclude that the witness is lying based on circumstantial evidence. Circumstantial evidence of a lie might include evidence that tends to show that the witness must be lying because:

1) her testimony is not consistent with other reliable evidence in the case;

2) her testimony is unsupported by an ability to observe or remember important events at issue;

3) the witness has a motive to lie in this case; and/or

4) the witness is generally a liar.

When you contend that the witness is lying, you will want to show all of the available circumstantial evidence of the lie to the jurors. In other words, you will not select just one technique or type of circumstantial evidence of impeachment. You will pile it on.

8.2 Revealing Weakness: Attacking the Witness's Competence

To be considered competent to testify, all non-expert witnesses must have personal knowledge of one or more events at issue in the trial.[1] They must have perceived something through their own senses that is relevant to the case. Even expert witnesses must have informed themselves about issues or events relevant to the case. And all witnesses must be able to remember and relate those events to the jurors. Because there is no perfect perception, no perfect memory, and no perfect telling of an event, these areas of "competence" provide fertile ground for impeachment.

---

1. *See* FED. R. EVID. 601.

Generally, attacking a witness's competence involves revealing the gaps or inadequacy of the witness's ability to perceive or remember the events that are at issue. You will use this form of impeachment whether your theory is that the witness is simply mistaken or that the witness must be lying.

8.2.1 *Inability to Perceive*

Many questions intended to demonstrate the weak spots in a witness's testimony[2] are designed to show the witness's lack of personal knowledge or inability accurately to perceive the things about which he testified. Evidence supporting the inference that a witness could not accurately perceive the things he testified about may be elicited on cross-examination or introduced by other witnesses. Questions may relate to the difficulty or impossibility of perception generally. For example:

Q: The only light available was a single street lamp?

Q: There were more than 500 people in the bar that night? It was loud? It was crowded?

Q: The cell phone connection was weak? There was a lot of static?

This kind of question develops the scene or circumstances surrounding the events in a way that persuades the jurors that any observer could not have very accurate or complete information about the events.

In addition to questions that relate to the circumstances, you may ask questions that relate to the witness's specific inability to perceive.

Q: You saw the defendant only for a split second, didn't you?

Q: You were standing at the back of the crowd? And you are five feet, one-inch tall?

Q: Your driver's license is restricted because you have poor night vision?

Q: At the time you say you heard the conversation in the restaurant, you were seated four tables away, weren't you?

Some questions will relate to what the witness did *not* perceive:

Q: Inspector, you didn't arrive at the scene until approximately thirty minutes after the incident. Isn't that right?

Q: Dr. Smith, you don't know whether this patient had a previous neck injury, do you?

Q: You didn't follow Mr. Jones when he left the bar, did you?

---

2. *See* chapter seven.

National Institute for Trial Advocacy

It is often very effective to develop a long series of questions that demonstrate the limits of the witness's perception of the events. If the witness is a police officer, medical doctor, or expert witness, this series of questions will often include a long litany of the things that the witness did *not* do. For example:

Q: Officer Jones, when you arrived on the scene, there were five or six people milling about, weren't there?

A: That's right.

Q: And some of those people left while you were waiting for backup to secure the scene, didn't they?

A: I made every effort to speak to each one of them.

Q: But you didn't, did you?

A: No.

Q: You didn't get all of their names, did you?

A: I got some of their names and addresses.

Q: But not others'?

A: That's right.

Q: So, you did not have an opportunity to interview those others, did you?

A: No.

Q: And you don't know why they were there?

A: I assumed they were just passing by.

Q: But you don't know that, do you?

A: No.

Q: And if you did not interview them, you don't know if any of them had any relationship to the victim, do you?

A: No.

Q: And you don't know if any of them had any criminal record, do you?

A: No.

Q: And you don't have any description of these other people who were present, do you?

A: No.

Q: You didn't get their fingerprints either, did you?

A: Of course not.

Q: Then there is no way to tell if their fingerprints might match any found in the car, is there?

A: No.

In addition to questioning the witness about gaps or weaknesses in his perception of the events in the case, you will also want to explore factors that may have distorted the witness's perception. When you explore the realm of witness perception, remember that perception may be influenced by state of mind. There may be good reasons not to trust the perceptions of a person who is distracted, in a hurry, angry, drunk, or taking medication. Remember also that people often see what they expect to see. Perception may similarly be shaped by hopes, fears, or prejudices.

We do not see things as they are. We see them as we are.

—Talmudic saying

When you cross-examine to establish a weakness in perception, remember not to attempt to have the witness acknowledge the weakness. Rather, you should establish circumstances that, one fact at a time, will persuade the jurors that the witness's perception was flawed. For example, in a case in which your theory is that the witness was in too much of a hurry to notice the new sign at a particular intersection, you probably will not ask the witness if she was in a hurry. Instead, ask the witness a series of questions that show she was in a hurry:

Q: At the time of the accident, you were on your way from a dentist appointment to a meeting with the school counselor?

A: That's right.

Q: And you had just had two teeth drilled?

A: Don't remind me! Yes.

Q: That took a little longer than you had expected, didn't it?

A: Well, I'm not sure what you mean.

Q: You went to the dentist expecting to have one filling and you ended up with two?

A: Right.

Q: And the appointment took longer than you had planned, didn't it?

A: Well, yes, I guess it did.

Q: You left the dentist's office a few minutes after three o'clock, didn't you?

A: Right.

Q: And the meeting with the school counselor was supposed to take place at 3:15, wasn't it?

A: Yes, but I missed it because of the accident.

Q: But that is where you were going?

A: Yes.

Q: And the school is on Roland Avenue and Deep Creek Road?

A: Yes.

Q: That address is about six miles across town from the dentist's office?

A: I guess that's about right.

You can now successfully argue to the jury that the witness was rushing across the town from one appointment to the next.

8.2.2 Inability to Remember

Witnesses testify primarily from memory, but memory is never perfect. Flaws in the witness's memory will often provide fertile areas for cross-examination. Your goal is to call attention to details that reveal the witness's memory to be incomplete or inaccurate. If the witness cannot recall important details about the events or if the recalled details are inconsistent with other reliable information about the events, the jurors may conclude that the witness's testimony is not credible.

It is singular how soon we lose the impression of what ceases
to be constantly before us. A year impairs, a luster obliterates.
There is little distinct left without an effort of memory,
then indeed the lights are rekindled for a moment
—but who can be sure that the Imagination is not the torch-bearer?

—Lord Byron

Think about the factors that affect memory. Events that are unremarkable or routine often fade from memory very quickly. Did the witness have any reason to remember the specific events? Could he be confused about dates or times? Did he give any statement to a police officer at the scene? Plan your impeachment to reveal why the witness's memory is likely to be flawed.

Q: Mrs. Wilson, you are Marvin's aunt, are you not?

A: Yes.

Q: He calls you Aunt Willie, right?

A: Yes.

Q: You've seen Marvin coming and going from Debbie's apartment many times, haven't you?

A: Yes.

Q: In fact, he was there quite often, wasn't he?

A: Yes.

Q: So many times that you could not possibly list them all?

A: I'd say so.

Q: He was there often enough, in fact, that you would not be able to recall the dates of each one of his visits. Isn't that true?

A: Yes.

8.3   Revealing Mistakes or Lies: Prior Inconsistent Statement

Often during a trial, a witness will say something that contradicts his earlier statements. Because you know the record well, you can spot the inconsistency immediately. You know that one of the statements must surely be either a mistake or a lie. If you think the difference is attributable to an honest mistake and the information is not important, it may make sense to let it go. But if the witness has a motivation to lie and the inconsistency is important, revealing that inconsistency to the jurors in the courtroom will be powerful impeachment.

If a witness[3] has made a statement at some time before he testifies that is at odds with his trial testimony, you may use that statement to attack his credibility.[4] The applicable Federal Rule of Evidence is 613, which contains only three restrictions on the use of prior inconsistent statements to impeach. First, you must show the prior statement (or disclose it, if it was oral) to opposing counsel. Second, you must give the witness an opportunity to explain *or* deny the statement if you introduce extrinsic evidence of it. And third, the court must afford opposing counsel an opportunity to interrogate the witness about the statement.

Rule 613 specifically states that you do not have to show the prior statement to the witness before you question him about it.[5] You may gain a distinct tactical advantage if you do not show the witness the document first because you know exactly what the witness said and the witness may not be able to remember. Nevertheless, we recommend that you generally show the witness the document before asking about the statement contained in it. This is a matter of strategy. To ask first, without showing, may appear to be taking unfair advantage of the witness. Because in this fencing match with the witness you always must strive to be the "good guy," you should normally show the statement to the witness before questioning him about it. Another important practical reason to show the witness the document before asking about the statement is to ensure that the jurors see it. By showing it to the witness first, you make sure that the jurors understand that the written document actually exists.

Rule 613(a) requires that you give the witness an opportunity to explain *or* deny the statement. It does not require you to allow him to explain *and* deny it. Never give him the opportunity to explain it. That is a job for the redirect examiner. Give the witness only the opportunity to admit or deny making the prior statement.

---

3. Fed. R. Evid. 607 grants the direct examiner the right to impeach his own witnesses. Though it rarely makes sense to impeach your own witness, the technique employed in impeaching one's own witness with a prior inconsistent statement is generally the same as that used when impeaching the opponent's witness on cross-examination, except that the lawyer's manner should be more solicitous and friendly. Generally, if your own witness testifies in a way that is contradictory to his previous statements, you should assume that the witness is merely mistaken or has forgotten something. A subtly leading question may be enough to get the witness back on track. If the witness has forgotten something important, use the technique of refreshing recollection discussed in section 6.3.3.

4. Under certain conditions, prior inconsistent statements may be considered by the jurors for their truth, as well as merely for the purpose of weighing the witness's credibility. The Federal Rules of Evidence allow such substantive consideration only if the statement was given under oath in a judicial proceeding or deposition. Fed. R. Evid. 801(d)(1)(A). State rules governing the substantive use of witnesses' prior inconsistent statements vary. The variation contained in the Revised Uniform Rules of Evidence imposes the foregoing restriction only in criminal cases. In civil cases, the Revised Uniform Rule allows any prior inconsistent statement used to impeach to be considered for its truth as well as for credibility assessment. *See* Ark. R. Evid. 801(d)(1)(i).

5. At common law, a rule developed that required a cross-examiner to show the witness any prior out-of-court statement before questioning the witness about it. *See* The Queen's Case, 2 Br. & B. 284, 129 Eng. Rep. 976 (1820). Some jurisdictions have not abandoned the common law requirement, and some judges have not yet become aware of the rule's demise in jurisdictions where it no longer applies.

When impeaching, it is only the inconsistent *statement* that is admissible, not the *document* that contains it. The document, be it deposition, police report, or informal memorandum, is inadmissible hearsay unless made admissible by some exemption from or exception to the hearsay rule. You do not have to introduce a document into evidence to impeach with a statement contained within it. In fact, many documents that contain statements admissible for impeachment purposes are themselves inadmissible.

What kills a skunk is the publicity it gives itself.

—Abraham Lincoln

The inconsistency you use to impeach must be glaring enough to impress the jury. If you impeach with a minor, picky point, the jury is likely to think you are being unfair to the witness. If a witness stated in a deposition that a car was red, then on direct examination said it was blue, you have the ingredients for a pungent impeachment. On the other hand, if a witness says on direct that he was "about two feet" from someone, but in his deposition said he was "two or three feet," and if the precise distance is unimportant, impeachment with the insignificant inconsistency may appear to be a low blow.

8.3.1 Method

In theory, you can accomplish impeachment with a prior inconsistent statement in a single question. "Isn't it true that you testified at your deposition that the car was red?" technically constitutes impeachment of the witness who testified on direct examination that the car was blue. However, there are two glaring practical flaws in this approach. First, the jurors, unfamiliar with the role or stature of a deposition, will not appreciate the significance or magnitude of the witness's departure from the deposition testimony. Second, impeachment through a single question is too quick and too mundane. Some jurors simply may be inattentive to the question and answer. Those who are following will not readily perceive from the lack of theatre of the interchange that something quite dramatic has just occurred. If you choose to impeach with a prior inconsistent statement, you must commit to ensuring that the jurors recognize that the witness is saying something different at trial, and must understand that the difference really matters.

The method of impeaching with prior inconsistent statements that we suggest here will ensure that you accomplish the task with maximum impact on the jurors. This method has three steps: 1) *Confirm* the witness in-court statement; 2) *Credit* the prior inconsistent statement; and 3) *Confront* the witness with the prior inconsistent statement.

Step One: *Confirm* the witness's in-court statement. The first step in the method of impeaching with a prior inconsistent statement is to have the witness reaffirm his in-court statement. The testimony you are going to impeach may have been given much earlier during direct examination. Even where you are impeaching an answer the witness gave in response to a one-fact question you just posed on cross, you have to ensure the witness did not misspeak. Consequently, you must have the witness confirm the in-court statement that you are about to impeach.

The language and tone of the question confirming the trial testimony should reveal your doubts about the in-court statement. A useful technique is to begin the question with the word "Today." "*Today,* when asked what color the car was, you said it was blue."

It is critical to be precise in confirming the in-court testimony to avoid giving the witness an opportunity to muddy the waters. State the exact words the witness used in his testimony. And do not make the mistake of asking the witness if he remembers making the statement at trial. You are embarking on a journey toward impeachment, not a much different and less useful exercise in refreshing recollection.

There is a variation on the commit that you may employ in situations when you want the jurors to be impressed with the accuracy of the prior statement and convinced that the witness's present testimony is false.[6] It involves one additional step, added after you commit the witness to his in-court statement. At that point, you ask whether the fact as stated in his out-of-court statement isn't *really* the truth. For example,

> Q: Today when Ms. Billings was asking you questions,[7] you testified that the yellow car was traveling at sixty miles per hour, didn't you?"
>
> A: Yes.
>
> Q: *The truth is that the yellow car was only going thirty miles per hour. Isn't that right?"*
>
> A: No.

Step Two: *Credit* the prior inconsistent statement. The second step in the impeachment protocol is to get the witness to acknowledge that he made a statement earlier concerning the same matter: "This is not the first time you have talked

---

6. Technically, when you use a prior inconsistent statement only to impeach, it is not being offered to prove the truth of matters contained in it; it is offered merely to diminish the witness's credibility. Therefore, you cannot argue to the jurors that the prior statement is the truth. If, however, the prior statement was made under oath in some sort of judicial proceeding or deposition, you may argue that it is the truth. *See* FED. R. EVID. 801(d)(1)(A). In some jurisdictions, this limitation applies only in criminal cases. *See, e.g.,* ARK. R. EVID. 801(d)(1)(i).

7. We recommend that you avoid using terms like "on direct examination" because jurors often do not understand them.

about the accident, is it?" Do not yet confront him with the prior inconsistent statement itself; merely make him concede that he gave a statement.[8]

You then must make sure the jurors understand the solemnity or importance of the out-of-court statement. This task would be easy if the judge would allow you to interrupt the cross-examination to make a speech to the jurors explaining why a deposition or a statement to a police officer is as sacred as testimony at trial. Because judges will not permit a speech during cross-examination, you instead must educate jurors through one-fact questions to the witness that lets the jury plainly see why the prior statement must be 1) truthful, 2) accurate, and 3) comprehensive because of its importance and the circumstances under which the witness made the earlier statement. Crediting the prior statement should render implausible all excuses the witness may invoke to explain away the inconsistency when confronted with the earlier statement.

Because of our own familiarity with the context of the prior statement and the adrenaline coursing through the body, the tendency is to rush through the crediting of the earlier statement. Instead, you must treat the giving of the earlier statement as its own story, one that leads the jurors to conclude that the witness surely would have spoken truthfully, accurately, and comprehensively. Cathy Bennett, currently the Director of Training for the Massachusetts Committee for Public Counsel Service, impeccably summarizes the mindset you should bring when crediting the prior statement on cross-examination:

> Try to create a visual image in the jurors' minds about what it looked like at the place and time when the witness made the statement. In order to do that for the jury, you will find it helpful to imagine and picture the physical circumstances of the prior statement and then walk through the process step by step in your mind. This will help you visualize and baby step the accreditation picture in your mind whether you are dealing with a transcript of previous testimony, police report, 911 call, witness statement or conversation. Then when you cross-examine the witness you can do it from the picture in your head and there will be no need to meander or stumble through the details. The jurors will see it as you describe it. This is the best way to persuade.[9]

---

8. Many trial lawyers advocate marking every document referred to in the course of trial with an exhibit number for identification, even though you do not intend to introduce the document into evidence. Indeed, some judges require it. They believe that marking every document helps to create a clear record. The authors disagree with this practice because documents with numbers have a way of finding their way into the jury room, either because the judge simply admits them though you did not offer them or because they get mixed up in the exhibits. If you mark only the documents you intend to offer into evidence, you avoid the possibility of this occurring. Of course, if the judge requires marking of all documents referred to, you must comply.

9. Cathleen Bennett, *Marry Storytelling and Technique in Impeachment by Inconsistent Statement* (unpublished).

For example, if the statement is contained in a deposition, you may ask a series of questions such as:

Q: Mr. Alexander, this is not the first time you testified about the collision, is it?

Q: You recall coming to my office to testify about how the collision happened?

Q: You gave this testimony at what is called a deposition, isn't that correct?

Q: This deposition was four months after the collision occurred?

Q: Obviously your deposition testimony was given much closer to the time of the collision than the testimony you gave this morning?

Q: You came to the deposition with your lawyer, Mr. Nolan, isn't that right?

Q: Your lawyer, Mr. Nolan, was present the whole time you were testifying?

Q: You took an oath to tell the truth before testifying here today, didn't you?

Q: Just as you took an oath to tell the truth before testifying here today, you took the same oath to tell the truth before answering questions at the deposition?

Q: Of course, you did tell the truth at the deposition, didn't you Mr. Alexander?

Q: The whole truth?

Q: You are aware the court reporter here today is taking down all my questions and your answers?

Q: There also was a court reporter present at your deposition, wasn't there Mr. Alexander?

Q: Just as the court reporter here today is taking down all my questions and your answers, the court reporter took down all the questions and answers at the deposition?

Q: And the court reporter typed out all the questions and answers in a transcript?

Q: In fact, Mr. Alexander, you had the opportunity to review the transcript of the questions and your answers given at the deposition?

Q: You did review the transcript to see if there were any mistakes in your answers?

Q: You also checked the transcript to make sure your answers were true and accurate?

Q: You signed the transcript only after making sure that your answers recorded on that transcript were true and accurate?

If the statement is a police report, you may wish to ask the officer:

Q: Officer, you made a report of your investigation of this crime, didn't you?

Q: You make these reports every time you investigate a crime as an ordinary part of your work, don't you?

Q: The reports collect and document the important facts in your investigation?

Q: That is where you preserve your observations?

Q: And the important information you learn?

Q: You make the report soon after the investigation, while it is still fresh in your mind, don't you?

Q: Officer, these reports you make are important, aren't they?

Q: You receive training in how to make them truthfully, don't you?

Q: You receive training in how to make the reports accurately, don't you?

Q: And to include the important details of the investigation?

Q: Of course, when you make your reports, you follow your training to be truthful, to be accurate, and to include the important details of the investigation?

Q: The report is an official document?

Q: Your reports are kept in files at the police department, aren't they?

Q: Other officers sometimes rely on your reports?

Q: And the higher-ups in the department?

Q: The prosecutor takes your report into consideration in determining whether to bring charges, right?

Q: You investigate a lot of crimes, don't you?

Q: And you can't remember the details of every one clearly, can you?

Q: You use your reports to refresh your recollection before you testify, don't you?

Some lawyers may find these examples to be too lengthy, boring, and perhaps confusing to the jurors. On the other hand, the effectiveness of impeachment turns on the jurors understanding that the circumstances under which the witness made the earlier statement was as significant and solemn as the surrounding in which he is testifying at trial. You must make your own assessment in determining the detail of your crediting of the prior statement.

Some lawyers advocate crediting the prior statement before confirming the in-court statement. The impeaching power of a prior inconsistent statement comes from its contrast with the witness's in-court testimony. The jurors will be more likely to recognize the inconsistency if you present the in-court statement and the prior inconsistent statement side by side. Consequently, you may choose to establish, explain, magnify, and solemnify the occasion on which the witness made the prior statement as the first step in impeachment.

Step Three: *Confront* the witness with the prior inconsistent statement. You now have taught the jurors why the prior statement is truthful, accurate, and comprehensive, and have placed on a pedestal the in-court testimony that is to be impeached. The final step is to show the jurors that the witness' in-court testimony is inconsistent with the earlier creditworthy statement by confronting the witness with that statement.

The witness may have been unaware of the direction of your cross when you were crediting the prior statement. However, the witness is now fully alert to the fact that impeachment is imminent and will instinctively resort to "fight or flight" mode. You cut off many of the escape routes by your thorough crediting of the prior statement. Now you must execute the confrontation step in a manner that prevents the witness from explaining away the inconsistency.

The witness's first and most plausible means of attempted escape will be to state that he does not remember every detail of what he said in his prior statement. To thwart this dodge, you must put the statement in front of the witness. Pick up the document that contains the prior statement, refer opposing counsel to the page and line where the statement is located, ask to approach, and show the statement to the witness. At this stage of impeachment, be careful not to get into a private conversation with the witness, ignoring the jurors. Do not huddle with the witness with your body positioned between the witness and the jurors. Stand to the side of the witness with your face to the jurors. If you have a copy of the document for yourself and another for the witness, you may hand the witness a copy. If you only have one copy, keep it in your hands, stand beside the witness, and show it to the witness.[10] Have the witness identify this document as the deposition, statement, or report that he has just acknowledged having made: "This is a copy of your sworn statement, isn't it?"[11]

Because the prior statement is sitting right in front of him, the witness can no longer evade impeachment by invoking an inability to recall his earlier statement. Instead, the witness will desperately search for any opportunity to explain away the inconsistency. If you confront the witness by asking "Isn't it true that at your deposition you testified the car was red?," the witness will seize on the word "testified" as calling for an explanation of the mental processes by which he heard and interpreted the question, and processed and communicated the answer. To eliminate this mode of evasion, you should confront the witness by a simple reading of the prior inconsistent statement.

You will be sorely tempted to have the witness read the prior statement to the jurors, believing impeachment will be enhanced if the words summon from the lips of the person who testified inconsistently at trial. Asking the witness to read his prior statement to the jurors, however, empowers the cornered witness to offer the explanation for the inconsistency in the course of the reading.[12]

To maximize the control over the witness during the confrontation, you should read the impeaching statement and ask the witness only to affirm the accuracy of your reading. In addition to retaining control, you will be able to place proper emphasis on the words of the prior statement that are inconsistent with the in-court testimony. Direct the witness's attention to the specific page and line where the inconsistent statement is found. Tell the witness to read along with you.

> Please read along with me on page 47, lines 12 through 16 of your deposition. "Question: How fast was the yellow car going? Answer: Not very fast. Question: How fast is that? Answer: Less than thirty miles per hour." [*Now, look back at the witness.*] Did I read that correctly? Answer: Yes.

Stop! When the witness has admitted making the prior inconsistent statement, it is time to quit. Never ask the witness to explain the inconsistency. Resist the temptation to ask the conclusory "so" question. Do not ask the witness whether he was lying then or now. Just stop. Immediately move on to another area of inquiry. Or, if you have finished cross-examining, sit down.

---

10. With the permission of the court, you may display the document to the jurors using available courtroom technology.

11. If the witness will not acknowledge the earlier statement, you may have to authenticate it by other evidence before reading it into evidence. In the case of a deposition, the court reporter is an obvious authenticating witness.

12. Impeached witnesses also tend to mumble. Although we recommend reading the statement yourself, some seasoned trial lawyers prefer to let the witness read the statement aloud, so the jurors will hear the inconsistent words from the witness's own lips. Devotees of this practice point out that the witness's mumbling or embarrassment only detracts from his credibility. You should utilize whichever method you believe, in your best professional judgment, will best impress the inconsistency on the minds of the jurors.

8.3.2 *Impeachment with Prior Inconsistent Oral Statements*

As we mentioned earlier, the Federal Rules of Evidence do not require you to show the witness anything before asking whether he made the prior statement.[13] In fact, you may impeach with a prior inconsistent statement that has never been written. Although this is somewhat unusual, the method would be the same. For example:

[Confirm *the testimony just given.*]

Q: Today, you claim that the yellow car was going sixty miles per hour.

A: That's right.

[Credit *the prior statement.*]

Q: Robert, you talked to Suzy Almeida immediately after the accident, didn't you?

A: Yeah.

Q: She's a good friend of yours, isn't she?

A: Yes.

Q: A person you often confide in?

A: I guess so.

[Confront *the witness with the prior statement.*]

Q: And you told Suzy Almeida that the yellow car was going about thirty miles per hour, didn't you?

Notice that it is much more effective to present prior inconsistent statements that are contained in documents. If Robert denies making the statement to Suzy, the court will not allow you to adjourn the cross, immediately call Suzy as a witness to recite Robert's prior inconsistent statement, and then return Robert to the stand and resume the original cross-examination. Rather, you will have to complete the cross-examination of Robert without the ability to confront him with the inconsistency. You then will have to wait for the later stage of the trial where you are permitted to call your own witnesses, and call Suzy to testify to the statement Robert made to her immediately after the accident.

8.4 Impeachment by Omission in the Prior Statement

While you will prepare your cross-examination before trial, one of your most important skills in cross-examination is your skill at listening to what the witness says during direct examination. Witnesses often say unexpected things on direct

---

13. FED. R. EVID. 613(a).

examination. These unexpected statements may be pearls the witnesses cast before you. The witness may reveal new favorable facts that will contribute to chapters of a constructive cross-examination. The witness may offer testimony that is squarely contradicted by her deposition, in which case you must consider the necessity and wisdom of adding impeachment by prior inconsistent statement to your planned cross. More commonly, the witness may offer details on direct examination that were never included in statements she made before trial. In such instances, you must consider whether to impeach the witness by omission in the prior statement.

As with impeachment by the prior inconsistent statement, you must first decide whether impeachment by omission is advisable. Are the newly disclosed facts harmful to your story of the case? Are the facts sufficiently significant that the jurors would expect that they would and should have been included in the prior statement? Is it plausible to argue that the witness was lying or mistaken when she testified to these facts on direct examination?

Assuming that you choose to attack the witness testifying to facts on direct that were not disclosed in earlier statements, the steps in impeachment by omission are the same as in impeachment by the prior inconsistent statement: 1) *Credit*, 2) *Commit*, and 3) *Confront*. The one difference is in the execution of the *Confront* step of the impeachment.

As with impeachment by contradiction, you must recognize that the witness now is in über-fight-or-flight mode. Once again, to prevent the witness from feigning lack of recollection of the content of the prior statement, you must put the document in front of her. Hand the witness a red pen and ask her to circle where in the statement she included the facts she stated in court.[14] Then revel in, and be prepared to accommodate, any and every excuse she proffers for the difficulty in circling the words.

Example

The investigating officer in the prosecution of Mr. Mills for knowingly receiving a stolen boat and trailer testified on direct examination that Mr. Mills refused to tell the officer the name of the person who gave him the boat.

Credit Circumstances under which the Prior Statement Was Made

> Q: You investigate a lot of crimes over the course of a year, correct?
>
> A: Correct, sir.
>
> Q: You can't remember every detail of every crime, isn't that right, officer?

---

14. Special thanks to Philadelphia Defender Mary DeFusco for the "red pen" technique.

National Institute for Trial Advocacy

A: That's correct.

Q: However you recognize that as part of your professional duties, you may be called upon to testify in court recalling details from one or more of these crimes?

A: Yes, sir.

Q: You do fill out an investigation report at the time of each investigation, is that correct?

A: That's correct, sir.

Q: You write down in that report the important circumstances of what you observed?

A: Yes, sir.

Q: It's important to be very thorough in those reports, isn't that right?

A: Correct.

Q: Is it fair to say that you make it your practice to try to put everything that is significant in those investigation reports?

A: To the extent that it is possible, yes.

Q: You also make it your practice to be accurate in your reports?

A: Of course.

Commit Witness to the Direct Examination Testimony

Q: Today it was your testimony on direct examination that Mr. Mills twice refused to give you name of the person who gave him the boat in New Jersey, correct?

A: That's correct, sir.

Confront the Witness with Prior Statement to Elicit Omission

Q: May I approach the witness Your Honor? Sir, this is the copy of the investigation report you filled out in this particular case, isn't that right?

A: Yes, sir.

Q: Can you please take this red pen and circle where in that report you indicated that Mr. Mills refused to tell you the name of the person who gave him the boat in New Jersey?

A: That is a very long report, sir.

Q: Officer, it was important enough for you to testify on direct examination that Mr. Mills refused to tell you the name of the person who gave him the boat, so take as much time as you need to circle that portion of your report.

A: The report is six pages long, sir.

Q: Officer, would you prefer that I ask the Court to take a recess so you can carefully read the report? When the jurors returns to the courtroom, you can show them where you used the red pen to circle where in the report you documented that Mr. Mills refused to tell you the name of the person who gave him the boat in New Jersey.

You must appreciate that time is working in your favor. The longer the witness takes before acknowledging that the facts he testified to on direct are not in the report, the more significant he makes the omission.

8.5 Exposing the Liar: Attacking the Witness's Character for Truthfulness

Often, you will not be able to catch the witness in a lie on the witness stand. You may not be able to prove that any particular thing the witness has said about your case is a lie. You may still, however, be able to prove that the witness is a liar.

A liar will not be believed, even when he speaks the truth.

—Aesop

The Rules of Evidence are quite leery of introducing evidence of other bad acts to prove a person's character,[15] but when a witness takes the stand, his character for truthfulness becomes relevant and the law of evidence partially opens the door to allow some proof of a witness's behavior that is probative of truthfulness.[16] In other words, every time a new witness testifies in court, a new issue is injected into the case: the credibility of that person. We are allowed to introduce evidence supporting an inference that this witness is the sort of person who is likely to lie on the witness stand. However, the law of evidence strictly circumscribes the kinds of evidence we may use for this purpose.

8.5.1 Opinion and Reputation Evidence

One method of offering evidence of a witness's untruthful character does not occur during cross-examination of the witness. That method is to call another

---

15. *See* FED. R. EVID. 404.
16. FED. R. EVID. 404(a)(3).

person to testify either that in her opinion the witness is an untruthful person or to testify that the witness has the reputation in the community of being an untruthful person.[17]

8.5.2 *Prior Convictions*

The fact that a witness has been convicted of a felony, no matter what the nature of the crime, has traditionally been considered relevant to an assessment of his credibility. This view is based on the assumption that anyone who has committed a felony is more likely to lie than a person who has not. The validity of that assumption, which holds that even serious violent crimes are relevant to truthfulness, is open to question to say the least. Nevertheless, the rule that prior felony convictions may be used to impeach credibility is firmly established in the law of evidence. The extent to which prior convictions are admissible to impeach credibility varies among jurisdictions. You must familiarize yourself with the evidence rule in the jurisdiction where your case is tried. For purposes of this discussion, we shall refer to Federal Rule of Evidence 609.[18]

---

17. FED. R. EVID. 608(a).
18. Rule 609. Impeachment by Evidence of Conviction of Crime
    (a)   **In General.** The following rules apply to attacking a witness's character for truthfulness by evidence of a criminal conviction:
    (1) for a crime that, in the convicting jurisdiction, was punishable by death or by imprisonment for more than one year, the evidence:
    (A) must be admitted, subject to Rule 403, in a civil case or in a criminal case in which the witness is not a defendant; and
    (B) must be admitted in a criminal case in which the witness is a defendant, if the probative value of the evidence outweighs its prejudicial effect to that defendant; and
    (2) for any crime regardless of the punishment, the evidence must be admitted if the court can readily determine that establishing the elements of the crime required proving–or the witness's admitting–a dishonest act or false statement.
    (b) **Limit on Using the Evidence After 10 Years.** This subdivision (b) applies if more than 10 years have passed since the witness's conviction or release from confinement for it, whichever is later. Evidence of the conviction is admissible only if:
    (1) its probative value, supported by specific facts and circumstances, substantially outweighs its prejudicial effect; and
    (2) the proponent gives an adverse party reasonable written notice of the intent to use it so that the party has a fair opportunity to contest its use.
    (c) **Effect of a Pardon, Annulment, or Certificate of Rehabilitation.** Evidence of a conviction is not admissible if:
    (1) the conviction has been the subject of a pardon, annulment, certificate of rehabilitation, or other equivalent procedure based on a finding that the person has been rehabilitated, and the person has not been convicted of a later crime punishable by death or by imprisonment for more than one year; or
    (2) the conviction has been the subject of a pardon, annulment, or other equivalent procedure based on a finding of innocence.
    (d) **Juvenile Adjudications.** Evidence of a juvenile adjudication is admissible under this rule only if:
    (1) it is offered in a criminal case;

1) **Convictions for crimes involving dishonesty or false statement.** Evidence of a witness's unpardoned and unannulled conviction for a crime involving dishonesty or false statement (but not a juvenile adjudication) is admissible. This is true no matter whether the crime is a felony or a misdemeanor. Other misdemeanor convictions are not admissible.

2) **Convictions for other felonies.** Evidence that the witness has been convicted for a felony not involving dishonesty or false statement is admissible in the court's discretion. If the witness is a criminal defendant, the court must find that the probative value of this species of felony conviction outweighs its prejudicial effect to the accused. If the witness is anyone other than a criminal defendant, the court should admit the evidence unless it finds that the evidence's probative value is substantially outweighed by one of the negative factors listed in Federal Rule of Evidence 403 (unfair prejudice, confusion of the issues, misleading the jury, undue delay, waste of time, needless presentation of cumulative evidence).

3) **Age limitation.** As a general rule, the court should not admit evidence of any conviction if more than ten years have elapsed since the date of conviction or of release from confinement, whichever is later. However, a court may allow evidence even of these ancient convictions if it finds that their probative value *substantially outweighs* their prejudicial effect.[19]

4) **Method.** Although you are not required to ask a witness about her prior convictions on cross-examination as a prelude to introducing extrinsic evidence of them, you should always do so. This evidence is most damaging to the witness's credibility when she is stung with it during cross-examination. Indeed, that is why the lawyer who called the witness should elicit this information during direct examination, a process commonly referred to as "drawing the sting."[20] Be aware, though, that even if your opponent has not brought out the fact of a prior conviction on direct examination, you may nonetheless inquire about it on cross-examination.

It is the fact of the former conviction, and not the facts surrounding the crime, that is admissible. Therefore, you are quite limited in the scope of your questions.

---

(2) the adjudication was of a witness other than the defendant;
(3) an adult's conviction for that offense would be admissible to attack the adult's credibility; and
(4) admitting the evidence is necessary to fairly determine guilt or innocence.
(e) **Pendency of an Appeal.** A conviction that satisfies this rule is admissible even if an appeal is pending. Evidence of the pendency is also admissible.
19. In some jurisdictions, the ban on such ancient convictions is absolute. *See, e.g.*, ARK. R. EVID. 609(b).
20. A criminal defendant waives any objection if his lawyer "draws the sting" of his prior conviction during direct examination. Ohler v. United States, 529 U.S. 753 (2000).

You may generally only elicit the fact and date of conviction, the jurisdiction, and the crime for which the witness was convicted.

If the witness denies the conviction, you must prove it by extrinsic evidence. Rule 609 places no limitation on the form of evidence that may be used prove a prior conviction or on the time during trial when the evidence may be offered. The usual, preferred form of proof is a certified copy of the judgment of conviction. Unless you are prepared to give a compelling reason why you cannot obtain a certified copy of the judgment of conviction, that is the form of extrinsic evidence you should offer.

8.5.3 *Prior Unconvicted Bad Acts*

What if a witness has committed some bad act that did not result in a criminal conviction? Can you ask her about it on cross-examination? If she denies it, can you introduce evidence to contradict her denial?

The answer to the first question is that you may ask the witness about the prior bad act only if the act was one that is probative of untruthfulness.[21] For example, if the witness was expelled from college for cheating, or lied on a job application, you can ask about it. You may not ask about a prior, unconvicted act involving violence, such as assault, or one involving conduct that is merely errant and does not involve an element of falsehood, such as public drunkenness.

You must, of course, have a good-faith basis to ask a question about a prior bad act. Because a sustained objection to your attempt to ask it can be devastating, you should always inform the court of your intentions before you sail into these waters. Show the court your evidence and obtain the court's blessing on your venture.

And what if the witness denies the act? The answer to this second question may seem strange, but Rule 608(b) leaves you stuck with the witness's negative answer. You may not introduce extrinsic evidence to contradict her answer.[22]

However, all is not lost. The law of ethics may come to our rescue where the law of evidence leaves us hanging. A lawyer must not present or allow anyone else to present false evidence.[23] Therefore, if you disclose your intention and basis to the court in advance and allow opposing counsel an opportunity to object, the court will recognize the falsity of the witness's answer and may take appropriate disciplinary action. Further, the opposing lawyer is required to instruct her witness to answer truthfully. If the court allows you to ask this question but says that you do so at your own risk

---

21. FED. R. EVID. 608(b).
22. *Id.* Note that Rule 608(b)'s prohibition of extrinsic evidence only applies when your purpose for offering the evidence is to support an inference of untruthful character. You may offer extrinsic evidence of other acts to prove bias. As in other instances when evidence is admissible for one purpose but not for another, the court must balance its probative value for the permissible purpose against the danger that the jurors will use it to support the impermissible inference.
23. *See* MODEL RULES OF PROFESSIONAL CONDUCT 3.3 (2003).

of a denial by the witness, at least you know where you stand. You can then exercise informed judgment about whether to ask the question. The act may be so distasteful that the mere fact of asking the question may serve to impeach the witness, despite a denial. However, unless you are sure that the witness will admit the conduct, it is usually best to avoid this line of questioning.

8.6 Revealing Reasons to Shade the Truth or Lie: Attacking the Witness for Bias, Prejudice, Interest, or Corruption

Witnesses are people with motives. From the jurors' perspective, the ideal witness would be entirely impartial. But no witness is entirely impartial. Each witness will, consciously or unconsciously, slant his testimony in one party's favor. Any partiality that may affect the witness's testimony may be brought to the jurors' attention during cross-examination and through the introduction of other evidence. We generally refer to this method of attacking a witness's credibility as impeachment for bias. Impeachment for bias is not mentioned in the Federal Rules of Evidence, although it is referred to in the Advisory Committee's Notes. Nevertheless, it is a time-honored method of impeachment.

Though a witness's partiality may derive from any of a number of sources, four categories of influence that tend to affect a person's objectivity are the traditional subjects of impeachment: bias, prejudice, interest, and corruption.

Bias, in this narrower sense, connotes a disposition to feel undue affinity toward one party. It does not necessarily impute an evil motive to the witness. Each of us is inevitably and irreversibly biased in favor of some people and that fact is admissible. The obvious examples are witnesses who are closely related to a party, such as a party's parent, child, or spouse.

You should usually approach bias gingerly. If the relationship is a particularly intimate and affectionate one, such as mother and son, and the jury knows of it, the relationship can often be ignored on cross-examination and only mentioned in passing during summation. On the other hand, in a case in which a party's close relative or friend testifies, it can sometimes be very effective to bring out the bias on cross-examination.

> Q: Mrs. Taylor, you are the defendant's godmother, isn't that right?
>
> A: Yes, I am
>
> Q: No further questions.

If the relationship is less intimate, such as employer and employee, it should probably be brought out during cross-examination. Simply have the witness acknowledge the relationship and do not attempt to force the witness to admit bias. Instead, expose the facts that might make the witness feel more inclined to testify favorably for your opponent.

Q: You've been employed by the defendant for six years?

A: That's right.

Q: You like your job?

A: Yes.

Q: You are hoping for a promotion next year?

A: Yes.

You will argue during summation that the admitted relationship must necessarily have colored the witness's testimony.

Some relationships can be attacked head-on. For example, if the witness and a party are fraternity brothers, members of the same police force, or members of the same charitable organization or other small group, bring out the group membership. Find out whether the fraternity or group oath or tradition requires loyalty to the organization, brotherhood, or club. If, for example, the Aryan Brothers take an oath not to say anything that would harm another brother, the jurors need to know about both the membership and the oath.

Prejudice is the converse of bias: a dislike of one party. It may result from bigotry or from bad experiences. Bigotry is difficult to attack because it is usually buried deep within the soul of the bigot and will rarely be acknowledged. Only when the bigotry has manifested itself in some overt way, such as words or violent acts toward the hated class or membership in intolerant groups, can it be successfully brought out on cross-examination. Prejudice born of bad experiences, though less odious than bigotry, is much more accessible to cross-examination. For example, if the witness was sued last year by your client and lost, the witness may bear a grudge. On cross-examination you should be able to explore any reason that the witness might harbor bad feelings about the people or events that form the subject matter of her testimony. If, for example, the witness testifies that Billy hit Jimmy first, you should be able to explore any reason why the witness might not like Billy. This evidence would support an inference that the witness might be inclined to make up bad things about Billy.

Q: You were engaged to be married to Billy, weren't you?

A: Yes.

Q: And he broke it off with you in May?

A: Right.

Q: After you had already bought a wedding gown and sent out invitations?

A: Yes.

As a general rule, you should not ask a witness whether he is prejudiced. Merely inquire about the underlying facts from which the jury may conclude that the witness is prejudiced and argue the inference of prejudice during closing. However, if the prejudice has manifested itself in some overt act of which you have independent evidence, you may ask the witness if he is prejudiced, and when he denies it, introduce evidence of the act to contradict his denial.

For example, assume that the witness is a Klansman and you represent an African American. Assume further that you have a photograph in which he can clearly be identified as a participant in a cross burning. You may ask him, "Sir, you don't like African Americans much, do you?" After he makes some waffling denial, such as, "Oh, I don't really have anything against anybody," you can present the photograph and force him to admit that he is the person depicted.

Nobody speaks the truth when there's something they must have.

—Elizabeth Bowen

Interest refers to a witness's stake in the outcome of the case. Any association with one of the parties that might give the witness such an interest raises an inference that the witness's testimony may lean toward the party from whose victory he may receive a dividend. The stake may be something as subtle as the prospect of future employment as an expert witness. Therefore, an expert witness is always subject to being asked on cross-examination whether he is being paid. The fact of his being a hired gun supports the inference that he understandably wants to justify his pay. He may also be asked whether he works for a particular class of persons, such as personal injury plaintiffs or defendants, on a regular basis. Similarly, the state's witness who has been granted immunity or a reduced sentence in exchange for his testimony may be cross-examined about the grant of immunity.

Corruption refers to the deliberate falsification of testimony as a result of payment, threat, coercion, or other evil influence. The opportunity to utilize this means of impeachment arises infrequently. But if the occasion does arise and if you are able to prove corruption, no other means of impeachment is so devastating to a witness's credibility. When you have the independent evidence to back up a charge of corruption, you may ask the witness about it on cross-examination and, no matter whether he denies it, introduce the extrinsic evidence that proves it.

Chapter Nine

Expert Witnesses

"Professor," John began with a look of dismay, "My senior partner just asked me to prepare our expert for trial. I am absolutely not the right person to do it. The guy is an expert in inferential statistics. For Pete's sake, I don't know anything about inferential statistics and my eyes glaze over when I hear the first thing about numbers. Should I ask the partner if she can find somebody else?"

"Oh no," said the Professor. "The fact that you know almost nothing about the topic is an asset. Your challenge will be to remember what you do not know."

"Remember what I do not know? You're doing it again, Professor. You're talking in circles."

"Like you, the jury who hears your case probably won't know anything about inferential statistics. When the case goes to trial, if you can remember what you do not know now, what you do not understand, what makes your eyes glaze over, then you will be able to ask the right questions to help the jurors learn about it for the first time."

"But how do I prepare a witness when I don't know anything about the subject?"

"Let the witness teach you."

"So, I just go into this preparation session and let the expert teach me? That's all?" John looked incredulous.

"No, of course not. The expert will teach you about inferential statistics. You will teach the expert about this case. Together, you will explore how inferential statistics may help you prove your theory of the case."

9.1   Interviewing Your Expert Witness before Trial

A non-expert witness generally tells the jury only what he knows from personal experience.[1] A non-expert must stick to the facts: tell the jurors what he perceived and refrain from characterizing the evidence or expressing an opinion about it.

---

1. *See* FED. R. EVID. 602.

For example, a non-expert in a criminal case may testify, "I saw Fred come running out of Joe's Bar with a gun in his hand and a fist full of money." He will not be permitted to go on and express his opinion: "In my opinion, nobody would run out of a bar like that unless he had just robbed the place." The non-expert is limited to relating what he saw or heard because it is the jurors' job to evaluate the information, make inferences, and draw the conclusion that Fred just robbed Joe's Bar.

The public do not know enough to be experts,
but know enough to decide between them.

—*Samuel Butler*

In many situations, however, the jurors will be unqualified or unable to interpret the information provided by the perceptions of a witness. In a medical malpractice case, for example, if a non-expert witness testified, "I watched from the gallery as Dr. Botchco cut open Marcie's chest and used a saw to cut through her chest bones," the jurors would have no way of knowing whether Dr. Botchco had completed a surgery or committed an act of butchery. In those cases where the training, education, or experience of a witness will help the jurors understand testimony that is out of the realm of everyday experience, an expert witness may be called.[2] The kinds of matters that may be out of the realm of the jurors' experience may include a wide variety of technical, scientific, economic, or historical fields. If the issue in the case involves the habits of bees, a beekeeper might be an appropriate expert. If the issue involves the appropriate technique for digging the foundation of a building, a builder or architect or even an experienced ditch-digger might be an appropriate expert. Any area in which a person may have specialized knowledge that will assist the jurors in deciding the issues in the case may be appropriate for expert testimony.

Once qualified as "expert," these witnesses become a special species of witness: because of their expertise, knowledge, training, or experience, they are allowed to evaluate the evidence in the case, make inferences, draw conclusions, and give the jurors their opinions on what the evidence means. The expert witness can tell the jurors not only what Dr. Botchco did during the surgery, but also explain to the jury why Dr. Botchco did what he did, whether his surgical technique met accepted standards of care in the medical community, and how long the patient is likely to live after the surgery.

---

2. FED. R. EVID. 702. Testimony by Expert Witnesses.
    A witness who is qualified as an expert by knowledge, skill, experience, training, or education may testify in the form of an opinion or otherwise if:
    (a) the expert's scientific, technical, or other specialized knowledge will help the trier of fact to understand the evidence or to determine a fact in issue;
    (b) the testimony is based on sufficient facts or data;
    (c) the testimony is the product of reliable principles and methods; and
    (d) the expert has reliably applied the principles and methods to the facts of the case.

Expert witnesses play an important role in most trials. Indeed, in many cases it is not possible to meet your burden of proving each and every element without the presentation of expert testimony. Carefully choosing and preparing your expert may be the key to winning your case. You will want to find an expert who possesses impressive qualifications, who is able to communicate well with the jurors, and who is convinced of the merits of your cause. To find the right expert, you might have to interview several.

Interviewing an expert witness is a two-way street. Each of you must teach the other. You must let your expert know what the legal issues are and advise her of the subjects upon which her opinion is needed. You must tell her exactly what opinions you need, but you must not try to tell her what her opinions should be. In other words, inform the expert about the legal standards that apply to the case. Tell her your theory of the case, give her the facts, be absolutely honest, and conceal nothing. You do not want the following exchange to occur during the cross-examination of your expert at your trial:

Q: Doctor, you just stated that in your opinion the amount of anesthetic administered to the plaintiff during surgery was inappropriate.

A: Absolutely.

Q: Doctor, isn't it true that drug addicts have a higher tolerance for certain anesthetics and therefore may require a different dosage?

A: Yes.

Q: Are you aware that the plaintiff in this case is a Valium addict?

A: No, I was not. That changes everything.

To avoid this disaster, you must not whitewash your case. Reveal the bad along with the good. Give the expert witness the unvarnished raw materials with which you are asking her to work, complete with all the wormholes, knots, and cracks.

During the interview, the expert's side of the exchange of information is to evaluate the information you provide about the case and tell you what her opinion is on each subject you delineate. Often it will be necessary to provide the expert with extensive data, files, or documents relevant to the case. The expert may need significant time before your first meeting to read the files and become familiar with the facts of your case. In forming an opinion, an expert witness may rely on information that may not be admissible in the trial as long as it is the type of information that experts in that field generally rely on.

If the expert's opinions will be helpful to your case, you will probably call her as a witness. But before deciding to call this expert to the stand, you must find out *why* she formed whatever opinions she holds. The Rules of Evidence require that the expert's conclusions be based on the kind and quality of information that experts in that field reasonably rely on.[3] Further, that information must have been evaluated using reliable methods and must be applied reliably to the facts in the present case.[4] Beyond the evidentiary standard, however, your expert will only be persuasive if she can explain how and why she reached her conclusions. Moreover, your opponent will often call an expert witness whose opinions are dramatically different from those of your expert. Therefore, it is vitally important to find out why your expert disagrees with the opponent's expert. Ask her. Learn from her the fallacies in the other side's position.

Have your witness explain the process she used to reach her conclusion. Ask her to explain the process used by the opponent's expert. Explore the assumptions both experts have made and ask why her assumptions and analysis are more reasonable than those of the opposing expert. You will have access to copies of your opponent's expert witness report.[5] Have your expert go over it with you in great detail. Make sure your witness can explain why she is right and the opponent's expert is wrong. Make sure that your expert can back up her opinion and every step of her analysis with authority from her field. This is important. You do not want a Lone Ranger expert. You want the most mainstream expert you can find. If your expert is too far from the mainstream of her field or if her methods or conclusions are not supported by the work of other experts in the same field, your opponent may be able to convince the judge that the opinion is "unreliable" and therefore inadmissible under Rule 702. Pretrial motions to exclude expert witness testimony are increasingly common as trial judges take seriously their responsibility to act as "gatekeepers" to keep out unreliable opinion evidence. Of course, you, too, should consider whether your opponent's expert witness might be excluded through a pretrial motion.

In most situations, exclusion of the expert will not take place and the two experts will agree on basic methodology, but disagree on the specific application to the case at hand. Most often, the two experts look at the case differently because they have based their opinions on slightly (or even vastly) different versions of the facts. You have presented the facts of the case as you believe them to be to your expert. These facts become the assumptions on which the expert's opinion is grounded. As you prepare your expert for trial, warn her that the cross-examiner may ask her to admit

---

3. Rule 703. Bases of an Expert's Opinion Testimony.

    An expert may base an opinion on facts or data in the case that the expert has been made aware of or personally observed. If experts in the particular field would reasonably rely on those kinds of facts or data in forming an opinion on the subject, they need to not be admissible for the opinion to be admitted. But if the facts or data would otherwise be inadmissible, the proponent of the opinion may disclose them to the jury only if their probative value in helping the jury evaluate the opinion substantially outweighs their prejudicial effect.

4. *See* FED. R. EVID. 702.

5. *See* FED. R. CIV. P. 26(a)(2), requiring disclosure of information relating to experts to be presented at trial.

that her opinion would be different if different assumptions were made. Advise her to acknowledge that fact if it is correct. Instruct her to seize any opportunity offered during cross-examination to explain why her assumptions are more likely to be valid than those of the opposing expert. Assure her that you will give her the opportunity to defend her assumptions on redirect examination.

This two-way approach to interviewing your expert will enable each of you to prepare for an effective presentation of her direct testimony. She will have taught you what questions to ask on direct examination to effectively present the testimony. She will be prepared to successfully defend her opinions from the attacks of the cross-examiner and you will learn what questions to ask the opponent's expert witness on cross-examination.

9.2   Preparing the Expert for the Courtroom

Imagine yourself sitting in a courtroom after lunch trying to stay awake while an expert witness drones on and on, answering endless questions with incomprehensible words. The lawyer asking questions and the expert answering them are using language only they understand. When the witness finally finishes testifying, nobody in the courtroom is sure exactly what she said or why she testified, unless it was to prove that the examining lawyer had mastered the expert's jargon.

Most of the fundamental ideas of science are essentially simple, and may, as a rule, be expressed in a language comprehensible to everyone.

—Albert Einstein

The direct examination of an expert witness does not have to be that way. An expert's function is to teach and clarify, not confuse. You must make sure that your expert witness speaks in terms the jurors can understand. Every trade and profession has its jargon, and many experts have difficulty expressing their knowledge in language devoid of technical terms that are incomprehensible to the lay listener. When an expert witness uses terms of art that are understandable only to other members of her calling, you must interrupt and make the expert explain in ordinary language what the words mean. For example, jurors will probably not know what a patella or femur is, but they all will be familiar with a kneecap and a thigh bone. This is not to say that the expert should refrain from using the technical terms. To the contrary, the expert should use the language of her field because it will often be more accurate and impressive to the jurors. But the expert must also explain. A juror expects a physician to say things like, "The patient presented with an acute upper respiratory infection." While your expert should not avoid using technical language, she should add the explanation, "In other words, she came into the office with a common cold."

Your expert witness must state her opinions simply, forcefully, and unequivocally. Many experts who are inexperienced witnesses do not understand that, in most situations, the evidentiary standard for expressing an expert opinion is reasonable degree of professional certainty. She does not have to be certain to state an opinion. If an expert, using her professional judgment, is able to reach a conclusion, she may testify that, in her opinion, the conclusion is the fact. For example, the pathologist who conducted an autopsy may not be certain whether a death resulted from homicide, suicide, or natural causes. Nevertheless, if the pathologist concludes to a reasonable degree of medical certainty that the death was more likely than not a homicide, she may simply state as her opinion that it was a homicide. Experts who are experienced witnesses know this. But the inexperienced witness often will be quite tentative in offering her opinions. She may try to be scientifically objective and say something like, "We can't really be sure, but we think the cause was homicide." You must prepare that overly cautious witness to respond simply and forthrightly to your question concerning cause of death. The key exchange should go like this:

> Q: Based on your autopsy and post-mortem investigation, have you formed an opinion to a reasonable degree of medical certainty as to what was the cause of death?
>
> A: Yes.
>
> Q: Doctor, what is that opinion?
>
> A: It was a homicide.

Then your witness can explain the basis for her opinion and, in the process, explain why she discounted the possibilities that the death could have been a suicide or the result of natural causes.

The best way to prepare your expert witness for the courtroom is to practice. Put your expert in the "witness stand," explain how the courtroom will be set up, and designate a place in the room as the "jury box." You can then take a seat in the "jury box." Go through the formalities of swearing in your witness. Have one of your colleagues play the role of direct examiner and have him ask the direct examination questions in the same way that you will ask them at trial. Listen to your expert respond and take notes. After a few questions or a few minutes, interrupt the mock-direct examination to give your witness some feedback.

Be sure to tell the witness what she is doing well. Encourage your witness to speak directly to the jurors. Encourage your witness to take time to explain things and to teach the jurors about her field. Tell her to watch out for "weasel words." Many experts habitually phrase their opinions in tentative terms, tending to include words and phrases such as "I think," "could have," "possibly," or "might have." Remind the witness to speak in more definitive terms. This expert has an opinion or she would not be on the witness stand, so be sure she states it forcefully, confidently, and with an air of certainty.

Next, practice a mock cross-examination. Encourage your witness to continue to direct her remarks to the jurors, rather than to the opposing lawyer. Encourage your witness to answer questions as forthrightly as possible, but to be assertive about areas which may need explanation or matters on which she disagrees with the cross-examiner.

Finally, remember that your witness is an expert in a field because she has a passion for that field. Do everything you can to make sure that the expert communicates her energy, passion, and intensity about her subject to the jurors. Use hands-on demonstrations, exhibits, and the witness's ability to teach. Find reasons for the expert to step down from the stand and work in front of the jurors. Incorporate a chalkboard, diagram, or a model into the testimony. Encourage your expert to be as animated and enthusiastic as the subject allows.

9.3 Presenting the Direct Testimony of Your Expert Witness

As you begin direct examination of your expert witness, you will have several technical things you need to ask about. You will want to introduce the witness as an expert in the field, but you also want the jurors to feel like this is a person they know and care about. The expert witness is on the stage and you have to put on a good show.

It's showtime, folks!

— *From* All That Jazz

9.3.1 *Emphasize the Expert's Opinions and Conclusions*

Until the Federal Rules of Evidence were adopted in 1975, the common law of evidence required lawyers to establish the expert's qualifications, link the expert to the case, and establish the basis for the opinion. Only then could the lawyer elicit the expert's opinion. By that time, the jurors were often asleep, bored, or distracted, and the opinion could easily be lost in a haystack of technical lingo. The lawyer's hands were tied. You either did it that way and risked losing the impact of the opinion in the process, or you were unable get the opinion into evidence at all.

That is no longer the case. Federal Evidence Rule 705 provides:

> The expert may testify in terms of opinion or inference and give reasons therefore without prior disclosure of the underlying facts or data . . . .

Given this flexibility, you should structure an expert's direct testimony to maximize the jurors' understanding of, and willingness to accept, the opinion.

Read literally, Federal Rule 705 would enable you to completely eliminate testimony concerning the basis for the expert's opinion from your direct examination. However, you should *never* eliminate the basis because it is the foundation of the opinion's credibility. When the expert explains the basis of the opinion, she explains to the jurors why her opinion is correct. The practical effect of Rule 705 is to allow you to present your expert's opinion at an earlier juncture of the direct examination for maximum impact on, and retention by, the jurors.

9.3.2 A Basic Outline for the Direct Examination of an Expert Witness

The following topical outline of the chapters of the direct examination of an expert witness contains all the necessary components, and arranges them in the order that is usually most persuasive.

1) Introduce the witness and alert the jurors about what type of opinion the expert will offer

2) Establish the expert's qualifications

3) Connect the expert witness to the case and elicit the opinion

4) Teach the jurors how to reach the opinion

5) Disclose the facts underlying the opinion

6) Reiterate the opinion and explain the basis for the opinion

7) Disprove the opinion of the opposing expert

The outline assumes that you have called the expert witness for the purpose of eliciting a single opinion. Of course, you will sometimes need to elicit several opinions from the same expert witness. When this is the case, you may simply adapt the outline to accommodate the number of opinions you need to elicit.

Step One: Introduce the witness and alert the jurors about what type of opinion the expert will offer. As with every direct examination, ask the witness to introduce herself to the jurors. Unlike lay witnesses, you should follow the introduction with questions that alert the jurors to the type of opinions the expert will offer during the direct exam. She cannot state the opinion yet, but this "headnote" serves to educate the jurors to the witness's purpose for being in the courtroom.[6] For example, after the expert has introduced herself, you might ask,

> Q: Dr. White, have you come to court prepared to offer your expert opinion on the diagnosis of Mr. Malloy's present injuries?
>
> A: Yes.

---

6. This technique is sometimes referred to as "foreshadowing." *See* chapter six.

Q: Dr. White, are you also prepared to offer your expert opinion as to the cause of Mr. Malloy's present injuries?

A: Yes.

Q: Doctor, before getting into these opinions, let's discuss what qualifies you to reach these opinions.

This colloquy previews the subject of the opinions Dr. White will share with the jurors. The questions also will motivate the jurors to be interested in the next chapter of the direct: Dr. White's qualifications.

Step Two: Establish the expert's qualifications. The rules of evidence relax the ordinary competence requirement by allowing expert witnesses to offer opinions even where they have no personal knowledge of the underlying facts.[7] On the other hand, the rules of evidence impose an additional competence requirement for experts, mandating that you satisfy the court that the witness is sufficiently qualified in the field to render opinions.[8] Consequently, you must have the witness testify to the specialized knowledge, skill, experience, training, or education that qualifies her to offer an opinion on the subject. Aside from being required, this step allows the expert to convince the jurors that she is someone worth listening to.

Do not assume that all jurors understand the nature of the expert's profession or the prerequisites to practicing that profession. Lay persons often do not know. For example, few people understand the medical specialties. For years, one of the authors has illustrated this point by asking third-year law students (a fairly enlightened group) whether an anesthesiologist and a psychiatrist are medical doctors. Usually, at least half do not know. Take heed of this general ignorance and after the expert states her profession, ask her to describe it to the jurors. For example, after Dr. White says she is an orthopedic surgeon, your initial follow-up questions could be: "Doctor, what is orthopedic surgery?" "Doctor, is an orthopedic surgeon a medical doctor?"

If your expert had to complete years of education and pass rigorous examinations before becoming licensed or certified in her field, be sure the full extent of the expert's background is communicated to the jurors. Many jurors have had no experience with higher education and simply do not know the extent of the training physicians, scientists, and other learned professionals are required to complete. For all they know, these professionals only take a six-week correspondence course after graduating from high school.

Additional qualifications you should establish when they are applicable include:

- specialized certification in the field

---

7. *Compare* Fed. R. Evid. 602 *and* Fed. R. Evid. 703.
8. *See* Fed. R. Evid. 702.

- practical experience

- employment

- teaching positions

- publications

- offices in professional societies

- honors

- awards

- memberships

- previous acceptance by courts as an expert witness in the pertinent field of expertise

Seeing the witness's qualifications in writing will impress the jurors and help them remember your expert's qualifications. Introduce the witness's curriculum vitae as a summary exhibit.[9] Give each juror a copy and have the expert point out and explain the most important qualifications, honors, and achievements as she testifies.

While it is important to help the jurors understand the witness's professional education, training, and experience, do not neglect the human side of her story. Ask "Dr. White, what led you to decide to become an orthopedic surgeon?"[10] When the jurors see the authenticity of Dr. White's motivation to pursue her profession, they will put greater stock in the substance of the opinion she is offering at trial.

Dealing with Offers to Stipulate to Qualifications

You also must prepare to counter opposing counsel's offer to stipulate to the qualifications of your expert witness. At first blush, this may seem to be a sporting and time-saving proposition. However, you may rest assured that the offer is made for the sole purpose of preventing the jurors from hearing the full extent of your expert's qualifications. Graciously refuse the offer to stipulate to your expert's qualifications. You are not required to accept a stipulation, and it is of utmost importance that the jurors learn why this witness is a true expert, a person whose opinions should be accepted.

You also must prepare to respond to pressure from the judge to accept the stipulation, or to abbreviate the time spent on the qualifications chapter of your direct.

Direct Examiner: Dr. White, can you tell us about the formal education needed to become an orthopedic surgeon?

---

9. *See* FED. R. EVID. 1006.
10. Thanks to trial lawyer extraordinaire William Caroselli for this invaluable tip.

Opposing Counsel:	Your Honor, the defense stipulates that Dr. White is qualified to render an opinion about the diagnosis and cause of Mr. Malloy's injuries.
The Court:	Counsel, given that stipulation, is there any need to spend time asking Dr. White about his qualifications?
Direct Examiner:	Yes, Your Honor. While opposing counsel has stipulated to the admissibility of Dr. White's opinion, it is important that the jurors hear the qualifications to decide what weight to give that opinion. The defense is calling its own expert to give an opinion on diagnosis and causation. The jurors are entitled to learn and compare the qualification of the experts in deciding which opinion to accept.
The Court:	Very well, counsel. But could you try to move more quickly through qualifications in light of the stipulation?
Direct Examiner:	Your Honor, I will proceed as quickly as I can to share Dr. White's qualification with the jurors.

Just as you rejected opposing counsel's stipulation, you must not alter your planned direct or withhold Dr. White's important qualification from the jurors in response to the court's urging.

Formally Tender the Witness as an Expert

When you have concluded your questions regarding qualifications, you should formally tender the witness as an expert witness in the requisite field.

Your Honor, plaintiff tenders Dr. White as an expert in the field of orthopedic surgery, including diagnosis and treatment of injuries to the back.

Just as the court must rule on the admissibility of an exhibit before its content is shared with the jurors, the court must determine the expert is qualified before the jurors can hear her opinion.[11] Before ruling on the tender, the court is likely to turn to opposing counsel and ask whether she wishes to voir dire, or question the witness on qualifications.

Opposing counsel must respond strategically to the court's invitation. If you believe the witness is truly unqualified, you should conduct a full-throated cross-examination on qualifications at that juncture. Given the liberal standard for

---

11. *See* FED. R. EVID. 104(a).

qualification and the availability of pretrial hearing to exclude unreliable expert testimony, your voir dire of the expert on qualifications will rarely result in preclusion of the opinion. You nonetheless could choose to voir dire the expert to show the jury weaknesses in qualifications before the jurors hear the opinion. However, any doubts the jurors may harbor about credentials are likely to be erased by the judge's proclamation at the conclusion of your voir dire accepting the witness as an expert. In most cases, then, you should wait until your full cross to bring out deficiencies in the expert's qualifications that the jurors should consider in evaluating the weight to give those opinions.[12]

Step Three: Connect the witness to the case and elicit the opinion. Ask the witness how she became involved in the case and generally what she has done to gain familiarity with it. This step is technically required in order to establish the relevance of the witness's expert testimony.[13] Even if this step were not required, it would be necessary in order to inform the jurors how the witness came to be involved in the case and what her role is. If your witness has extensive involvement, this testimony serves to build her credibility, particularly if the witness was not hired for purposes of the litigation and was involved as an expert outside the context of the lawsuit. For instance, the plaintiff's treating physician should be given an opportunity to fully describe the extent of her involvement with her patient. Even if your witness was hired solely for the purpose of testifying in the lawsuit and contradicting the opponent's expert witness, you should bring out her limited involvement, including the fact she is being paid for her time. If you do not, your opponent can severely damage your witness's (and your) credibility by bringing out the limited involvement and payment during cross-examination.

In some cases, you will find that the best strategy is to ask only the questions that are absolutely necessary to establish the relevance of the expert's testimony at this stage and then immediately elicit the opinion. You can double-back to fill in the details of the witness's involvement in the case when you get to "Chapter Five," which is disclosing the facts underlying the opinion. This technique will enable the jurors to hear the opinion early in the expert's testimony, when the jurors are most curious and interested.

The jurors will be eager to hear the opinion when your expert takes the stand. Satisfy their curiosity by delivering the opinion to them before they become impatient or lose interest. Immediately after qualifying the witness and establishing her

---

12. Opposing counsel must take pains to avoid inadvertent waiver of cross-examination on qualifications. When the court asks if you wish to voir dire the expert, you should reply as follows:
> Your Honor, the defense has no objection to Dr. White offering opinions on direct examination. However, we reserve the right to ask Dr. White questions about his qualifications during our full cross to aid the jurors in determining what weight to give Dr. White's opinions.

Of course, if the court responds by saying "now or never," you should cross-examine Dr. White on qualifications immediately following the tender.

13. *See* Fed. R. Evid. 402 and 702.

connection to the case, ask whether she has formed an opinion on the relevant subject and have her tell the jurors that opinion. This early statement of the opinion, after having alerted the jurors in Step One that it is coming, underscores the opinion in the minds of the jurors.

To be relevant, the expert must hold the opinion to the available degree of professional certainty. Consequently, asking an expert witness for her opinion consists of two questions: "Have you formed an opinion, to a reasonable degree of professional certainty, on . . . ?" and "What is that opinion?" During your witness preparation session, you should alert the witness to answer the question in two stages, just as you ask it. The answer to the first question should be a simple yes. When the second question is asked, the witness should express the opinion in her own words.

This set of questions is often crucial, particularly in a case where surviving your opponent's motion for directed verdict and getting the case to the jurors depends upon admission of the expert's opinion. Therefore, carefully word the question to ensure that its answer meets any applicable legal standard of proof. Write it out if necessary. For example, in a medical malpractice suit, the law in the jurisdiction may require a physician to testify "to a reasonable degree of medical probability" that the defendant failed to act in accordance with a specific standard of care. In such a case, a precise question is essential. After examining the applicable law, your question might be, "Doctor, have you formed an opinion, to a reasonable degree of medical probability, whether the defendant applied with reasonable care the degree of skill and learning ordinarily possessed and used by members of his profession in good standing, engaged in the same specialty in the locality in which he practices, or in a similar locality?"[14]

Step Four: Teach the jurors how to reach the opinion. The rules of evidence permit you to call an expert witnesses only if the expert can "assist the trier of fact to understand the evidence or determine a fact in issue."[15] Your direct examination should do exactly what the evidence rule contemplates: teach the jurors the information they need to know to be able to reach the opinion they just heard from the expert.

In most issues of significance, the opposing party will call its own expert to offer an opinion different than the one proffered by your expert. You will argue in closing that your expert is better qualified to render an accurate opinion, based that opinion on more reliable or comprehensive information, and/or is a more credible witness. But the jurors are most likely to accept the opinion offered by your expert if they have reached the same conclusion of their own accord.

---

14. *See, e.g.*, ARK. CODE ANN. § 16-114-206(a)(1), (2) (2002); Williamson v. Elrod, 372 S.W.3d 489 (Ark. 2002).
15. FED. R. EVID. 702.

The direct examination should take the jurors to school, with your expert serving as the likeable, interesting, accessible teacher who knows and can clearly explain the subject. With the court's permission, have the expert stand in front of the jurors where she can refer to anatomical models, diagrams and other demonstrative evidence to help the jurors understand what she is teaching. Simply by leaving the witness box, your expert will establish a personal connection with the jurors, unlike all other witnesses who testify at a remove.

While the expert will lead the class, you must serve as the most curious but least intelligent student. Ask the witness to define any technical terms that invariably seep into her answers. Never hesitate to ask follow-up questions to clarify potential confusion about the material. Ask any question you believe the jurors would want to ask the expert.[16]

Keep in mind the ultimate goal of the teaching chapter of the direct. The expert shortly will share the underlying information to which she applied the specialized knowledge she has just taught the jurors. You will have properly done your job teaching the jurors if they are metaphorically raising their hands and saying, "I will answer that question," when you then ask the witness to reiterate her opinion.

Step Five: Disclose the facts underlying the opinion. While no longer required by the rules of evidence in some jurisdictions,[17] the rules of persuasion require that you share with the jurors the facts on which the expert relied to formulate his opinion. The jurors will be more willing to accept the opinion of the expert if they are confident that she used reliable, accurate, and comprehensive information to reach that opinion. Equally importantly, the jurors will need the underlying data to exercise their newly acquired expertise. This chapter of the direct should set forth the facts of the final examination question that will allow the jurors to prove by their verdict that they understood and successfully applied the courtroom teachings of the expert.

Step Six: Reiterate the opinion and have the expert explain the basis of the opinion. You previewed the subject matters on which the expert would opine in the introduction to the witness. You elicited the opinion after qualifying the expert and explaining her connection to the case. For several reasons, you should have the expert again state the opinion after teaching the jurors and discussing the facts on which the opinion is based.

You have taken the jurors on a somewhat lengthy journey since they first learned of the opinion. By re-asking the opinion question after the expert has taught the

---

16. In some jurisdictions, jurors may be allowed to ask questions, not only of experts but of any witness. Regardless of this practice, you should try to put yourself in the jurors' minds and ask the questions the jurors would ask.

17. *See* FED. R. EVID. 703.

jurors, you remind them of the expert's opinion. But you also create the precise "a-ha moment" at which the jurors will reach that same conclusion. Now owning the opinion, the jurors will be unwilling to be shaken in their conclusion by whatever the opposing expert has or will offer to the contrary.

The expert's explanation of the basis for the opinion should use the same tools the expert taught the jurors and apply them to the underlying facts. If you have done your job well, the jurors should be mentally, and maybe even visibly, nodding in agreement as the expert explains how and why she reached her conclusion.

Step Seven: Disprove the opinion of the opposing expert. As will next be discussed, under no circumstance will your cross-examination of the opposing expert intend to comprise, or devolve into, an attack on that expert's opinion. On the other hand, you can and should use the direct examination of your own expert to squarely explain why she (and the jurors who are her students) rejects the opposing expert's contrary opinion.[18]

Lawsuits are composed of disputed facts. In forming her opinion, every expert makes assumptions that some disputed facts are either one way or another. The difference between the opinions of the opposing experts in a case can often be attributed to different factual assumptions they have made.

You and your opponent often will have similarly qualified expert witnesses who will offer different opinions based on essentially the same facts. They reach different conclusions because they make one or more different assumptions about those facts. Whether the jurors accept your expert's opinion over that of your opponent's expert may depend on which witness's assumptions appear most reasonable. Have your expert compare and contrast her assumptions of fact with those made by the opponent's expert and explain why hers are more valid. Anticipate the cross-examination by having the expert describe her assumptions and the reasons she made them. Then have her explain why the opposing expert's assumptions are unlikely.

9.4   Cross-Examining an Expert Witness

Your opponent's expert witness is as dangerous as a coiled rattlesnake, and you should approach him as gingerly as you would a viper. No matter how much time you spent educating yourself, the witness will have greater expertise about the subject matter. And in many cases, the expert will have more experience in the courtroom than the lawyer conducting the cross. Because of his expertise, he can communicate

---

18. If you represent the plaintiff, the defense expert will not have testified before the direct examination of your expert. Nonetheless, the court is likely to give you latitude to conduct an anticipatory rebuttal of the defense expert's opinion. Judges are fully cognizant of how expensive it is to hire experts and how difficult it is to get even highly compensated experts to come to court and testify. The court is not likely to insist that you bring your expert to court a second time as a rebuttal witness.

with the jurors as a teacher communicates to students. Unrestricted by the rule limiting ordinary witnesses' testimony to matters personally observed, he may offer his opinion even though he has no personal knowledge of the facts in the case at hand. When he offers his opinion, telling the jurors what inferences and conclusions they should draw from the evidence, he makes part of your opponent's closing argument.

On the other hand, this witness's potent direct testimony cannot be left unchallenged. He must be cross-examined. However, he *must* be handled with extreme care because, like the rattlesnake, he will strike with devastating effect given the slightest opportunity. Nevertheless, your careful cross-examination can defang the rattler and sometimes even make it strike your opponent.

Under no circumstances should you argue with the opposing expert about his opinion. This witness undoubtedly knows more about his area of expertise than you do. Even if you know he is wrong on a particular issue, you will never get him to acknowledge his error and your every attempt will allow him to reinforce his testimony. If you fight him on his turf, he will beat you every time. When it comes down to your word against his, the jurors will accept his. Therefore, do not ask an expert "How can you say . . . ," "Can you explain why . . . ," or "Why do you feel . . . ?" Save the argument that the expert's opinion is worthless for your summation.

Arguing with an expert witness in his area of expertise is like hog wrestling. Both you and the pig get dirty. And the pig loves it.

— Bob Vanderlaan

When examining the opposing expert, you must slavishly adhere to all the precepts for cross-examination of lay witnesses.[19] Ask only questions to which you know the answer and have the means to unambiguously impeach if the expert offers a different response. Structure your questions precisely. Ask intensely leading, one-fact questions—those in which you make statements and force the witness to agree with you. All you want from the witness is the word "yes." Do not give him any room to wiggle. Non-leading, open-ended questions (who, what, when, where, why, how) are safe only when you know what the answer has to be and you have the ammunition to discredit the witness's answer if he says anything other than what you want or if any other answer will be so ludicrous that the jurors will consider the witness a liar or a fool. This will rarely be the case when cross-examining the expert.

While being vigilant to keep a healthy distance from the expert's opinion, your cross-examination of an expert witness can take one or more of several tacks: you can bring out matters favorable to your theory of the case; you can elicit differences in the qualifications between the expert and your expert; you can force him to admit

---

19. *See* chapter seven.

differences in the quality and quantity of information used in reaching his opinion compared to your expert; or you can impeach his credibility.

9.4.1 *Elicit Favorable Facts from Your Opponent's Expert*

The safest chapters of a cross-examination of the opposing expert will be those where your purpose is constructive.[20] Eliciting information favorable to your factual story of the case from the opponent's expert witness is sometimes overlooked because it is so obvious. When you prepare the cross-examination, the first question you should ask yourself is whether there are matters helpful to your case with which the opposing expert must agree. These powerful facts should be the first thing you extract when you cross-examine, and they allow you to establish early control over the expert. Favorable testimony that flows from the lips of your opponent's witnesses can become some of the most digestible morsels of your argument.

Sometimes the favorable facts you bring out on cross-examination have nothing to do with the opinion the expert offered on direct examination. These facts are just waiting for you to elicit as if you had called the expert as your witness.[21]

Imagine a case where the plaintiff calls an emergency room physician as a damage witness to describe the nature and extent of the plaintiff's injuries. Representing the defendant, you discover that the doctor noted in the hospital records that the patient had been drinking. Although this fact has nothing to do with the doctor's direct testimony and does not diminish his credibility, you should bring it out on cross-examination. (The plaintiff's lawyer should cushion the jurors from the shock of this evidence by eliciting it gently on direct examination. If he does, you should still bring it out on cross.) In this situation, you are using the doctor as a fact witness to help establish your case on the issue of liability.

In addition to bringing out facts that favor your client, bring out any facts that support your expert's opinion. These may include acknowledgement of your expert's qualifications, endorsement of your expert's methods, acknowledgement of the validity of the data your expert relied on, acknowledgement of the validity of your expert's assumptions, or acknowledgement of your expert's reputation in the field. If your expert was trained at the famous Mayo Clinic, ask the opponent to acknowledge the worldwide reputation of the Mayo Clinic. If this expert witness once cited an article by your expert, bring out the fact that he relied on your expert's work.

---

20. *Id.* at 7.2.1.
21. FED. R. EVID. 611(b) limits the scope of cross-examination to "the subject matter of the direct examination and matters affecting the witness' credibility." This rule will rarely present a problem. First, the court will often broadly define the "scope of direct examination." Secondly, even if the court finds that the new matter is beyond the scope of the direct examination, the rule allows the court to permit inquiry into it "as if on direct examination," meaning you might have to elicit new, favorable information using non-leading questions.

You must read every document and report the opposing expert reviewed. Those documents typically will contain facts on which your own expert relied. You should constructively cross the expert to elicit an admission as to each fact on which your expert relied that is codified in these documents. By using cross-examination of the opponent's expert carefully and as an opportunity to bring out facts that favor your case, you can effectively milk the rattler without giving him an opportunity to sink his fangs in you.

9.4.2 Establish Why the Expert Is a Less Reliable Source of the Conclusion than Your Expert

After extracting all the available concessions of facts that are consistent with your story of the case or supportive of your expert's opinion, you may then let the jurors see why the expert is a less reliable source for the conclusion than your expert. There are three principal areas of differentiation: 1) respective qualifications of the experts, 2) the quality and quantity of information on which the experts relied, and 3) the comparative credibility of the experts.

Qualifications

In our daily lives, we make choices about those whose services we are willing to purchase and whose advice we are prepared to follow—salespersons, real estate and stock brokers, plumbers, electricians, lawyers and doctors. Often our decision is based upon whether the person is the most qualified for the job. You may help the jurors choose whose opinion to accept by using cross-examination to bring out the areas in which your expert is more qualified by "knowledge, skill, experience, training or education."[22] Any deficiencies in an expert witness's education, licensure, or work history should be brought out. The expert may have lesser "paper qualifications" than your expert. Even if more well-credentialed generally, the expert may have less hands-on experience in the specific field in which he is offering an opinion. Even though these deficiencies may not have been serious enough to disqualify the expert from testifying, they are still highly relevant to assist the jurors in deciding how much weight to give the expert's testimony.

A classic example is the general rule that any medical doctor may testify regarding any medical specialty so long as she can say that she received some training or has some experience practicing in that area. The foregoing rule of admissibility, however, does not mean that the testimony of a general practitioner concerning a particular medical specialty must be accepted by the jurors. The jurors are empowered to discount his testimony to the degree that they do not believe he knows what he is talking about. Consequently, you may always bring out the fact that the physician is not a board-certified specialist in the area his testimony concerns. You should

---

22. FED. R. EVID. 702.

also consider using cross-examination to limit the areas of the witness's expertise. For example, if the witness is an expert pathologist who testified that the cause of death was suicide, you might ask:

Q: Doctor, you did not complete a residency in psychiatry, did you?

A: No.

Q: You are not a member of the American Board of Psychiatry, are you?

A: No.

Q: You are not an expert in the field of psychiatry, are you?

A: No, I'm a pathologist.

Your cross-examination need not suggest that the expert was wholly unqualified to render an opinion. Assume the jury panel would prefer the services of the best qualified person if they needed help in a matter of utmost importance in their personal lives. Your cross will show that your expert is best qualified in this case to assist the jurors in their new duty of utmost importance: arbiters of the facts in this trial.

Quality and Quantity of Information

The expression "garbage in, garbage out" applies to the testimony of experts. The reliability of the most immaculately qualified expert's opinion is only as good as the quality of information that forms the basis for the opinion. Your cross, then, may elicit the areas in which the quality or quantity of the information used by the expert is inferior to the data your expert used to formulate her opinion.

Information the Expert Failed to Consult in Reaching the Opinion

The first category to consider is whether information your expert used in reaching her opinion was considered by the opposing expert. If your expert was the treating physician and you are cross-examining an "independent medical examiner" who saw your client one time at the request of defense counsel, use a series of one-fact, leading questions have the expert concede each occasion on which your expert examined the plaintiff. Then point out that the witness saw the plaintiff on but a single occasion. Identify every report and document that your expert consulted that was not reviewed by the witness. You also may get the witness to concede tests that she did not, but could have, conducted. However, this line of cross will be ineffective if your expert similarly did not conduct the same available test.

The opposing expert may have rejected or ignored facts that can help your case. In this instance, your cross-examination serves to elicit those facts (or underscore them if they have been brought out on direct). These facts will not alter his opinion—he has already discounted them—so do not give him a chance to explain why they are not important. Just make him acknowledge the existence of those facts and move on.

For instance, assume a murder prosecution in which the state's psychiatrist has given his opinion that the accused was sane at the time of committing homicide. Psychiatric evaluation records reveal that during the year preceding the shooting, the accused suffered delusions that he was President of the United States and hallucinations in which he saw people trying to assassinate him. Your cross-examination as defense counsel might go something like this:

Q: Doctor, what is a delusion? [*Safe, non-leading question to which there is only one correct answer.*]

A: A false belief brought about without appropriate external stimulation and inconsistent with the individual's own knowledge and experience.

Q: In ordinary language, thinking you're somebody you aren't would be a delusion, wouldn't it?

A: Yes.

Q: For instance, if I thought I was George Washington, that would be a delusion, right?

A: Right.

Q: During the year before this shooting, Mr. Wright suffered delusions, didn't he?

A: Yes.

Q: Doctor, tell us who he thought he was when he had these delusions?

A: He thought he was the President of the United States.

This line of questioning has established valuable factual data for your closing argument on the affirmative defense of insanity. Equally important, and without overtly attacking the psychiatrist's credibility, you have set up a strong argument that his opinion is not credible because it flies in the face of reason.

Reliance on Information Provided by Other Sources

You also will want to point out where the expert has relied on information produced by others: if the supplied information is not correct, then neither is the conclusion. Who compiled the information for the expert? Did the expert rely on information that was compiled by a biased source? For example:

Q: Dr. Robinson, you testified that the plaintiff in this case lost approximately $2 million in future profits.

A: Correct.

Q: And that opinion is based, in part, on your economic analysis of the viability of the business in the current market?

A: Yes.

Q: And it is based, in part, on the list of past sales and current customers that the plaintiff provided to you?

A: Right.

Q: And if the plaintiff gave you past sales figures that were inflated, that would change your conclusion as to the amount of the lost profits, wouldn't it?

A: Well, of course, but I have no reason to believe the figures were inflated.

Q: And if the list of current customers included customers of other companies that the plaintiff only "hoped" to woo away to his business, that would change your calculations on the issue of lost profits, wouldn't it?

A: Certainly.

If you can demonstrate to the jury (through other witnesses) that the plaintiff *did* inflate the past sales figures, or include "customers" who were not yet customers, you can argue that the jury may safely ignore the plaintiff's expert's calculations.

Assumption of One Version of Disputed Facts

The difference between the opinions of opposing experts often is not the result of applying different principles or methodologies. The opinions differ simply because each expert *assumes* that the disputed facts are as the side that employed him wants them to be. A bona fide expert will admit that he made such assumptions and concede that his opinion is not based on the alternate version of these disputed facts. These concessions allow you to argue to the jury that if they find the facts as you hope they will, the opposing expert's opinion will not be helpful in deciding the case.

A slightly more risky approach is to ask the expert witness if the underlying fact he assumed to be true is changed, would the expert's conclusion change? In some areas, like mathematics, you can proceed safely with this line of cross. For example, if the expert has calculated the market value of some asset using a 3 percent inflation factor, point out how the final value will change if the inflation factor were

5 percent. In less objective areas, you risk undermining the entire line of cross if the expert answers that his opinion would not be different even if the underlying assumption were different. Some lawyers prefer to ask the expert whether his opinion "might," rather than "would," change if what he assumed to be true was in fact not true. A third, and much safer, option is simply to get the expert to identify the underlying facts he assumed to be true. In closing, you can argue that the jury does not know what the expert would have concluded if the jury rejects the version of the disputed facts on which the expert relied.

Challenging the expert's assumptions is often the most essential and extensive area of cross-examination of an expert witness. It is often the only area available to you: he may have nothing to say that is favorable to your case and his credibility may be unimpeachable. Yet, if the jury has been persuaded of the truth of an underlying fact that differs from what the expert assumes, the jurors may reject the expert's conclusions. Make the contingent nature of the expert's opinion clear to the jurors.

Credibility

An expert witness is subject to impeachment on the same bases as any other witness.[23] Because an expert is required to be qualified in the area upon which he speaks, and because he is allowed to base his testimony on matters other than those he personally perceived, some special tools and techniques are available to impeach him that are not available to impeach an ordinary lay witness.

Contradiction by Learned Treatise

You may contradict the witness's testimony with passages from learned treatises in his area of expertise. Federal Rule of Evidence 803(18) states that the following kinds of statements are excepted from the hearsay rule:

A statement contained in a treatise, periodical, or pamphlet if:

(A) the statement is called to the attention of an expert witness on cross-examination or relied on by the expert on direct examination; and

(B) the publication is established as a reliable authority by the expert's admission or testimony, by another expert's testimony, or by judicial notice.

If admitted, the statement may be read into evidence but not received as an exhibit.

After you have taken the opposing expert's deposition or know what the essence of his trial testimony will be, research the literature in his field of expertise to learn

---

23. *See* chapter eight.

if his views can be contradicted. Your own expert witness can provide invaluable assistance by telling you whether such authority exists and by leading you to it. If you take the deposition of the opposing expert in his office, notice any books on his shelves and ask whether they are considered reliable authority. He will probably acknowledge their reliability and will thus be forced to admit during cross-examination that they are reliable.

Rule 803(18) provides four methods of establishing reliability. First, if the witness has testified on direct examination that he relied on the authority or agrees that the text is an authority as in the example above, you are home free. Here is where your questions during the deposition in his office regarding the treatises on the shelf may serve you well. The expert now must either admit that the treatise you call to his attention is reliable, or he will face impeachment with his prior inconsistent statement in the deposition. If the expert will not acknowledge the text's authority, ask the court to take judicial notice of the work's reliability. However, the somewhat restrictive rule governing judicial notice[24] usually prevents the court from taking judicial notice of the reliability of any but the most generally familiar publications. If the opponent's expert refuses to concede reliability and the judge is not inclined to take judicial notice of your text, you can still have your own expert witness testify to the work's reliability.

Once you have found a passage in an authoritative treatise that contradicts the opposing expert, prepare to use it at trial. The treatise itself may not be introduced as an exhibit. Rule 803(18) provides that the contradictory statement may only be read into evidence. Do not ask the witness if he agrees with it, or to explain his disagreement with it or anything else about it. Instead, you should establish that the treatise is reliable and then read it into evidence.

> Q: Dr. Bingo, you are familiar with the *Physician's Desk Reference?*
>
> A: Yes, of course.
>
> Q: It is considered an authority in the field of drug interactions and side effects, isn't it?
>
> A: Yes. It describes most known drug interactions and side effects.
>
> Q: In fact, doctors rely on it daily to provide the most accurate drug information?
>
> A: Yes.
>
> Q: On page 2072, the Physician's Desk Reference states, and I quote, "Amoxicillin is indicated in the treatment of . . . ."

---

24. FED. R. EVID. 201(b) allows judicial notice only of facts "generally known within the trial court's territorial jurisdiction" and facts that "can be accurately and readily determined from sources whose accuracy cannot reasonably be questioned."

Prior Inconsistent Statements

Any prior statements made by the expert can provide a treasure trove of information helpful to your case. Having said one thing before, the expert witness will have a difficult time saying something different in the present trial. Here, you are on safe ground. If he does deny his prior observations, you have the prior statement to impeach him. Carefully search every pretrial deposition, report, or record made by your opponent's expert for statements favorable to your side of the case, and then bring them out on cross-examination.

Likewise, you may use any statements he has made in any published works. Obtain a copy of the transcript of his deposition or trial testimony from other trials, or a copy of the pertinent article or book, and use it to impeach him.[25] Testimony the expert has given in previous trials may provide an excellent source of insight and impeachment material. Often a particular expert will testify on cases with similar issues. Use discovery to find in what cases the expert has appeared. Contact the lawyers who have previously cross-examined this expert. Tell that attorney what the expert contends in your case. Ask your colleague for the benefit of her experience with this witness. What worked and what did not work in cross-examination? If the expert had a different theory in an earlier case, get a copy of the trial transcript of the earlier trial.

Attacking the Expert Personally

The two permissible areas of inquiry concerning an expert's personal reliability are bias and character for truthfulness. However, the opportunity to attack the expert on either of these bases does not present itself in every case. You should consider the matter carefully before deciding to attack an expert witness personally, as it may be perceived as an unjustified assault. For example, a highly qualified expert who is not habitually identified with the opposing party, attorney, or class should not normally be attacked for bias. Nevertheless, if there is something in the expert's background that will likely sour the jurors' attitude toward his testimony, press on.

Bias

Any of the expert witness's associations that may raise an inference of bias may be explored on cross-examination if you decide that knowledge of those associations will dampen the effect of the expert's testimony on the jurors.

A question often heard during cross-examination of an expert witness is, "You are being paid for your testimony here today, are you not?" The question is proper as a matter of evidentiary law because it is relevant to the jurors' assessment of the witness's partiality. However, the question is often counterproductive. In modern

---

25. For the technique of impeaching with a prior inconsistent statement, see chapter eight.

National Institute for Trial Advocacy

litigation, both parties usually have paid expert witnesses and the jurors know it. If both lawyers ask the "payment" question, the result is usually only to make the lawyers appear to be vexatious. The "payment" question may be effective if your expert witness is a public servant such as a medical examiner testifying to the results of an autopsy as a part of her duties and your opponent's expert witness has been hired to give an alternative opinion.

Another potential area of bias is the expert's own interest in maintaining certain positions or opinions. If the expert has built a reputation contending that a person may be identified by his shoeprint, he will have a vested interest in continuing to assert the truth of that position. In this kind of situation, the expert's reputation in a particular field may operate as a potential source of impeachment for bias.

Similarly, if the witness has worked many times with opposing counsel, or better still, habitually represents only plaintiffs or defendants in similar cases, the fact can have a deflating effect on the witness's believability. The professional witness—such as the physician who makes his living testifying in lawsuits—is a deserving target for cross-examination questions that illustrate his preference for obtaining lawsuit results for his clients over practicing in his profession.

Character for Truthfulness

The opportunity to attack an expert witness's character for truthfulness is particularly unlikely because opposing counsel will probably not present an expert witness who is vulnerable to this line of impeachment. The Federal Rules of Evidence provide only three ways of impeaching a witness's character for truthfulness. You may present opinion or reputation evidence that the witness has an untruthful character.[26] Additionally, you may ask the witness on cross-examination to admit having committed unconvicted acts that the court finds are probative of untruthfulness. However, you may not contradict the witness's answer with extrinsic evidence if he denies committing these acts.[27] Finally, you may impeach the witness with certain prior criminal convictions.[28]

---

26. FED. R. EVID. 608(a).
27. FED. R. EVID. 608(b)
28. FED. R. EVID. 609.

CHAPTER TEN

EXHIBITS AND ILLUSTRATIVE AIDS

"Big day in trial today!" she said to her husband at breakfast.

"Why's that?" he answered.

"I get to show Denny's gun to the jurors and let them hold it!"

"How do you know it's Denny's gun?"

"That is what the police officer will say."

"And how does the police officer know?"

"Because the gun whispered 'I belong to Denny' to the police officer," she said with a wry smile as she came to the grim realization that she would have to review how to lay a foundation for an exhibit.

10.1   Introduction

Exhibits are often your most powerful evidence. You know this from your earliest experiences. In kindergarten, you learned by "show-and-tell," not "tell-and-tell." More importantly, with advances in technology, it is now possible to display information to a jury in ways that are fast, compelling, and memorable. Showing your trial story to jurors through exhibits supports your words and ideas with a tangible reality. Real or computer-assisted exhibits make the information you are trying to convey more persuasive. You have heard the old expression "Seeing is believing." It is true. Something in our human nature makes us more likely to accept events we have seen on video. We are less likely to question words we have seen in print and things we have held in our hands. When you put a document or an item taken from the scene into the jurors' hands, you improve the believability of your witnesses' statements immeasurably.

Exhibits also make your story more memorable. Jurors are apt to forget much of what a witness says, but they will remember more about things they have seen as well as heard. Even more important, jurors do not have to remember the information contained in admitted exhibits because they can take them to the jury deliberation room. When you introduce exhibits, you are building a show-and-tell demonstration that can be repeated by jurors during deliberations. You put the tools of your argument in their hands.

Modern trials are often paper chases. Computers, word processors, photocopiers, email, and fax machines have created so much written information that it is possible to overwhelm the courtroom with documentary exhibits. The advent of sophisticated electronic courtroom technology has created both opportunities to present evidence more effectively and dangers that a lawyer will detract from the overall impact of her case by its overuse or clumsy use.

Sing me no song! Read me no rhyme!
Don't waste my time, Show me!

—*From* My Fair Lady

The ability to handle physical evidence smoothly and efficiently has become an increasingly essential element of the art of advocacy. Today's successful trial lawyer must be a proficient selector and manager of exhibits. In the courtroom, the lawyer who appears to be more in control of the paper flow and other visual information is more likely to gain the confidence and respect of the jurors. Further, if the case is appealed, a clear, understandable record of the exhibits is essential. Therefore, while handling exhibits you must remain constantly aware of your two audiences: the jurors and the court reporter. Here are some basic guidelines for marshalling, introducing, and using your exhibits.

10.2   Types of Exhibits

Exhibits can be divided into three broad classes: real evidence, demonstrative evidence, and illustrative aids. Real evidence includes documents and things that played an actual role in the events at issue in the trial. An item of real evidence is the thing itself: the offer letter, the murder weapon, or the defective product. Demonstrative evidence, on the other hand, includes exhibits that have been created for the purposes of the trial to help the jury understand other relevant evidence. Examples include charts, diagrams, and models. Demonstrative evidence requires foundational testimony that it fairly and accurately represents whatever you claim it does.

The term "illustrative aid" is more inclusive than the term "demonstrative evidence."[1] An item is "evidence" only if it is introduced into the record of the case. Sometimes you will use an exhibit to clarify, simplify, or illustrate evidence

---

1. *See generally* P. Corboy & R. Clifford, "Demonstrative Evidence," *Docket* 5 (Summer 1986). The authors make no distinction between demonstrative evidence and demonstrative aids. They actually discuss the use of demonstrative aids, but denominate them all as demonstrative evidence. This fine semantic distinction makes little difference and the article packs much useful information into a few pages. *See also* M. Dombroff, "Demonstrative Evidence: Setting the Stage for Outstanding Trial Performance," *Compleat Lawyer* 14 (Winter 1984).

in the case, but will not introduce the exhibit as evidence. A witness's sketch on a chalkboard or physical demonstration of the way something happened, though not subject to introduction into evidence, can be enormously helpful to the jury's understanding of the witness's oral testimony. Similarly, a witness may identify a diagram of the trial scene on a projected video, a whiteboard, or on a paper chart and may mark on either while testifying. Charts and diagrams of various sorts are often utilized as illustrative aids without being introduced as exhibits.

A lawyer is limited in the way he uses exhibits mainly by his imagination. This is the "show-and-tell" of trial. Some lawyers use computer-generated slides during their opening statements to emphasize exactly what must be proved.[2] These embellishments may be the difference between victory and defeat. The more you do to guide the jury through the factual maze, the greater the likelihood that they will reward you with a verdict. While witnesses testify using visual aids, do not forget your second audience, the court reporter. As a witness marks a diagram, make an oral record describing what is being drawn so a future appellate court will be able to decipher the exhibit. If you ask the question, "Where was the truck?" and the witness answers while drawing the truck on the diagram, "Right here," an appellate judge will have no way to know which of several markings is intended to represent the truck. Say, "Please draw a rectangle where you saw the truck," and follow up with "Now, in that rectangle, please write a T to indicate 'truck.'" The appellate court will have no doubt which of the markings on the diagram represents the truck. Rehearse this testimony with the witness before turning her loose with a magic marker or computer screen. It is also important to rehearse using whatever technology you will be using in court, get to the courtroom in time to set it up, and have a backup presentation method in case your technology fails.

10.3   Make and Use a Checklist of Exhibits

Before trial, organize all the exhibits you intend to introduce and give each one a number. Prepare a list containing the following columns:

Number/Description   **Witness**   **Stipulated**   **Offered**   **Received**   **Refused**

Your list will be placed in the front of a notebook that contains a hard copy of all the documentary exhibits. If the trial will have many documentary exhibits, create a computer file with a link to each document. You then can easily view each document on your computer from your master list by clicking on the link. In an electronically equipped courtroom, you will easily be able to display documents

---

2. An excellent guide to using technology in the courtroom may be found in Federal Judicial Center, *Effective Use of Courtroom Technology: A Judge's Guide to Trial and Pretrial*, http://www.fjc.gov/public/pdf.nsf/lookup/CTtech00.pdf/$file/CTtech00.pdf (last viewed May 11, 2016).

from your list to witnesses and jurors. Be sure, however, to keep a hard copy of all documents and your index list with you during trial.[3] If the courtroom technology (or your own computer) fails, you can always use the paper version of documents.

The exhibit list should contain a brief description of the exhibit. It should also have columns for tracking the status of each exhibit. Before trial, you will check on the courtroom technology available and any local rules on the use of technological exhibits. You will then meet with opposing counsel to review proposed exhibits. Generally, the relevance and authenticity of most of the documents that were exchanged during discovery is obvious. Counsel can usually stipulate to the admissibility of most exhibits. This is good practice. Stipulating to the evidentiary foundation of exhibits will save time during trial and will win you the good will of the judge.[4]

Note in your exhibit list each exhibit that your opponent has stipulated to be admissible. These may be introduced without laying a foundation by simply offering the exhibit into evidence along with the statement that opposing counsel has stipulated to its admissibility. You can then go on to examine the appropriate witness about the exhibit and use it in front of the jurors. Even when an exhibit is introduced pursuant to a stipulation, you should ask a witness questions that will explain the significance and relevance of the exhibit. Use every exhibit as a storytelling tool. Make sure the jurors understand how this piece of evidence fits into the events of the trial.

Keep your exhibit list with you during trial. As each exhibit is received or refused, place a check in the appropriate column. The list will enable you to keep track of the numbers and status of your exhibits. It will also remind you to offer each one into evidence—a necessary detail that is easy to overlook in the heat of trial. We cannot overemphasize the importance of making sure each of your exhibits is formally introduced. If an exhibit is not offered and received, it is not part of the record of the case. Before resting your case, check the status of the exhibits on your checklist against the court's understanding of its rulings. If the court believes you neglected to offer an exhibit into evidence, reoffer that exhibit.

---

3. Some lawyers prefer to have a separate file folder for each exhibit. Each folder will contain five copies of the exhibit: one for the witness, one to give to opposing counsel, one for the court, one for the law clerk, and one for herself.

4. Fed. R. Civ. P. 26(a)(3)(A)(iii) requires that at least thirty days before trial, counsel provide to the other party an identification of every document or other exhibit she expects to offer or may offer if the need arises. Within fourteen days after receipt of this disclosure, the party must file any objections, together with the grounds for the objection, to the listed exhibits. Unless excused for good cause, any objection not raised, other than objection under Federal Rules of Evidence 402 or 403, is waived.

If one of your exhibits is refused admission, proffer it into the record as an offer of proof so the record will be complete on appeal.[5] To make an offer of proof, you will ask to approach the bench and say, "Your Honor, I'd like to make an offer of proof." When the judge acknowledges you, either give a copy of the document to the clerk or court reporter or read the relevant portion into the record at sidebar. If the exhibit is not a document and cannot be easily maintained with the record, you can have the court reporter take down your description of the exhibit for the record.

Check the local rules or individual judge's rules as to 1) who marks exhibits (counsel, court reporter, other court official), and 2) in what manner exhibits are to be marked (e.g., does the court want counsel to use numbers or letters, are exhibits to be marked "for identification" with those words stricken once the exhibit is admitted into evidence). If permitted by rule or practice, pre-number and mark all of your exhibits before you go to court. Unless the judge insists that exhibits be introduced in numerical sequence (a senseless requirement), you may number and introduce your exhibits in any order you choose. Pre-printed stickers that say "Plaintiff's Exhibit," "State's Exhibit," or "Defendant's Exhibit" are available in office supply stores. When several documents are related, you may identify them in a way that indicates the relationship. For example, a series of letters between two persons may be numbered Exhibits 3A, 3B, and 3C, rather than Exhibits 3, 4, and 5. During the trial, refer to each exhibit by its number or letter. Although this may sound awkward, it is important for the record. An appellate judge will be able to locate "Plaintiff's Exhibit 3" in the record, but will have no way of knowing what you meant if you referred to the exhibit as "this letter" or "this document."

10.4   Observe the "Ritual of Foundations"

It is likely that your opponent will not agree to stipulate to the admissibility of all of the exhibits you would like to use. These exhibits will require an evidentiary foundation before they may be admitted. The "ritual of foundations" is a protocol designed to assure that you make a clean record, lay an appropriate foundation, and look good doing it. We suggest that you make a habit of observing the ritual every time you offer an exhibit. Drill yourself until it becomes so much a part of your behavior pattern in trial that you do it unconsciously.

The ritual consists of the steps that follow.

10.4.1   *Step One: Qualify the Witness and Establish Relevance*

Every witness must establish personal knowledge of the subject matter of her testimony before being allowed to relate that knowledge. Personal knowledge is not

---

5. When evidence is excluded, an offer of proof is required by Fed. R. Evid. 103(a)(2) to preserve the issue for appeal.

only an evidentiary requirement, but also a prerequisite to credibility. Therefore, before asking a witness foundational questions concerning an exhibit, establish the witness's competence to answer by allowing the witness to tell how she gained familiarity with the exhibit. Your qualification of the witness will also place the exhibit in the story of the trial and establish how the exhibit is relevant to the case. Do not skimp on the build-up to an exhibit. Make the jurors want to see that exhibit. For example, in a wrongful discharge case your introduction of a letter from the defendant might begin as follows:

Q: Ms. Matsos, tell us how you learned you were fired.

A: A security guard appeared at my desk at 9:15 a.m. on Monday morning and told me that I was to pack up all personal items in my desk and leave the premises with him.

Q: How did you react?

A: I was shocked. I asked, "Why? What's going on?"

Q: What did the guard say?

A: He said something like, "I don't know the details, ma'am, but you have been fired." That's when he handed me the letter from Mr. Boniface.

The jurors' curiosity is now raised about the exhibit. You would like to be able to show it to them right away. But you must lay additional foundation before the exhibit may be admitted and shown to the jurors. These additional steps (steps two through six) should be accomplished quickly and smoothly.

10.4.2 Step Two: Show the Exhibit to Opposing Counsel and the Judge

Your opponent is entitled to see whatever you plan to ask a witness about. Besides, common courtesy dictates that you show it. Perform this step even though your opponent has seen the exhibit before, has a copy, and knows exactly what you are talking about. You should not make a statement like, "Let the record reflect that I'm showing the exhibit to opposing counsel." This step is not important for the record. Just smile and hand a copy to the judge and your opponent. If you have prepared a book of exhibits for the judge (and this is our recommended practice), refer the judge to the page or exhibit number in the trial notebook.[6]

When the roles are reversed and your opponent is laying foundations, you should insist on seeing every exhibit. If she neglects to show you one, stand and politely ask the judge to see the exhibit. This is not a rude or frivolous practice. Exhibits

---

6. You may also offer the court a copy of the book of exhibits—or a copy of the individual exhibit—for the judge's law clerk.

or exhibit numbers may have been altered between the time of their discovery and their introduction into evidence. You need to make sure you are looking at the same document that the witness is looking at so that you can follow the testimony and make appropriate objections.

10.4.3 Step Three: Have the Witness Identify the Exhibit

Now ask the judge if you may approach the witness.[7] When the judge nods, you will walk up to the witness with the exhibit in your hand. Refer to the exhibit by its exhibit number so that the record will reflect which exhibit the witness is looking at, show the exhibit to the witness, and ask him what it is. Say something like, "I'm showing you what's been marked for identification Plaintiff's Exhibit 1. What is it?"

At this point, the witness should give an answer that identifies the exhibit but does not disclose its contents.[8] For example, the witness will say, "This is the letter the security guard gave to me." Or, "This is a letter from Mr. Boniface dated June 10." You should practice with your witness so that he can identify documents appropriately.

10.4.4 Step Four: Ask the Necessary Questions to Lay the Evidentiary Foundation

The questions you ask here depend on the evidentiary prerequisites that apply to the particular item of evidence you are introducing. Relevance and authenticity are part of the evidentiary foundation of every piece of evidence.[9] Some exhibits require additional evidentiary foundation to establish a hearsay exception or overcome another evidentiary barrier to admissibility. We will look at some of the special problems of evidentiary foundations below.

You will always have to establish the exhibit's authenticity. Federal Rule 901, which governs authentication, simply requires some evidence that an item is what you claim it is.[10] Therefore, the questions you are required to ask depend upon what you contend that the exhibit is. For example, after the witness identifies the item as a letter from Mr. Boniface, you will ask, "How do you know that?" The witness will then provide the information that authenticates the document: "It is on his stationery and is signed 'Harold Boniface.'" Federal Rule of Evidence 901(b) gives examples of the types of evidence that will satisfy the requirement of authentication. Federal Rule of Evidence 902 sets forth categories of evidence that are self-authenticating, eliminating the need to ask questions of the witness to authenticate the exhibit.

---

7. Many judges prefer for attorneys to ask permission to approach the witness. Some do not. If the judge indicates that you need not ask, then stop asking.
8. Until the exhibit is admitted into evidence, its contents should not be disclosed to the jurors.
9. FED. R. EVID. 401, 402, 901(a).
10. FED. R. EVID. 901(a).

10.4.5   *Step Five: Offer the Exhibit*

As we mentioned before, an exhibit does not become evidence until it is received by the court. Therefore, when you have completed your foundation, turn to the court and say, "Your Honor, the plaintiff offers Exhibit 1." Unless an objection is made and sustained, the judge will say "Admitted" or "Let it be received." At that moment, what was before merely one of innumerable objects adrift in the universe becomes that magical creature of the law—an item of evidence in this case. It is now eligible to be considered, scrutinized, and analyzed by the jurors. You can now use it just about any way you please to enhance your case.

10.4.6   *Step Six: Publish the Exhibit to the Jury*

"Publish" is a legal word that means "show," "give," "pass," "read," or "demonstrate." Once an exhibit becomes evidence, you have a license to use it. Exploit that license to make the point for which you introduced the exhibit. Do not forget the jurors. It makes no sense to go through the process of laying a foundation and finally getting an exhibit introduced, only to place it on the table and never mention it again. When that happens, jurors rightly wonder what all the fuss was about and why they were not let in on the secret. If you do not publish your exhibits, the jurors will never forgive you for being so inconsiderate of their curiosity.

How you publish is up to you and depends on the best tactical use of the exhibit at that moment in the trial. If the exhibit is an item from the scene of the trial events—a gun, a bullet, or a bag of clothes—most lawyers will take time to pass the item to the jurors and let each juror handle and examine it. Be sure not to continue with your examination of the witness until the jurors have finished examining the exhibit. If the item is a document, many lawyers make a photocopy for each juror so that the jurors can follow along as the witness reads from it. If the court is equipped with computer screens visible to the jurors, you may also put the document up on the screen. You may also create blow-up copies of documents and display them to the jurors.

The point is that introducing an exhibit is only the threshold task that enables you to use the exhibit to your client's best advantage. For each exhibit you offer, you must plan how to most effectively share its content with the jurors. If you propose to publish the exhibit by any means other than asking the witness a question about the exhibit, tell the court exactly what you would like to do with the exhibit and obtain the court's permission.

10.5   A Review Script

The foregoing six-step process may seem overwhelmingly complicated. Most of the steps, however, are more difficult to describe and explain than they are to do. For this reason, we are including a bare-bones script of the ritual without the explanation of each step. The words you will say are printed in bold text below.

1) Examine the witness who will introduce the exhibit in a way that establishes competence and relevance and makes the introduction of the exhibit become part of the story of the trial.

2) Show the exhibit to opposing counsel, the judge, and the witness.

   Say to opposing counsel and the judge, **"I'm going to show the witness the exhibit marked as Plaintiff's Number 1."** Show them a copy.

   Say to the judge, **"Your Honor, may I approach the witness?"**

   Say to the witness, **"I am showing you what has been marked for identification as Plaintiff's Exhibit Number 1."**

3) Have the witness identify the exhibit.

   Show the exhibit to the witness. Say, **"Please tell the jury what it is."** Or, **"What is it?"**

4) Lay any necessary evidentiary foundation:

   Authenticate the exhibit through testimony that shows that the exhibit is what you say it is.

   Complete the foundation with testimony that shows that the exhibit is not excludable on any other grounds.

5) Offer the exhibit.

   Say, **"Your Honor, I move plaintiff's exhibit Number 1 be admitted into evidence."**

   Or, **"Your honor, I offer plaintiff's exhibit Number 1 in evidence."**

6) Publish the exhibit to the jurors. Don't forget to use it!

Notice that steps two, three, four, and five are no more than formalities—indispensable formalities, but still formalities. The heart and soul of the exhibit ritual are found in steps one (showing how the exhibit fits into the story and getting the jurors interested in seeing the exhibit) and six (actually showing the exhibit to the jurors). You should practice the formalities so that they come naturally to you during trial, but always put the focus of your creative energy, thought, and effort into the storytelling steps of the process, steps one and six.

10.6   Special Problems in Evidentiary Foundations

In step four of the "ritual of foundations," you authenticate the exhibit and lay any other foundation necessary to show that the exhibit is not excludable on other grounds. What does that mean? There are many rules governing the admissibility of evidence, any of which may stand in your way until you ask the proper foundational questions.

Your exhibit may draw an objection based on relevance,[11] its potential prejudice or other negative effect on the trial process,[12] a specific relevance/prejudice rule applicable to the type of evidence at issue,[13] lack of originality (the "best evidence" rule),[14] hearsay[15] (including hearsay within hearsay[16]), privilege,[17] the confrontation clause of the United States Constitution,[18] or incompetence of the witness.[19] To avoid these objections, you must engage in a pretrial preparation process. Before trial, take a look at each exhibit on your list. Imagine what objections your opponent may raise to the exhibit and then plan to ask questions to avoid the objection. In other words, if the document you plan to introduce might be hearsay, plan to ask the witness (during step four of the ritual) questions that will show that a hearsay exception applies. Draft the series of questions that you will need to ask to establish the foundation and attach it to your exhibit or exhibit list.

Usually, you can derive the formula for the foundation by turning each one of the requirements of an exclusionary rule of evidence into a question or series of questions. For example, Rule 803(16) provides a hearsay exception for "statements in a document that is at least 20 years old and whose authenticity is established." If you are trying to introduce a statement from an old letter, you can ask the witness, "When was this letter written?" If there is any issue about its authenticity, you will ask, "How do you know who wrote it?" You might also ask, "How do you know it hasn't been changed since then?" Your witness's testimony, for example, that the letter was written in 1957 by Thurgood Marshall and has been kept among the official papers of Thurgood Marshall, available in the Library of Congress, will undoubtedly satisfy the rule.

There is no need to use a specific formula to avoid each evidentiary objection. Many lawyers feel more comfortable, however, having a foundation formula that they use every time they have an exhibit that raises certain issues. They may have a "business records" formula and a "public records" formula. There is nothing wrong with that. In fact, there are some evidentiary problems that arise so frequently that

---

11. FED. R. EVID. 401–402.
12. FED. R. EVID. 403.
13. FED. R. EVID. 404–415.
14. FED. R. EVID. 1001–1008.
15. FED. R. EVID. 801–802.
16. FED. R. EVID. 805.
17. FED. R. EVID. 501 and various applicable statutes and court decisions.
18. *See* Crawford v. Washington, 541 U.S. 36 (2004).
19. FED. R. EVID. 601, 602, 701, and 702.

National Institute for Trial Advocacy

it makes sense to have a simple strategy to address them.[20] We will address some of those problems here.

10.6.1 *Problems of Authenticity*

As we noted above, unless an exhibit is self-authenticating under Rule 902, Rule 901 requires you to show that the exhibit is what you claim it is. Your witness can often establish the exhibit's authenticity through her own personal knowledge.

> Q: Officer, I'm showing you what has been marked as Plaintiff's Exhibit 2. What is it?
>
> A: This is the .38-caliber pistol I found at 22 Hobble Street on the night of the shooting.
>
> Q: How do you know?
>
> A: When I picked it up off the floor, I put it in an evidence bag marked with my initials. Here are my initials on the bag, right here.

Sometimes, however, the witness will not have personal knowledge that the exhibit is what you claim it is. For example, if your witness received a letter in the mail, your witness has no firsthand knowledge of who wrote the letter. In that situation, you must use circumstantial evidence that tends to prove that the item is what you say it is. Notice that "what you say the exhibit is" is not simply "a letter." To be relevant, it must be "a letter from Mr. Boniface." Your authentication of this exhibit must tie the letter to its author. Here are two examples of common situations where circumstantial evidence is used to authenticate documents:

1) **Letters received.** If you seek to prove only that person "A" received a letter, it is a simple matter to have "A" so testify, and that proof should be sufficient to support the letter's introduction. However, if you seek to prove that person "A" received the letter from person "B," you must offer additional evidence to support the inference that "B" sent it. If "A" is familiar with "B's" signature, his identification of the signature is sufficient.[21] The fact that the letter is on "B's" letterhead may also be sufficient. Likewise, the contents of the letter may reflect knowledge that only "B" would be likely to have or may contain matters earlier discussed by "A" and "B." Any of these circumstantial links provides an adequate connection between the letter and "B."

2) **Letters mailed.** If you seek to prove that your client mailed a letter, the foundation must include proof of mailing. If the author of the letter

---

20. If you are one of those people who likes a formula to deal with each kind of potential exclusionary rule, we recommend Edward J. Imwinklereid, *Evidentiary Foundations* (9th ed. 2014), which contains detailed scripts to address each evidentiary problem.
21. *See* FED. R. EVID. 901(b)(2).

personally placed it in the mail, she may so testify. However, in the business environment, writers of letters rarely mail them personally. Rather, they or their secretaries typically place all letters in an "outgoing mail" receptacle, from which a mail clerk picks them up, affixes postage, and places them in a mailbox. One could call all of these people to complete the foundation. Even if one did so, however, the mail clerk, and maybe even the secretary, probably could not testify under oath that he remembered the particular letter in question. To resolve this dilemma, the law of evidence allows an inference to be drawn that a letter was mailed upon proof of a routine mailing practice of the business, followed whenever a letter is mailed.[22]

Another problem arises when the opponent claims that no letter was received. Requests for admissions will have been denied and motions to produce will have generated only denials of having ever seen any such letter. Having mailed the original, your client will have only a copy of what he claims to have mailed. Thus, the authenticity of the original having been questioned, you are faced with the necessity of complying with the "best evidence" rule before introducing the copy.[23] Normally, a duplicate is admissible to the same extent as its original.[24] When the authenticity of the original is questioned, however, the proponent must account for its absence before introducing secondary evidence. Generally, the proponent must offer foundational evidence sufficient to justify an inference that the original was lost, destroyed, not obtainable, or in the possession of the opponent.[25] In the case of a letter mailed, this proof normally consists of testimony concerning the routine practice of addressing envelopes, typing letters on office letterheads showing the return address, and affixing proper postage, plus testimony that the letter in question was not returned by the postal service.

Chain of Custody

Another special authentication problem arises when the relevance of a piece of real evidence depends on its being "the exact same item" or an item "in the exact same condition" as it was at the time of the events at issue. In these situations, it may be necessary to present a "chain of custody" to demonstrate that the exhibit is the same in all relevant respects as it was at the time of the trial events. A chain of custody is most likely to be required when there is a danger of substitution or adulteration of the evidence or when the condition, appearance, or weight of the

---

22. FED. R. EVID. 406 states: "Evidence of a person's habit or an organization's routine practice may be admitted to prove that on a particular occasion the person or organization acted in accordance with the habit or routine practice. The court may admit this evidence regardless of whether it is combined or whether there was an eyewitness."

23. FED. R. EVID. 1002.

24. FED. R. EVID. 1003.

25. FED. R. EVID. 1004.

evidence is relevant or in dispute. In a prosecution for drug possession, for example, the plastic bag of cocaine would not be relevant if it were not the same item that was taken from the defendant by the police. Further, the testimony of the state's chemist that the substance in the bag is cocaine would not be relevant if the chemist did not test the very same item. The prosecutor does not merely claim that the item is "cocaine." He claims that this is the same cocaine taken from the defendant and tested in the state laboratory.

In these situations, the item of real evidence can be shown to be authentic—that is, what you claim it is—only by showing that there has been no substitution, alteration, or tampering with the item that would alter its relevance. You can do this by establishing a "chain of custody." You call to the witness stand every person through whose hands the item has passed. Each must, in essence, tell how and where she received the item, describe what she did with it while it was in her possession, and relate how and to whom she passed it on. By accounting for the whereabouts and condition of the item from the moment it was taken from the defendant to the moment it appeared in the courtroom, you demonstrate that the item has not been substituted or altered.

Demonstrative Exhibits and Illustrative Aids

We have said that the authentication process requires you to produce some evidence that the item is what you claim it is. When you work with demonstrative exhibits or illustrative aids, you do not claim that the exhibit is the gun that was used in the shooting, or the bullet that was taken from the body, or the purse that was stolen by the purse-snatcher. You do not assert that it is a piece of real evidence. So, what exactly do you claim that the exhibit is, and how can it be authenticated? When you are using a demonstrative or illustrative exhibit, your claim is that the exhibit will be helpful to illustrate the witness's testimony and that the exhibit is a fair and accurate representation of the thing that you are trying to illuminate. Therefore, when using a chart or diagram as a visual aid—even if you do not intend to introduce it into evidence—you must authenticate it by demonstrating its helpfulness, accuracy, and fairness.

No matter what kind of illustrative aid you employ, the court must first decide that it will be helpful to the jurors' understanding of the witness's testimony. Therefore, before using an illustrative aid, always ask the witness whether it would help the jurors understand his testimony. For example, "Mr. Davis, would it help the jurors understand your testimony if you were to step down here and show them just exactly how you were standing when the defendant stuck the gun in your face?"

You will also ask questions to establish the fairness and accuracy of any model, map, chart, or diagram. For example, before using a drawing of the crime scene, you might ask the witness:

Q: Are you familiar with the parking lot at the corner of 12th and Vine?

A: Yes.

Q: Can you describe it?

A: Yes. It has streetlights on the west side, a line of trees on the east, and the cars park perpendicular to Vine Street.

Q: I'm showing you what has been marked as Plaintiff's Exhibit 17. Do you recognize it?

A: Yes, it is a drawing of the parking lot at 12th Street and Vine.

Q: Does it fairly and accurately reflect the layout of the parking lot on the day of the murder?

A: It does.

Q: Would using the drawing help you to illustrate your testimony about what you found there?

A: Yes.

Q: [*To the judge.*] Your Honor, may the witness step down to use this exhibit as a demonstrative aid?

Court: Any objection? Hearing none, the witness may step down and use the exhibit.

At this point, you may have the witness mark on the exhibit the things he found at the scene. Technically, all marks on an exhibit at the moment of introduction should remain and no additional marking on the exhibit should be allowed after its introduction. Therefore, it is sometimes advantageous to use an object as an illustrative aid before introducing it into evidence as an exhibit. For example, consider the diagram of an intersection that was the scene of an automobile accident. You may wish to have one or more witnesses draw on the diagram to illustrate their testimony. It is a simple matter to have the first witness establish that the diagram fairly and accurately represents the intersection on the day of the accident. Each succeeding witness may then use the diagram as a visual aid as she testifies, drawing on it various things she observed. (It is often helpful to have each witness use a marker of a different color to clearly differentiate their drawings.) Alternatively, if you have the equipment, you may use a computer slide and have the witnesses mark on that.

After the exhibit has been marked by all of your witnesses, you may offer it into evidence to preserve it in the record. You should object if your opponent attempts to mark or alter one of your exhibits after you have placed it into evidence. An effective way to handle the logistical problem that arises when several witnesses will mark the same diagram is to number and introduce the unmarked diagram (as, for example, Exhibit 2). You can then have a clear plastic overlay for each witness to mark, number these overlays Exhibits 2A, 2B, and so forth, and offer each as the witness completes using it to elucidate his testimony. If you are using computerized exhibits, the same document may be saved with several different file names—one for each witness who will mark changes on the document.

10.6.2 Hearsay: The Business Records Exception

Every document that is not an admission of a party opponent creates a hearsay problem. The document is a statement. It is not made by a witness in court. If you are introducing the document for the truth of the matters contained in the document, it is hearsay. Therefore, each time you want to introduce a document, you must decide which hearsay exception fits and prepare to lay a foundation that shows the elements of the exception. The most commonly used hearsay exception is the business records exception.[26]

Every competent trial lawyer must know how to lay a foundation to get business records into evidence. Admittedly, these documents are often stipulated to be admissible, and such a stipulation relieves the proponent of the necessity of laying a foundation. Indeed, the Federal Rules of Evidence now provide that business records may be introduced without a live authenticating witness if a person qualified to be such a witness certifies their authenticity.[27] The rules require that you give adverse parties notice of your intention to introduce the records sufficiently in advance to give them an opportunity to challenge the admissibility of the records. Many states' evidence laws have similar provisions dispensing with the necessity of a live authenticating witness.

Nevertheless, you must know how to lay the foundation when the need arises. Moreover, the testimony that constitutes the foundation can be important for the jurors to hear so they can understand the significance of the record and accord it the weight it deserves.

---

26. FED. R. EVID. 803(6) defines an admissible business record in the following language:
    A record of an act, event, condition, opinion, or diagnosis if:
    (A) the record was made at or near the time by–or from information transmitted by–someone with knowledge;
    (B) the record was kept in the course of a regularly conducted activity or a business, organization, occupation, or calling, whether or not for profit;
    (C) making the record was a regular practice of that activity;
    (D) all these conditions are shown by the testimony of the custodian or another qualified witness, or by a certification that complies with *Rule 902(11)* or *(12)* or with a statute permitting certification; and
    (E) the opponent does not show that the source of information or the method or circumstances of preparation indicate a lack of trustworthiness.
27. FED. R. EVID. 803(6), 902(11), 902(12).

Laying the foundation will require the following.

1) **A qualified witness.** Rule 803(6) requires that the elements of the foundation be "shown by the testimony of the custodian or other qualified witness . . . ." Therefore, your first task is to select a witness who has personal knowledge of the way the records of the business are kept and who can identify your exhibit as one of those records. The witness must be able to testify to all of the following elemental facts.

2) **When the entries were made.** Your witness must testify that each entry in the record was "made at or near the time" when whatever it records occurred.

3) **Knowledge of the person who furnished or recorded the information.** The entries must have been made "by, or from information transmitted by, a person with knowledge . . . ." After testifying to when the entries were made, the witness must testify that the person who made the entries either had knowledge of the matters recorded or made the entries based on information furnished by someone who had knowledge of those matters.

4) **Kept in the course of a regularly conducted activity.** The rule only excepts from the hearsay rule records "kept in the course of a regularly conducted activity of a business, organization, occupation or calling." This requirement simply means that the entity that kept the record must have been a "business." The exception does not include personal notes, records, or diaries. Because this issue is often so clear, asking this question is usually redundant. You really do not need to ask, "Is First National Bank a regularly conducted business?" However, you do need to establish that the record was "kept" in the course of a regularly conducted activity of that business.

5) **A regularly made record.** Rule 803(6) treats the "keeping" and "making" of the record as separate foundational requirements. The rule requires you to establish that the making of the record "was the regular practice of that business activity."

10.6.3   *Should You Elicit Underlying Facts or Parrot the Rule?*

The business records rule states its components in conclusory terms. The witness who has personal knowledge of the facts that satisfy the exception's requirement should be able to testify to those facts.

Actually, to simply ask the witness about the conclusory elements by leading questions may be technically objectionable and is not as effective as asking the witness for the facts that lead to that conclusion. To illustrate, assume that witness Drudge is asked, "Was this record prepared at or near the time of the matters recorded?" Such a question and answer will probably have minimal impact on the jury. It is better to ask Drudge about each relevant entry: "When is that entry made into this kind of record?" Then the witness can give a knowledgeable, credible answer, such as, "When the order clerk receives the phone call ordering merchandise. When the call comes in—and while the customer is on the phone—the clerk enters into the computer the customer's name, address, and account number, and the description, catalogue page number, and stock number of the merchandise ordered."

In spite of what we have just said, some judges listen for the "buzz words" of an 803(6) foundation and sustain objections unless they hear them. If you are before such a judge, throw in the conclusory, boilerplate questions to assure admissibility of your business record. However, do not omit the non-leading, informational questions that give the witness the opportunity to establish his knowledge and the jurors to understand the significance of the record.

10.6.4 A Sample Business Records Foundation

Let us lay a good, clean, informative foundation for a simple business record: a telephone message pad.

The issue: whether Nugent had a telephone conversation with Oliver, the sales manager of Manual Lawn Sprinkler Company, on the morning of September 3. Nugent has testified that he called Oliver that morning and they discussed an important matter. Oliver has testified that he was out of the office all that day and did not talk to Nugent. Manual Lawn Sprinkler Company wants to introduce its telephone message log to show that Oliver was not there when Nugent tried to call.

> Q: Mr. Drudge, where do you work?
>
> A: For Manual Lawn Sprinkler Company.
>
> Q: Is that a regularly conducted business?
>
> A: Yes, sir.
>
> Q: What's your job there?
>
> A: I'm office manager.
>
> Q: Are you responsible for the company's records?
>
> A: Yes, sir.
>
> Q: In that job, is it necessary for you to be familiar with the procedures for preparing all of the company's records?
>
> A: Yes, sir.

Q: Does your company have a procedure for recording incoming telephone calls when the person called is unavailable?

A: Yes, sir.

Q: Tell us about that procedure.

A: Well, all incoming calls come in through the switchboard and the receptionist answers the phone. If the person called is available, the receptionist transfers the call and no record is made. If the person called is unavailable, the secretary either transfers the caller to the person's voice mailbox or takes a message. Mr. Oliver does not use voicemail because he prefers to have a written memorandum of every call that came in while he was out of the office.

Q: Does the company have a standard procedure for recording those telephone messages?

A: Yes, sir. We have pads of message forms. There are six message forms on each sheet. Each sheet is in duplicate, so that whatever is written on the form shows through on the second sheet. The top sheet is perforated, so that each of the six messages can be torn off. The second sheet is not perforated. As each message is recorded, the receptionist tears off the top sheet and places the message in the message box of the person called. When a pad of forms is used up, the second sheets form a permanent record of all the messages left.

Q: When does the receptionist fill out the message form?

A: Immediately. While the caller is on the phone. She asks the caller's name and phone number and writes down any message the caller wants to leave.

Q: Are the date and time recorded?

A: Yes, sir. She writes on the form the date and the time the call came in.

Q: Is it always done that way?

A: Yes, sir. That's our standard office procedure.

Q: What happens to those second sheets when the pad is used up?

A: Each pad of second sheets is placed in a file. They are kept in chronological order.

Q: Is it the regular practice of Manual Lawn Sprinkler Company to make and keep these telephone message records?

A: Yes, sir.

Lawyer: Your Honor, I have here what's been previously marked as Defense Exhibit 4. [*At this point, the lawyer walks over and shows the exhibit to opposing counsel.*] May I approach the witness?

The Court: Very well.

[*The lawyer approaches and hands the witness the exhibit.*]

Q: I've just handed you Defense Exhibit 4 for identification. Can you tell us what it is?

A: Yes, sir. It's a page out of the company's telephone message records.

Q: Where did you get it?

A: Out of the file where these records are kept.

Q: Why did you get this record out of the file?

A: Because you asked me to get the telephone message logs for September 3.

Q: Does this page contain messages recorded September 3?

A: Yes, sir.

Q: Does the name "Nugent" appear on any of those messages?"

A: Yes, sir. One that was recorded at 10:37 a.m.

Lawyer: Your Honor, the Defense offers Defense Exhibit 4.

The Court: Any objection?

Opposing counsel: No objection, your Honor.

The Court: Admitted.

Q: Mr. Drudge, would you now read to the jurors the name of the person whom Nugent called?

A: Oliver.

Q;   Sir, does the telephone log have anything written in the place for "message?"

A: Yes, sir. It says, "Sorry I missed you. Will call again next week."

Lawyer: Thank you, Mr. Drudge. Your Honor, may I pass Defense Exhibit 4 to the jurors?

The Court: Very well.

Lawyer: Your Honor, I pass the witness for cross-examination.

Chapter Eleven

Making and Responding to Objections

"Professor," John began, "Don't you think it is rude to interrupt people when they are talking?"

"Generally, yes, I do," the Professor responded.

"Well, in a trial, every time I stand up and say 'Objection,' I am interrupting a witness or my opponent. I feel like I am being rude. I don't see how it could possibly help my image with the jurors."

"You are right, John, the jurors may view your objections as rude lawyer behavior. But they also expect you to be your client's protector and advocate. They expect to see some confrontation."

"They expect a contest . . . like a football game . . . ." John mused. "And the judge is the referee!"

"Well," the professor began, shaking his head, "The trial is certainly a competitive match, but the judge is more like the judge of a skating competition than the referee in a football game."

"Now you lost me, Professor."

In a football game, a referee runs around and follows the play. When somebody does something wrong, he throws a flag and stops the play. The trial judge does not do that. Like the judge in a skating competition, the trial judge sits on the side and watches the two lawyers skate around and fall down. No matter how bad the skaters are, the judge does not stop the action."

"Yeah, right," said John, "But it's not like a skating match exactly, is it? Because if I don't want the other lawyer to skate right over my client, I can stop the action myself."

"Exactly," the professor concurred. "You are the only one who can prevent the other side from skating right over your client's rights. You do that by making an objection."

11.1   Introduction

An individual coming into court has almost no rights at all—unless an advocate asserts and protects those rights. The Federal Rules of Evidence place the responsibility for raising evidentiary issues squarely on the shoulders of the lawyers. You must object and respond to your opponent's objections. If you do not, your client's rights will be waived. On appeal, you may not complain of the trial judge's error in *admitting* evidence unless you made a timely objection or motion to strike and stated your specific ground.[1] Conversely, you may not complain of the trial judge's error in *excluding* your evidence unless you made an offer of proof.[2]

To preserve your client's rights on appeal, it is necessary to call those rights to the attention of the trial judge. It is even more important, however, to win your point at trial. You need to be able to raise and respond to objections in a way that convinces the trial judge that you are correct. It is better to win your case at trial than to lose at trial and hope for a successful appeal. If the judge rules against you and you lose the case, you are not likely to have the judgment reversed based on an erroneous evidentiary ruling. That is why it is extremely important to be able to raise your objections effectively and win the point at trial.

Even so, you must try your case for the benefit of two audiences. One audience, the trial judge and jurors, watches your live performance. The other, an appellate court, will see only a written record of the trial proceedings if the case is appealed. When an appellate court reviews the trial record, an incident that was not included in the record may as well not have occurred. Likewise, if the written record is unclear, the appellate court cannot determine whether error was committed. Therefore, you must always be conscious of the court reporter. Your every word must be directed not only to the jurors, but also to the reporter. For the jurors' benefit, your words must be simple; for the record, they must be precise.

11.2   How to Make Objections

While you should keep in mind the idea that it is rude to interrupt someone, it is also imperative to raise objections that will protect your client's rights. You will have to raise objections and you will have to do it well.

11.2.1   The Basics

Stand up. Always stand when you object (and, for that matter, whenever you speak during a trial). Because you must generally make your objection in the fraction

---

1. FED. R. EVID. 103(a)(1). You should not rely on the saving clause, "unless it was apparent from the context," found in Rule 103(a)(1)(b). That language simply emphasizes an appellate court's power to save litigants from the carelessness of their lawyers.
2. FED. R. EVID. 103(a)(2).

of a second after a question is asked but before the answer is given, you must be ready to pop up out of your chair quickly. As you listen to your opponent's examination of a witness, sit with both feet on the floor. As soon as you hear an objectionable question, stand up. It may take you another second or two to think of the proper grounds for the objection, but once you are on your feet, the trial judge will generally recognize that you are objecting and will stop the questioning.

Say "Objection!" Be firm and assertive; try to sound as if you know what you are doing. "Objection" should be your first word, followed by a succinct statement of the specific ground or grounds for the objection. For example, you will stand and say, "Objection! The question calls for a hearsay answer." Do not detract from the force of your objection by adding qualifying language such as "I believe" or "I think."

If there are multiple grounds for the objection, state all the grounds in the initial objection. For example, you will stand and say "Objection! The question calls for information in a document that has not been admitted into evidence, is hearsay, and is not relevant." Any basis you neglect to state in the initial objection is not preserved for appeal. You can be sure that the judge will not welcome hearing new grounds for your objection after entertaining argument on and overruling your original objection.

Ask to approach the bench, if necessary. Many objections can be raised and ruled on without extensive argument. For these objections, remain standing at counsel table until you get a ruling. On the other hand, when the grounds for your objection cannot be explained without talking about the very matters that you do not want the jurors to hear, then you should ask the judge if you may approach the bench. Both you and your opponent will then walk up to the bench and stand close to the judge so that you can make your evidentiary arguments without the jurors overhearing. Be sure the court reporter can hear and take down the sidebar conversations. It is important to make sure these sidebar arguments are on the record. It is equally important, however, to keep sidebar arguments to a bare minimum. Each sidebar argument appears to the jurors like a private conversation between the lawyers and the judge. These private conversations feed the jurors' suspicion that the lawyers are hiding something.

Insist on a ruling. Unless your objection is sustained or overruled, there will be nothing in the record to support an appeal. Some judges avoid ruling on objections, knowing that the absence of a ruling in the record will avert a reversal and you must ask the judge to state a ruling that the court reporter can record. This can sometimes be a touchy business. You cannot afford to incur the court's wrath or appear disrespectful. If the court fails to rule on an objection, say with unwavering courtesy, "May I have a ruling on my objection, Your Honor?"

Do not display emotion when your objections are overruled. To do so is inelegant and detracts from your image as a person in control of the trial proceedings. Some jurors will not know the difference between the words "sustained" and "overruled." Others may not be paying attention at the moment of ruling. Therefore, if you seem calmly assured as you resume your seat, as if your objection had been sustained, those jurors will likely assume that you won the point.

11.2.2 Do Not Object Unless the Evidence Will Hurt Your Case

With a few exceptions, you should make an objection only when the evidence, if admitted, will hurt your client's case. If your opponent offers objectionable but harmless evidence, do not object. A trial is more than an intellectual contest between lawyers; it is a struggle to occupy what the jurors perceives as the moral high ground. Jurors do not like lawyers who object too much. They expect and forgive a few necessary objections, but are offended by lawyers they perceive to be obstructionists. Too many objections, successful or unsuccessful, can make you look like a jerk. Even a single successful objection can damage your rapport with the jurors. Jurors seek "the truth" and are anxious to gather as much information as possible to guide them in their quest. They are likely to feel frustrated and subtly insulted when they are denied access to information because someone objected. They need to blame someone. Since they cannot blame the judge (after all, the judge is the law incarnate), they may form hostile feelings toward the lawyer who successfully objected.

An overruled objection hurts worst of all. Jurors who suspect that an objecting lawyer is being obstreperous have their suspicions confirmed by the judge's ruling. Moreover, every overruled objection detracts from the objector's credibility—and your credibility is your most indispensable asset. Your closing argument will be for naught if you have destroyed your credibility with groundless objections, so make every effort to have both a legitimate legal ground and a tactical reason when you object. Keep your ego in check and rise to object only when you have a good strategic reason to do so.

11.2.3 Object When Inadmissible Evidence Will Hurt Your Case

If a piece of evidence will harm your case more than an objection and if there is a legitimate ground to object, you should not let that evidence come in unchallenged. Federal Evidence Rule 403 gives judges wide discretion to allow or refuse evidence after weighing its probative value against its potential to harm the trial process. Though you will not often get a judgment reversed because the judge abused this discretion, you should object if the evidence is harmful and you can articulate a basis for its exclusion. After all, the judge might agree with you.

Even if the evidence will not hurt your case, there are some situations when you should make objections to inadmissible evidence that will not hurt your case. If you are a new trial lawyer, for example, your opponent may stretch the Rules of Evidence to find out whether you are ready and able to make appropriate trial objections. Be ready for the test. Show confidence and competence early by making an appropriate objection early in the case.

You should also object to protect your witness from harassing questions—even when the answers to the questions will not hurt your case. You brought the witness in to court. You must take responsibility to protect the witness from abuse.

11.2.4   Motions in Limine

Do not wait until trial to raise objections. The discovery process will give you a good preview of exactly what your opponent intends to introduce at trial. Before trial, go through everything that you expect your opponent to offer. Make a list of the pieces of evidence that you find objectionable. Where the evidence is very damaging and your chance of prevailing on the objection would be enhanced if the judge was given the opportunity to consult the language of the rule of evidence, advisory committee notes, and case law interpreting the rule, raise the objection before trial in a motion in limine. A motion in limine should be presented to the court in writing before trial. It does not have to be lengthy. It should briefly identify each piece of evidence you object to, state your objection to it, and give authority for its exclusion.[3]

If the motion is granted, your opponent will be precluded from mentioning the matter in opening statement or offering the evidence. Moreover, your opponent will be required to instruct witnesses not to blurt out the evidence. If the motion is denied, at least you will know where you stand and can plan your trial strategy accordingly. Even if the court reserves its ruling, the motion accomplishes the important objectives of helping you prepare to make well-supported objections at trial and alerting the court to the issues you will raise.

If your motion in limine is denied, you should renew the objection when the evidence is offered at trial.[4] If your motion is sustained but your opponent violates it

---

3. You also may file a motion in advance of trial seeking a ruling that evidence you propose to offer is admissible. As with the motion to exclude evidence, the judge will be positioned to make a more informed ruling if you arm her with the legal authorities that support admission of the evidence.

4. We advise this course of action although FED. R. EVID. 103(b) was amended in to provide that "Once the court rules definitely on the record—either before or at trial—a party need not review an objection or offer proof to preserve a claim of error for appeal." The problem is defining a "definitive" ruling. The comments to the amendment underscore the problem: "The amendment imposes the obligation on counsel to clarify whether an in limine or other evidentiary ruling is definitive when there is doubt on that point.

"Even where the court's ruling is definitive, nothing in the amendment prohibits the court from revisiting its decision when the evidence is to be offered . . . .

"A definitive advance ruling is reviewed in light of the facts and circumstances before the trial court at the time of the ruling. If the relevant facts and circumstances change materially after the advance ruling has been made, those facts and circumstances cannot be relied upon on appeal unless they have been brought to the attention of the trial court by way of renewed, and timely, objection, offer of proof, or motion to strike."

Bottom line: It is still wise to renew your objection.

at trial, you must object to avoid possibility that your failure to object may constitute a waiver of the objection raised in your motion.

If the court reserves ruling on the motion in limine until trial, ask the court to instruct opposing counsel to make no mention of the evidence in the opening statement and to approach the bench at the time she intends to ask the question that will elicit the questionable evidence. This will ensure that the jurors do not irreversibly learn of the objectionable evidence before the court issues its ultimate ruling.

11.2.5 *Object When the Question Is Asked*

If your opponent asks a witness a question such as, "What did people say about the defendant?" chances are you will recognize the question as one that calls for a hearsay response or as a question that calls for evidence that is more prejudicial than probative. Similarly, when you hear your opponent ask a lay witness a question like, "In your opinion, did the defendant tell the truth?" you will know the question calls for inadmissible testimony. Sometimes you will recognize a question that calls for inadmissible information because of your familiarity with the record. As soon as you hear such a question, stand up and object. Your goal is to interpose the objection before the answer is given. If you wait an additional second or two, the witness will have responded, "The word on the street was that the defendant was making methamphetamine," or "In my opinion, the defendant is a lying bum." Now it is too late to prevent the jurors from hearing the objectionable answer.

Some evidentiary material that your opponent seeks to offer may be intrinsically objectionable—that is, no foundation your opponent lays will make that material admissible. For example, unduly inflammatory photographs are inadmissible because of their inherent characteristics. You should object to these matters the moment you become aware that your opponent will attempt to introduce them. Always argue these objections out of the jurors' presence because the argument on admissibility will convey almost as much inflammatory information as the exhibit.

Sometimes your opponent will ask a question that does not give you a clue that the answer will be objectionable. For example, if your opponent asks, "When did you next see the defendant?" you will not expect the witness to say, "I next saw him lying in the gutter, half-naked and stinking like a brewery." Whenever you are unable to object in time to prevent the witness from making an objectionable answer, your only option is to move to strike.

A motion to strike is a questionable strategic weapon. If the court grants your motion, the judge will generally instruct the jurors to disregard the witness's statement. The jurors will certainly try to follow the judge's instruction, but it is very hard to disregard what you have already heard. Sometimes the admonition itself will serve to reinforce the offending testimony.

Picture the jurors, after lunch, with energy flagging, listening half-heartedly to your opponent's examination of Mr. Peabody. Question and answer follow question and answer. Blah. Blah. Nobody on the jury is tracking the testimony very carefully. By the time they go into the jury room to deliberate on the verdict, they may have forgotten Mr. Peabody completely. But suddenly, you are on your feet, breaking the monotony. You object and move to strike the witness's last statement. The jurors perk up. The judge sustains the motion and then turns to the jurors and says, "Ladies and gentlemen, I instruct you that the character of the defendant is not an issue in this case and you are to disregard the witness's statements that relate to character." Now the jurors start to think, "What are we supposed to disregard? Oh, the statement about the defendant's relationship with Mrs. Peabody! That must have shown bad character." Now the jurors will remember the witness, the statement, and the inference that you hoped they would not make.

Even so, there are at least two situations in which it makes sense to object after the excludable testimony has already been heard. First, if the objectionable testimony (or its exclusion) might be important in an appeal, make the motion to protect the record. Second, if your opponent is hitting below the belt by eliciting inadmissible information, make a motion to strike. Your motion will call to the jurors' attention the fact that your opponent is not playing fair.

Finally, if the inadmissible information is so prejudicial that an admonition will not cure the prejudice and justice cannot be served by continuing the trial, you should move for a mistrial.

Object as soon as your opponent attempts to read from documents that have not been admitted into evidence. It is generally improper to read the contents of a document that has not been admitted.[5] If an exhibit has not been formally introduced into evidence, the jurors should not see it or hear about its contents. If you plan to object to any of the contents of the document, do not let your opponent jump the gun and start reading from or discussing information contained in an exhibit before it has been introduced. Say, "I object, Your Honor, counsel is reading from a document that has not been admitted into evidence."

11.2.6 *Introduce Facts Showing Your Opponent's Evidence Is Inadmissible*

Before any evidence can be admitted, it must be relevant, authentic, offered through a competent and reliable source, and not subject to any exclusionary rule.

---

5. Exceptions to this rule exist. For instance, statements in documents offered as past recollection recorded pursuant to Federal Evidence Rule 803(5) may be read, but the document may not be introduced. A like rule applies to statements in learned treatises. FED. R. EVID. 803(18). Prior inconsistent statements offered to impeach a witness's credibility may be read into evidence without introducing the documents that contain the statements. *See* FED. R. EVID. 613

These requirements make up the "evidentiary foundation" for any particular piece of evidence. The party offering the evidence has the burden of establishing that foundation, but you are not required to sit back and accept whatever your opponent presents as an evidentiary foundation. If you believe that additional facts will render the tendered evidence inadmissible, you are entitled not only to object, but also to introduce additional testimony or information that demonstrates that the evidence should not be admitted. This is often done through a voir dire examination of the witness.

For example, your opponent may bring forward a witness who you believe should not be allowed to testify at all, perhaps an "expert" witness who you believe is not expert in the relevant field.[6] Your opponent will attempt to lay a foundation for this witness's testimony by eliciting testimony about the witness's expert qualifications. If you believe that the "expert" is unqualified, you should object to his testimony and ask to voir dire the witness.[7] You can then ask the witness cross-examination style questions relating to his qualifications: "Your license to practice medicine was suspended five years ago and has not been reinstated, has it?" Following your voir dire, you will ask the court to rule that the witness is unqualified and should not be permitted to testify.

Similarly, if your opponent attempts to introduce an exhibit that you contend is inadmissible, you have a right to raise factual questions relating to the admissibility before the exhibit is introduced. After your opponent has laid a foundation that appears to be sufficient and seeks to proceed with the witness's testimony or introduction of the exhibit, you have the right to cross-examine the witness at that time on the limited issue you raised in your objection.

Although this mini cross-examination is called voir dire, it should not be confused with the voir dire of the venire panel during the jury selection process. The purpose of this small segment of cross-examination, taken out of order and inserted in the midst of the opponent's direct examination, is to bring to light additional information that may bear on the issue of admissibility. If the exhibit were admitted without affording opposing counsel the opportunity to voir dire, thus postponing adverse examination on the issue of admissibility until the general cross-examination of the witness, the possibility of keeping the exhibit from the jurors would be lost. The same questions could be asked, but during regular cross-examination they could only affect the weight of the exhibit, not its admissibility.

---

6. You should, of course, raise this issue before trial in a motion in limine.

7. See chapter nine at 9.3.2 for a discussion of the strategic decision whether to voir dire the witness at the time she is tendered to the court or to wait until the full cross to bring out deficiencies in qualifications.

As a matter of strategy, you should consider conducting voir dire whenever there is additional evidence that could render a harmful exhibit inadmissible, even if that evidence may not be sufficient to prevent its admission. Though your voir dire examination may not prevent the exhibit's admission, it may well dramatically affect the weight the jurors give it. It is to your advantage to provide the jurors this weight-reducing information before they see the exhibit, so that they will view it in its proper context. In fact, the best strategy frequently is to point out the exhibit's limitations through voir dire questions, then agree not to object if the jurors are admonished that the exhibit should only be considered for certain limited purposes.

Consider for example a photograph of the scene of an intersection collision that shows the plaintiff's car parked in the proper lane. Assume that opposing counsel has asked the witness if the photograph fairly and accurately depicts the accident scene and the witness has said "yes." Opposing counsel moves to admit the photograph. Now, you tell the judge that you object to the admission of the "accident scene photograph" and ask the judge if you may voir dire the witness:

Q: The two cars involved in the collision were moved before the photograph was taken?

A: That's right.

Q: This photograph does not show their location at impact. Is that right?

A: Right.

Q: When you say that the photograph accurately depicts the scene of the accident, you mean that it shows debris in the intersection and a clearly marked center stripe. Right?

A: Yes.

Q: The photograph does not depict anything about the position of either car at the point of impact?

A: Right.

Unless you voir dire the witness, the jurors might be misled to believe that the photograph shows something about the positions of the cars at impact and you would have to wait until cross-examination to point out its potentially misleading characteristics. By then, the photograph may have already taken its prejudicial toll. On the other hand, if you bring out the potentially misleading characteristics of the photograph on voir dire, the court may refuse to admit it. If the court admits the photograph, as it probably will (to show the position of the debris and the center line), the jurors will have heard your voir dire questions and will be better able to weigh the photograph's probative value. After voir dire, the court will likely grant your request to admonish the jurors as to the limited purposes for which they may consider the photograph.

11.2.7   Object to the Judge's Questions Only When the Jury Is Out of the Room

The law of evidence generally requires an objection to be made contemporaneously when objectionable evidence is elicited.[8] Federal Evidence Rule 614(c) provides an exception to this rule when the judge questions witnesses. Recognizing that a lawyer risks alienating the jurors by objecting to the judge's questions, the rule allows these objections to be made at the first opportunity when the jurors are not present.

11.3   The Grounds for Objection

When appealing the erroneous admission of evidence, not only must you have stated the specific grounds for your objection, you must also have been correct on at least one ground. Therefore, it is important to know the grounds for objection. It is helpful to divide objections into three broad categories: objections to the form of interrogation, objections to non-responsive testimony, and objections to the admissibility of evidence.[9]

11.3.1   Form of Interrogation

Objections to the form of interrogation are aimed at the language or conduct of opposing counsel and the court's authority to sustain them is found in the general terms of Federal Rule of Evidence 611.[10] These objections rarely raise an issue that will be important in an appeal. They are available to keep the trial running smoothly, efficiently, civilly, and without overreaching by counsel. When an objection to the form of questioning is sustained, skilled counsel can usually rephrase the question. These objections do not prevent evidence from being admitted. Nevertheless, they can be very important tools to protect a witness or to keep opposing counsel from inappropriate argument to the jurors. Here is a list of the most common objections to the form of questioning.

Leading. Leading questions are those that suggest an answer to the witness. Generally, you are not allowed to ask leading questions on direct examination.

---

8. *See* FED. R. EVID. 103(a)(1).
9. Our coverage of evidentiary objections is only an introduction to the subject. For a more complete treatment of the rules of evidence, objections, and responses, we recommend *A Practical Guide to Federal Evidence: Objections, Responses, Rules, and Practice Commentary,* by Anthony J. Bocchino and David A. Sonenshein (NITA 2014).
10. FED. R. EVID. 611(c).

1) **Multiple or compound questions.** The judge should require lawyers to ask simple questions that are not confusing, bringing out one fact at a time.

2) **Argumentative questions.** Argumentative questions either assume or inquire about inferences that should properly be saved for closing argument. They may occur either on direct or cross-examination. Examples: "So, you have a good reason not to tell the truth today, don't you?" "Which story is a lie? The one you told in court today or the one you told the police last March?"

3) **Badgering a witness.** The judge should stop any attempt to bully, mistreat, or abuse a witness.

4) **Interrupting a witness.** Interruption usually occurs during cross-examination. A witness has the right to give complete answers if they are responsive to questions. The opponent may object, "She's not allowing the witness to answer the question," or "She's interrupting the witness."

5) **Assuming facts not in evidence.** The lawyer who assumes facts not in evidence is really attempting to testify and is not competent to do so.[11] The judge should not allow it. You must elicit every fact from a witness.

6) **Misstating or mischaracterizing prior evidence.** This prohibition is similar to the one against assuming facts not in evidence. For example, if the witness has testified that he was driving "about forty miles an hour," the question "As you were speeding down the road, what did you see?" misstates the witness's testimony.

7) **Inquiring beyond the scope of prior testimony.** To promote an orderly trial process, cross-examination in some jurisdictions is limited to matters covered on direct examination plus matters going to the witness's credibility.[12] Redirect examination is limited to matters covered on cross-examination.

8) **Asked and answered.** This objection asks the court to exclude evidence that is cumulative and a waste of time. Use it to prevent your opponent from getting witnesses to repeat their most favorable information over and over. If your opponent asks the witness to repeat, you may raise this objection.

9) **Calls for a narrative.** The trial process is premised on the assumption that lawyers will engage witnesses in an interrogative dialogue, drawing out each fact by asking a specific question. This process affords opposing counsel the opportunity to object before inadmissible testimony is blurted out by witnesses. Therefore, opposing counsel may object to witnesses giving

---

11. *See* FED. R. EVID. 602. *See also* ABA MODEL RULES OF PROFESSIONAL CONDUCT 3.7.
12. FED. R. EVID. 611(b).

their testimony in uninterrupted, narrative style. The narrative style is not objectionable per se, but may be halted in the court's discretion.

11.3.2   Non-Responsive Testimony

Witnesses are allowed to speak only in response to questions. They are not permitted to volunteer information not called for by a question. When a witness gives a non-responsive answer on cross-examination, your first recourse should be to repeat or restate the question. Tight, leading questions are the best tool for witness control.[13] If the witness persists in evading the question, you may object and ask the court to strike the non-responsive answer.

11.3.3   Admissibility of Evidence

Rulings on objections to the admissibility of evidence determine what evidence the jurors will hear. These objections are important at trial and may also be important on appeal. To maximize your chance of a favorable ruling on your objection and to preserve the record for appeal, you must state a specific ground for each objection.[14] The specific grounds for objecting to the admissibility of evidence are found in the Federal Rules of Evidence, the evidence codes of the various states,[15] and the common law.[16] Most of these rules are based on considerations of relevance and reliability, though some dictate exclusion of particular types of relevant, reliable evidence because it is unduly prejudicial or because its admission would be contrary to some public policy.

One way to think about the various exclusionary concepts contained in the rules of evidence is to consider them as a series of hurdles, all of which must be cleared before the evidence will be admitted. Each of these hurdles provides a ground for objection that is sufficiently specific to preserve error. The hurdles and the Federal Rules of Evidence dealing with them are below.

---

13. *See* chapter seven at 7.6, Use Only Leading Questions on Cross-Examination.

14. FED. R. EVID. 103(a)(1).

15. Check your own state rules of evidence. Many states have adopted the rules that follow the Federal Rules of Evidence almost verbatim, but some significant differences exist in the various states. Most, however, follow the section numbers, the basic organization and content of the Federal Rules.

16. For example, FED. R. EVID. 501, which covers privileges, defers to common law privileges, rather than codifying specific privileges. FED. R. EVID. 501 defers to state law as to privileges when the issue is one governed by state law. If federal privilege law applies, you must look to the Constitution, statutes, and common law.

Hurdle	Federal Rule(s) of Evidence
Relevance	401–415
Authentication and identification	901–903
Prejudice and other counterbalancing factors	403–415
Privilege	501
Competence of witnesses	601–606, 701–702
Hearsay	801–807
Originality ("best evidence" rule)	1001–1008

11.3.4 Relevance

Objections based on relevance assert that the evidence in question bears no logical relation to a fact in issue. All evidence must be relevant to be admissible.[17] Evidence is relevant if it tends "to make the existence of any fact that is of consequence to the determination of the action more probable or less probable than it would be without the evidence." You should object on relevance grounds when an item of evidence offered by your opponent has no probative value on any material issue in the case.

Notice that careful honing of the issues in the case may result in you successfully excluding evidence on relevancy grounds. If, for example, the judge has ruled in a pretrial motion that no punitive damages can be awarded in the case, then evidence on punitive damages, the defendant's ability to pay damages, and all related issues would be excluded.

11.3.5 Lack of Authentication or Identification

Authentication and identification rules are specialized applications of the requirement that all evidence be relevant.[18] For example, a tape recording of a confession to a horrible crime would not be relevant to the prosecution's case if the voice on the tape were someone other than the defendant. The tape will only be relevant if it is a recording of the defendant. Rule 901, which governs authentication, simply requires some evidence that an item is what the proponent claims it is.

The trick to raising authentication objections is to think through the question, "What does my opponent claim this is?" The answer is not always obvious. The

---

17. Authentication and identification are particular aspects of relevance. However, because they are typically considered as separate admissibility issues, we include them here as a separate barrier to admissibility.
18. FED. R. EVID. 402.

opponent's claim, which is what makes the exhibit relevant, may have several parts. For example, in a contract case involving offers and counteroffers, when your opponent presents a letter, he may claim that it is not a "letter from the defendant," but rather the specific letter the defendant wrote and mailed on a certain date. Any other letter, draft letter, or unmailed letter would be irrelevant. As you think through your objections on authenticity, ask yourself whether your opponent has presented something in support of each aspect of his claim relating to the exhibit. In the situation involving the letter, it would include some evidence to show who wrote it, when it was written, and whether it was mailed. If your opponent does not bring forth some evidence to show every essential component of what he claims the evidence to be, you may object.

Examples of objections based on improper authentication or identification are, "Objection, that document hasn't been properly authenticated," and "Objection, the witness can't identify the voice as that of the defendant." Some attorneys prefer to say, "Objection, no foundation." This objection covers a number of evidentiary foundation problems, but is generally not considered to be sufficiently specific to preserve an issue for appeal.

11.3.6 *Prejudice or Other Counterbalancing Factors*

Prejudice, as an evidentiary concept, refers to the danger that a relevant item of evidence may cause the jurors to decide the case on an impermissible basis such as sympathy or anger. The trial judge almost always has discretion to exclude otherwise admissible evidence if it is unduly prejudicial.[19] A number of the Federal Evidence Rules direct that specific categories of evidence be excluded on this ground.[20]

Objections Grounded in Rule 403

Rule 403 mentions several considerations, any of which may prevent the admission of evidence. Several of these considerations and the objections that effectively state them are set forth here.

You may object that an item of evidence is unnecessarily cumulative. Courts will often allow repetitive testimony two or even three times, but a time will come when the judge will sustain an objection that testimony is unnecessarily cumulative. Some judges try to limit each witness to testifying once concerning each point. A common objection to cumulative testimony is, "Objection, that's been asked and answered."

---

19. Fed. R. Evid. 403.
20. Fed. R. Evid. 404, 405, 608, and 609 (character traits, subject to several exceptions; note, however, that Rule 406 allows evidence of habit or routine business practice); Fed. R. Evid. 411 (liability insurance); Fed. R. Evid. 610 (witness's religious beliefs).

Even if the specific question or series of questions has not been asked and answered, evidence may be excluded if it is so repetitive of other evidence as to be a waste of time. Evidence may be excluded for the sole reason that its reception will cause undue delay. The objections can be simply stated, "Objection, that will cause undue delay," or "Objection, hearing this evidence will only be a waste of the court's time."

The most common objection grounded in Rule 403 is that evidence, though relevant, is unduly prejudicial. Prejudicial evidence is that which may cause the jurors to decide the case on an improper basis. The objection is often stated thus: "Objection, the prejudicial effect of that evidence will substantially outweigh any probative value it may have."

Evidence may also be excluded if it is misleading or confusing. Say, "Objection, that evidence tends to confuse the issues," or "Objection, that evidence is misleading."

Objections Based on Specific Relevance versus Prejudice/Policy Rules

The Federal Rules of Evidence include several specific rules that prescribe the result of the relevance-versus-negative-effect weighing process with regard to certain kinds of evidence.[21] When one of these rules applies, the judge's normal discretion to weigh the evidence is restricted by the rule. Each of these rules prohibits or severely restricts the admissibility of the kind of evidence it covers. When the evidence your opponent seeks to introduce is covered by one of these rules, you should base your objection on that rule. Categories of evidence excluded by these rules include proof of subsequent remedial measures,[22] settlement negotiations and settlements in civil cases,[23] payment or offers to pay medical expenses,[24] pleas and plea discussions in criminal cases,[25] and liability insurance.[26] Rule 412, the federal version of what are commonly called "rape shield" laws, imposes special restrictions when evidence of the prior sexual conduct of an alleged rape victim is offered.

11.3.7 *Privilege*

Federal Evidence Rule 501 simply recognizes all privileges created by the United States Constitution, statutes, or common law and recognizes state law privileges where state substantive law controls the issue. You must search the entire law of whatever jurisdiction's law governs an issue to determine whether any privilege applies and who is allowed to claim that privilege. Some common privileges are

---

21. FED. R. EVID. 404–412.
22. FED. R. EVID. 407.
23. FED. R. EVID. 408.
24. FED. R. EVID. 409.
25. FED. R. EVID. 410.
26. FED. R. EVID. 411.

those covering attorney-client communications, physician- or psychotherapist-patient communications, spousal testimony or communications, communications to the clergy, trade secrets, and political vote.

11.3.8   *Competence of Witnesses*

The evidentiary concept of competence refers to a witness's eligibility to testify to the things he is about to say. The law is first concerned with whether a witness has a minimal capacity to observe, remember, and relate. The testimony of a witness who does not possess this threshold level of competence would be worthless. Objections to a person's general competence to be a witness, usually based on age or mental capacity, are rarely successful except where children of extremely tender years are involved. Every person is presumed competent to be a witness,[27] and one's mental competence is generally considered to affect only the weight given to his testimony rather than its admissibility.

The law is next concerned with what things a mentally competent witness may relate. The basic guiding principle is that lay witnesses may testify only to matters of which they have personal knowledge.[28] Before a witness may testify on a particular subject, a foundation must be laid to show that the witness observed that which he is about to describe.[29] For example, you must establish that Linda was in a position to see the collision before Linda may tell what she saw.[30] Objections on this ground might be phrased, "Objection, the witness has no personal knowledge of that," or "Objection, that question calls for speculation." The concept of competence is also concerned with the circumstances under which witnesses should be allowed to give their opinions, rather than merely reciting "facts" they observed. Recognizing that all communication includes the expression of opinions and that the question is really whether a witness has a reasonable basis for the opinion expressed, the law allows lay witnesses to express opinions that are "rationally based on the perception of the witness and helpful to a clear understanding of the witness's testimony or the determination of a fact in issue."[31] Therefore, before eliciting a lay opinion, you should establish some foundation that the witness observed enough to form a rational opinion. Subjects upon which lay opinion is commonly allowed include whether a person was drunk or sober, sane or insane, traveling fast or slow, and sick or well. The objection to a lay opinion may be stated, "Objection, the question calls for an improper lay opinion."

---

27. *See* FED. R. EVID. 601.
28. FED. R. EVID. 602.
29. *Id.*
30. Under Rule 602, Linda may herself provide this foundation testimony.
31. FED. R. EVID. 701.

The opinions of witnesses qualified as experts in the field to which the opinion relates may be based upon expertise rather than personal observation of facts.[32] Therefore, once an expert's qualifications have been established, he may usually offer relevant opinions in his field of expertise with no further foundation.[33] Of course, if an expert's qualifications are not adequately established, you may object to his testifying as an expert at all. You should remain alert to object if an expert offers an opinion outside his field of expertise.

11.3.9 Hearsay

Out-of-court statements classified as hearsay are not admissible unless their proponent can show that they fall within one of the exceptions to the hearsay rule.[34] Rule 801 classifies many out-of-court statements as non-hearsay. When your opponent attempts to introduce an out-of-court statement that falls within the definition of hearsay, whether contained in a document or elicited from a witness, the proper objection is, "Objection, hearsay."

11.3.10 Originality

Objections based on originality are founded in what is commonly called the "best evidence rule." Its present-day version is found in Federal Rules of Evidence 1001 through 1008. The rule basically requires the original[35] of documents, photographs, films, and tapes[36] when seeking to prove their contents unless a foundation is laid for admission of a duplicate[37] or other evidence of contents.[38] The objection is usually stated, "Objection, best evidence rule."

11.4   How to Respond to Objections

The way you respond to objections can affect both the judge's rulings and the jury's comprehension of the evidentiary skirmish. We offer here several guidelines for responding when your opponent objects while you are questioning a witness.

---

32. FED. R. EVID. 602 and 703.

33. *See* FED. R. EVID. 705.

34. FED. R. EVID. 802.

35. FED. R. EVID. 1002, the modern version of the "best evidence rule." Rule 1001 defines the types of evidence subject to the rule. Rules 1003 and 1004 state the conditions under which duplicates and other secondary evidence of contents may be admitted. Rule 1006, a handy one, permits introduction of summaries of voluminous documents if the original documents have been made available to the opponent.

36. FED. R. EVID. 1001.

37. FED. R. EVID. 1003.

38. FED. R. EVID. 1004.

When a sustained objection keeps you from introducing important evidence, do not neglect to make an offer of proof.[39]

11.4.1 Anticipate Objections

If you are properly prepared, you will be able to predict many of your opponent's objections and have the correct and most persuasive responses at hand. If you can cite the applicable rule of evidence from memory, so much the better. Nothing is so intimidating to an opponent or so prized by a judge as a lawyer who knows the law. For instance, if you are able to respond to a hearsay objection by saying confidently, "Your Honor, it's the admission of the opposing party, admissible under Rule 801(d)(2)," your opponent will probably lapse into frustrated silence, futilely searching his memory for the long-forgotten knowledge of which you have so adroitly demonstrated your mastery. Not only will your opponent be rendered catatonic by your scholarly response, but the judge will also embrace you as a rare and appreciated gem in the gravel pit of the trial bar: a lawyer who can guide him knowledgeably to a correct ruling. Being able to cite rules inestimably increases the likelihood of obtaining favorable rulings.

No matter how well you know the rules, however, you should *not* rely solely on your memory. Always bring a copy of the applicable rules of evidence with you to court. When your opponent objects and cites a rule, flip to the rule and refresh your memory on its requirements. The exception that allows for the admission of your evidence may be there staring you in the face.

11.4.2 Do Not Withdraw Your Questions

Once you have asked a question, stick with it. Ask what you think are proper questions, seeking admissible information, and once you have asked them do not withdraw them. If the court sustains an objection, so be it. But do not sustain the objection yourself. Stand confidently expectant of the objection's being overruled until it is sustained.

11.4.3 Do Not Assume that Objections Will Be Sustained

Most of us tend to feel inadequate when trying a case. Our subconscious minds tell us that our opponents know more than we do. Therefore, when we hear objections it is as though we say to ourselves, "Oh, my God, she objected. I must have done something wrong." Then, while trying to think of another question, we may not hear the judge's ruling. Not realizing that the judge overruled the objection, we rush to another line of inquiry, leaving the jurors to wonder what the witness would have

---

39. *See* chapter eleven at 11.2.

said if only he had been given the opportunity to answer the question. Listen to the court's ruling. If the objection is overruled, repeat the question.

11.4.4 Carry on When Your Opponent's Objection to "Leading" Is Sustained

Most leading is harmless. Most objections to leading are useless. As we discuss in chapter six on direct examination, you should try to avoid leading your witnesses. Nevertheless, you will inevitably lead witnesses on unimportant matters and your opponent, filled with the lusty vigor that comes with judicial battle, may spring to his feet and make the technically correct objection that you are leading the witness. The judge may sustain the objection. At that point, everyone in the courtroom knows that your last question contained the answer you sought. When this happens, simply ask the witness for the same information, framing the question in unquestionably non-leading terms, and let the witness tell the jury what everyone knew before the objection was made. Consider the following example:

Q: Where did you go next?

A: To the house.

Q: When you got to the house, did you see Joe digging in the garden?

Opposing Counsel: Objection. Leading.

Court: Sustained.

Q: When you got to the house, what did you see?

A: I saw Joe digging in the garden.

[*Everyone in the courtroom chuckles.*]

11.4.5 Be Succinct and Act Confident

State the specific rule or evidentiary principle that justifies admission of the evidence you are attempting to extract and do not launch into a lengthy argument. If you are properly prepared, you will have thought through the question of admissibility with regard to each piece of evidence you offer. Presumably, you would not offer an item of evidence if there were not at least a legitimate argument supporting its admissibility. That being the case, you should feel confident. Even if you do not feel confident, act confident. If the objection is sustained, move on as though nothing had happened. Do not act like a whipped puppy.

11.4.6 Respond If You Have a Response

When your opponent objects, the judge will usually look at you and wait for your response. However, if the objection sounds clearly meritorious, the court will sometimes sustain it without giving you an opportunity to respond. When this happens and you have a legitimate response, ask the judge to allow you to respond. Simply say, "Your Honor, may I be heard on that point?" Most judges, hearing your request, will realize that there is more to the issue than met the ear when the objection was made and will grant your request. At any rate, that is what the judge *should* do. If the judge refuses to hear you, you must accept the ruling and move on. *Do not argue with the judge* after a ruling, *but do* make your offer of proof.

11.4.7   *Respond on the Same Basis as the Objection*

Judges roll their eyes in disbelief and frustration when lawyers display ignorance of the law of evidence by responding to objections on grounds other than those stated by the objector. The best way to assure that an objection will be sustained is to respond on a different basis than the one stated by your opponent. Always respond to the specific ground stated by your opponent. For example, if he says, "Objection, hearsay," respond either by explaining why the matter is not hearsay or by stating an exclusion from or exception to the hearsay rule. Do not, under any circumstances, respond to the hearsay objection by saying, "Your Honor, we think this testimony is clearly relevant to show . . . ."

11.4.8   *Responding to Hearsay Objections*

When a hearsay objection is made, the proponent of the evidence must state a reason why the hearsay rule should not exclude the evidence. These responses may be divided into two broad classes: that the evidence is not hearsay or that the evidence, though hearsay, is allowed by one of the exceptions to the hearsay rule.

Many kinds of out-of-court statements are not hearsay. One of the largest categories is statements not offered for the truth of the matter asserted.[40] When you offer such a statement, we suggest that you respond to a hearsay objection saying, "Your Honor, the statement is offered for a non-hearsay purpose." You can then go on and state the non-hearsay purpose, e.g., notice. This is preferable to saying that the statement is "not offered for the truth of the matter asserted." If you say that you are not offering the statement for its truth, the jurors will wonder why in the world you would offer something that is not true.

Other responses to hearsay objections are more straightforward. These include the out-of-court statement is not an assertion;[41] the evidence is a prior inconsistent

---

40. FED. R. EVID. 801(c). Out-of-court statements that are not offered for the "truth of the matter asserted" are not hearsay.
41. FED. R. EVID. 801(a).

statement given under oath;[42] the evidence is a prior consistent statement offered to rebut a charge of recent fabrication, or improper influence or motive;[43] the statement is one identifying a person;[44]or the statement is the admission of a party opponent.[45]

If the evidence is hearsay, the response must state an exception to the hearsay rule. These exceptions are enumerated in Federal Evidence Rules 803 and 804.[46] The exceptions listed in Rule 804 are applicable only if the person who made the out-of-court statement is unavailable to testify. Those exceptions listed in Rule 803 apply regardless of whether the person who made the statement is available to be witness.

Remember that every document you introduce at trial is an out-of-court statement and has the potential to raise a hearsay objection. Documents often contain statements from persons other than the author of the document that create a second level of hearsay.[47] Before trial, make sure that you know how to respond to a hearsay objection, including hearsay within hearsay, to every document on your exhibit list. Keep in mind that many of the documents are likely to be admissions—that is, statements of opposing parties—that are non-hearsay.

11.4.9   Make an Offer of Proof

When the judge sustains your opponent's objection, the evidence you sought to introduce is excluded. The jurors will not hear it. Nevertheless, you want the evidence to appear in the appellate record. Evidence that is excluded from the trial will be included in the appellate record if you make an "offer of proof." The Federal Rules of Evidence require only that the "substance of the evidence [be] made known to the court . . . ."[48] If the excluded evidence is an exhibit, you should make the offer by proffering the excluded exhibit into the record. Though the jurors will not see the exhibit, the appellate court will have it when deciding whether the exclusion constituted error. If the excluded evidence is testimony, it is usually sufficient for you to dictate the substance of the anticipated testimony into the record. To do

---

42. FED. R. EVID. 801(d)(1)(A).

43. FED. R. EVID. 801(d)(1)(B).

44. FED. R. EVID. 801(d)(1)(C).

45. FED. R. EVID. 801(d)(1)(2).

46. In addition, Rule 807 authorizes the court to admit hearsay to which no enumerated exception applies if it has "equivalent circumstantial grantees of trustworthiness" and you establish three things: (1) that it is evidence of a material fact; (2) that is more probative on that point than any other evidence you can reasonably acquire; and "(3) admitting it will best serve the purposes of these rules and the interests of justice." Rule 807 also requires notice to the adverse party of intention to offer such a statement and the particulars of the statement. State evidentiary rules, though often numbered differently, provide the same as Rule 807.

47. FED. R. EVID. 805.

48. FED. R. EVID. 103(a)(2).

this, you will speak directly to the court reporter out of the hearing of the jurors, summarizing what the witness would have said, if allowed. The rule gives the court authority to direct that the offer be made in question-and-answer form.[49] Although you have no absolute right to make an offer in question-and-answer form, you should not hesitate to request permission to provide the testimony in that form if that course of action will preserve a record more advantageous to your client.

---

49. FED. R. EVID. 103(b).

National Institute for Trial Advocacy

CHAPTER TWELVE

CLOSING ARGUMENT

"Oh, Professor, I'm a mess. I have to deliver my closing argument tomorrow morning, but I've been listening to the other side's evidence and, right now, I feel like I have a dog of a case."

"Well, can you remember what made you get involved in this case in the first place?" the Professor asked.

"I believed in my client. I think I still do. I just don't see how the jurors will."

The Professor smiled. "Sit down by yourself and—for a while—don't think about anything your opponent has been saying. Try to remember what made you believe in this client and in this case. Remember how you felt when you first heard your client's story. Find the thing that connected you to this case. Focus on the best aspects of your client and your case and let yourself be convinced of your client's cause all over again. Then you'll be ready to get up there and speak from your heart."

12.1 The Purpose of Closing Argument

Closing arguments are the lawyer's opportunity to tie all of the evidence together—to take all of the dangling, loose threads of evidence and weave them together into a coherent tapestry. Now is your chance to tell the jurors what it all means—to explain the facts in evidence and the law governing the case, reveal the path of justice, and demand a verdict in your client's favor. If you were a mystery writer, this would be your opportunity to write the conclusion and solve the mystery.

The closing argument is your moment to suggest to the jurors how to do the two jobs it is about to perform. First, the jurors must decide which version of the disputed facts is true (under the applicable burden of proof). Second, the jurors must apply the law to the facts, using the judge's instructions and ultimately filling out the verdict form. Your closing, then, must show the jurors why your factual story of the case is true. You separately must explain to the jurors how, in light of your story, the judge's instructions dictate that they fill out the verdict form in a manner that results in a verdict in favor of your client.

Lawyers' opinions about the importance of closing argument vary. Some argue that most cases are already effectively decided before closing arguments are given. Others feel that the closing argument often has a profound impact on the jurors. It is undoubtedly true that the facts are of paramount importance and that without sufficient evidentiary support the most magnificent closing argument will not prevail. However, closing argument does play an important role. No lawyer should fail to take full advantage of this final opportunity to persuade the jurors of the merits of her case.

I am confident that our clients have stories they want to tell
— and we are their story tellers.

— John Mauldin

First of all, although many jurors have made at least a tentative decision on most issues, many will still be subject to persuasion during closing arguments and after they retire to the jury room. Different jurors may have reached different tentative conclusions about the facts. They will argue the issues in the jury room. Your closing argument can give jurors who are persuaded to find in favor of your client the rationale to effectively argue your client's position. It can also give them the inspiration and conviction to take the trouble to convince their fellow jurors.

Secondly, because we human beings tend to remember most readily those things we have heard most recently, the first issues remembered and discussed during deliberations are likely to be those emphasized on closing argument. If you do not identify the strengths of your case and weaknesses in your opponent's during closing argument, the jurors may have forgotten them by the time they retire to deliberate.

Third, in a civil case, even if the jurors have reached a tentative decision on liability in favor of the plaintiff, they will not have considered how to calculate damages to be awarded. As the lawyer for the plaintiff, your closing argument must walk the jurors through each element of damages and suggest, in light of the evidence offered at trial, how the jurors should compensate plaintiff for that element.[1]

---

1. Assuming the defendant is contesting both liability and damages, defense counsel has three options for addressing damages in closing. First, you can ignore damages, exhibiting confidence that the jurors will find defendant is not liable. Of course, if you are wrong, the jurors will not have the benefit of your guidance on calculating damages. Second, you can argue liability and then address why the damages are not as significant as claimed by the plaintiff. However, this may send the message that you are equivocating in your argument that the defendant is not liable. Third, you can address damages first and segue to your argument on liability by stating that the jurors will not need to consider the issue of damages in light of your factual story of the case.

The primary difference between opening statement and closing argument is embodied in their titles. The opening "statement" must be confined to the facts that you expect will be presented; you may not suggest to the jurors what they should infer from those facts. The closing "argument," on the other hand, is not so limited. It is your opportunity to draw conclusions, including discussion of the flaws in your adversary's factual theory of the case, make inferences, explain the relevance of details or circumstantial evidence, make analogies or tell illustrative stories, comment on credibility and motives of various witnesses, refer to witnesses' demeanor, discuss the weight of the evidence, explain how to apply the law to the facts, and make a moral appeal. In closing argument, tell the jurors why the verdict must be in your favor and make them feel powerfully that they will be doing the right thing when they return the verdict you request.

12.2   How and When to Prepare Your Closing Argument

If you are not prepared to give your closing argument before the trial begins, you are not ready for trial. Early in your preparation of the case, you should outline the closing argument. By outlining the closing argument, you force yourself to analyze every aspect of the case: the evidence that will support each element you must prove, the shortcomings of your opponent's evidence, and the reasons your client should win. You will then have a game plan for conducting discovery and fact investigation, presenting your evidence, planning the cross-examination of opposing witnesses, preparing your opening statement, and conducting voir dire. You will revise this early version of your closing argument time and time again. You will refine it, add to it, delete some things, and finally modify it one last time after the evidence has all been presented. However, its essential content will normally be quite similar to your early draft.

Unlike the opening statement, the closing argument cannot be completely prepared and rehearsed before trial because you never know exactly what will happen in the evidentiary stage of the trial. No matter how well prepared the lawyers are, witnesses will say unexpected things, the evidence will take unexpected turns, and things will be revealed during the unfolding drama of the trial that no one could have predicted. You must remain alert and open-minded so that you can incorporate these matters into your argument.

Your trial notebook should have a separate section dedicated to closing argument. Before the trial begins, that section should contain an outline of your closing argument. Whenever anything happens during trial that you should consider adding to the prepared closing, make a note of that fact on a separate sheet of paper and put that sheet in the closing argument section of your trial notebook. You then will be positioned to use your notes in whatever time the judge grants you to make final revisions in your closing argument outline after all the evidence is in and the judge has informed you what jury instructions will be given.

12.3   The Contents of an Effective Closing Argument

In making a closing argument, you may be tempted to wander through all of the details and inconsistencies of the evidence that has been presented. It is nevertheless important to leave the jurors with a strong impression that the only appropriate outcome is the one you seek. While you must go into some detail and answer the questions they have, you must make the jurors want to act as you hope they will.

12.3.1   *Discuss Why Jurors Should Accept Your Version of the Disputed Facts*

This is your opportunity to explain inconsistencies and persuade the jurors to act in favor of the outcome you seek. Tell a story. Make the outcome imperative.

Appeal to Both Heart and Mind

Closing argument is not closing statement of facts. Closing argument is not closing restatement of the law. Closing argument is the time to argue, to lay it on the line, to pull out all the stops, to go to the mat for your client. It is the time to bring your passion into the courtroom and make the jurors feel. People are motivated by what they feel. Humans are not rational actors. We may try to find reasons for what we do, but we are usually finding reasons to support what we feel, what we believe, and what we want to do. That is why a recitation of the facts and the law are not going to cut it in a closing argument. To get jurors to do what you want them to do, make them feel something. If they feel something, they might believe something, and if they believe, they will act.

On the other hand, a purely emotional argument may come across as a cheesy ploy. An obvious appeal to sentiment may make the jurors suspicious. Jurors take seriously their duty to apply the rules of law diligently to the evidence. If your argument has provided them only with passion, its power may evaporate in the cold light of the deliberation room. You need an argument that will appeal to both heart and mind. You need to invoke the jurors' moral values and give them strong, logical reasons to do what they feel is right. So, how do you do that?

In closing argument, the story is your best asset. From the beginning of your involvement in the case, you have worked to develop and communicate a simple, understandable, logical story—the character, motive, and plot that caused each juror's System 1 brain to instinctively find your version of the disputed facts to be predicable, if not inevitable. You have put together a theory that makes sense, that is supported by evidence, and that conforms to the court's instructions on the law. Most importantly, you have put together a story with stakes that show how your cause is right and just. Now retell that story in an interesting and compelling way. You must bring the pieces of your story together powerfully and memorably.

You must resist the temptation to allow your System 2 lawyer brain to take charge of the closing. In preparation for and throughout the trial, you have made numerous individual tactical decisions designed to support your case and attack your adversary's positions. You have the mental capacity and physical stamina to review each one of these decisions. The law gives you leeway to do so by permitting argument in closing that was forbidden during the opening. But you must be vigilant not to abandon the factual story of the case as the driver of your closing argument.

Journalists and public speakers commonly adhere to a presentation formula: "Tell 'em what you're gonna tell 'em. Tell 'em. Then tell 'em what you told 'em." A jury trial roughly follows the same presentation structure. During your opening statement you "told 'em what you were gonna tell 'em." Then your witnesses "told 'em" during the evidentiary stage of the trial. (Hopefully, they "told 'em" what you predicted during opening.) In closing argument, you should "Tell 'em what you told 'em" and return to the story you began with in the opening statement. Do not be boring and stand up there and say, "Now you are going to hear a summary of everything you have already heard." Instead, tell the story in a way that sounds fresh.

Although you may discuss only the admitted evidence and the inferences that may legitimately be drawn from it, you should use analogies, stories, visual aids, appeals to common sense, and other rhetorical devices to persuade the jurors that justice demands a verdict in your client's favor. Draw from your own experience. Does the decision the jurors have to make remind you of any difficult choices you had to make in your life? Can you think of anything that happened to you that made you empathize with the client's situation? Take ideas or characters from fairy tales, parables, or popular culture. Is there a "prodigal son" in your case? A Homer Simpson? Help the jurors characterize and remember the evidence by connecting it to familiar characters, stories, or common experiences. You can even use ideas you have heard from other lawyers.

Let your personality and creativity come through. Be a preacher, a teacher, a shaman, a medicine man, a poet, a storyteller, or a troubadour for justice. Most of all, be a person—a real person, not just a "lawyer." Before you deliver your closing argument, revisit the evidence that makes you believe in the justice of your cause. Then speak directly to the jurors from your heart.

This means you have to believe what you say. Closing argument is no time for bullshit. If jurors perceive that you are shoveling them crap, they will run the other way. Nor should you overstate your case. Be absolutely certain that everything you say—every reference to evidence or law you make—is absolutely accurate. As we have emphasized throughout this book, your credibility, as well as that of your client and witnesses, is on trial. The jurors are looking for guidance and they will only follow the lead of a lawyer they can trust. For the jurors to trust you, make every one of your statements fair, honest, and accurate.

You must also deal with the weak points in your case. This is one of the most difficult, but most essential, tasks you take on in a trial. Do not emphasize the case's weak points during closing or make your closing argument defensive. Always emphasize the positive and discuss your strong points first. But you must also tell the jurors why the stumbling blocks in your case should not keep you from winning. You must give the jurors a rationale—a route—to get past those stumbling blocks if they are to reach the destination of a verdict in your client's favor.

Use the Facts in Evidence to Support Your Theory of the Case

Evidentiary details are essential to your argument. Details are persuasive. Your characterizations and conclusions are not. If, for example, an important issue in the case turns on the credibility of Mr. Jones's testimony, it is not very effective for you to get up and say, "Mr. Jones is a liar. You can't believe anything he says." A more persuasive tactic is to remind the jury of the specific information available to them from which they should conclude that Mr. Jones is lying about your client, Smith Construction:

> You saw what happened when I asked Mr. Jones about his own involvement in the Spondlewheel deal. He flushed red and didn't answer my question. Why did he blush? He blushed because he had bid on the same contract. Look. Here is a copy of his failed bid. Mr. Jones lost to Smith Construction. His business is in competition with Smith Construction. He doesn't want Smith to succeed. His testimony about what he calls the "low quality" of Smith's work is motivated by his own self-interest. Don't buy it. It is self-serving and not supported by the photographs or the logbooks of the subcontractors. Mr. Jones's opinion is also contradicted by the testimony of the CEO of Blakey Construction, whose firm does not compete in this area. Ms. Blakey testified that Smith's work on this project was high quality in every respect. . . .

Notice that the details to support the proposition that Mr. Jones should not be believed could be taken from many sources: an answer by one witness on direct examination, an admission on cross-examination by another witness, a sentence in a letter, an object that appears in a photograph, the contrast in credibility between two witnesses, a jury instruction. In closing argument, you must pull together the important details from all sources to show why the important factual disputes in the case should be resolved in your client's favor. Using details does not require you to recite all of the testimony of all of the witnesses. Focus on the essential fact or facts upon which the case will turn and explain why each should be decided in your client's favor. Stick with your strongest points and present them first. Most lawyers agree that the first few minutes of your closing argument are the most crucial. You should encapsulate during those first few minutes the essential points upon which the verdict will turn.

12.3.2 *Explain How Jurors Should Apply the Law to the Facts*

Except in rare instances where the jurors simply answer special interrogatories regarding disputed facts, the jury's job does not end with fact-finding. Instead, the jurors also will apply the law as given in the judge's final instructions to the facts as the jurors found them, filling out a verdict form that embodies both the facts and the law. Even the most carefully crafted jury instructions are difficult to understand. You must guard against the risk that the jurors will accept your factual story of the case but, by misunderstanding the governing law, enter a verdict in favor of your opponent. Without impinging on the province of the court, your closing must explain to the jurors how the judge's instructions, when applied to the facts of your story, dictate how they must answer the questions on the verdict form.

As far as the jurors are concerned, the law is what the judge tells them it is. There simply is no law other than what is contained in the court's instructions to the jury. Therefore, it is absolutely essential that your legal theory and closing argument dovetail precisely with the judge's jury instructions.

Some of the court's instructions will be favorable to your theory of the case and you should incorporate some of those key instructions into your closing argument. For example, in a criminal prosecution based upon circumstantial evidence, the prosecutor should incorporate the court's instruction that circumstantial evidence may be sufficient to convict into her closing argument. By doing so, the lawyer is emphasizing and underscoring that particular instruction. When the jurors later hear the judge saying the very same things you have said, their estimation of your credibility will rise. When you utilize jury instructions in your argument, you are placing your client's position in the case in the camp of justice.

Before you address the jury instructions, you must genuflect to the judge, acknowledging her role as the oracle of the law.

> Ladies and gentlemen of the jury, when we have completed our closing arguments, Judge Collier will give you instructions on the law. Of course, you will and should take your guidance on the law from Judge Collier. But she was kind enough to share with us the instructions on the law she intends to give you.

> Judge Collier will tell you that the first element we must prove is that Charles Shrackle was negligent. While Judge Collier will fully explain the definition of negligence to you, let me point out that negligence does not mean that Charles Shrackle intended to harm Katherine Potter—he most certainly did not. Negligence does not mean that Charles Shrackle is generally an unsafe driver—he is not. But as he made the left-hand turn on to Mattis Avenue, Mr. Shrackle's mind was on his business, not on his driving, a mistake that took the life of Katherine Potter, and in that moment, his actions were negligent.

A word of warning: Be absolutely accurate when you use jury instructions. Do not paraphrase. When you use the law as your ally, you must use it fairly and accurately. To misquote a jury instruction is devastating both to your personal credibility and to your client's case. When you know that a particular instruction will be given that favors your theory, it is quite effective to have that instruction blown up and to show the blow-up to the jurors as you mention it in your argument. Remember, however, that jury instructions are the responsibility of the judge. Always check with the judge before using a blow-up of an instruction in your closing argument.

12.4 A General Outline for Closing Argument

Every closing argument, no matter what kind of case you are trying, must cover the essential matters of liability and remedy.[2] In addition, you must reiterate your factual theory of the case, weave your theme in wherever it fits, identify the stakes, and tell the jurors what you want them to do. Here is a general organizational outline that can serve as a broad guideline for preparing every closing argument.

12.4.1 *Reconnect with Jurors*

Many trial lawyers will tell you to start your closing argument with a "grabber," an attention-getter, a catchy phrase or surprising demonstration. Certainly, you want to get the jurors' attention. But a catchy phrase is not always the best way to do that. The important thing is to connect with the jurors to make them want to listen to you.

You have listened to the evidence throughout the trial and watched the jurors' reactions to it. What are the jurors thinking and feeling as you get up to argue? Empathize with them and begin your argument where they are. If they seem weary and bored, pull out the surprising demonstration, the sentimental anecdote, or the catchy phrase. On the other hand, if the jurors still have tears in their eyes after listening to your opponent speak, they may not want to listen to you if you get up and start brightly. Take their mood into account. For example, the defense counsel in a particularly brutal rape and murder case knew that the jurors had been deeply disturbed by the evidence in the case. He began his closing by saying:

> It has been hard to listen to the evidence in this case. Some of it made me feel absolutely sick inside. The things we have heard about in this case are things that nobody should ever have to listen to, much less experience. A brutal crime has been committed and the person who did it should be punished. The person who did it should be punished. That's right. The person who did it. We need to remember that—because John Martin (the defendant) is not the person who did it.

---

2. In bifurcated trials, you will argue only the issue—liability or remedy—that is being considered in that stage of the trial. In a criminal case, you will discuss only guilt or innocence in the guilt phase of the trial.

12.4.2 Return to Your Theme and Factual Theory of the Case

In the first few minutes of your closing, remind the jurors of your factual theory of the case, echoing what you told them during your opening statement. Imagine that your favorite Aunt Betty has called you on the phone and asked you, "Oh, tell me about the case you are trying." You have only three minutes to tell Aunt Betty everything she needs to know to reach a verdict in your client's favor. This brief outline (which you will tell to the jurors, not to Aunt Betty) will provide a roadmap as you argue the various issues so that jurors will understand where every fact fits.

If it doesn't fit, you must acquit.

—*Johnny Cochran*

Early in your closing, you should also return to your theme. As you will recall from the chapter on case analysis for trial, your theme encapsulates the essence of your case in a few words. Johnny Cochran's theme in the O. J. Simpson trial, "If it doesn't fit, you must acquit," is a perfect example of how to make the most of a few words. In that trial, a key piece of prosecution evidence was a bloody glove found in the defendant's driveway. The defense contended that it had been planted by the police. The evidence presented during the trial included a dramatic moment when the defendant attempted to put on the glove and could not. That evidentiary point was so devastating that the defense lawyer was able to make it the theme of his closing argument. He stated it early and repeated it often as he reviewed every inconsistency and loose end in the prosecution's case. This catchy phrase is so memorable that it has become part of the lore of advocacy. It is also a sterling example of a lawyer's remaining flexible in order to adapt his closing argument to the evidence that developed during trial.

12.4.3 Argue Liability or Guilt

The body of your closing should separately address the two jobs the jurors must perform. As was true of the opening statement, in advocating your version of the disputed facts in closing, you should not engage in a witness-by-witness review of the evidence. Likewise, you should not use the legal elements as the organizing principle. Instead, you should continue to forward the story of the case, reviewing the evidence under the same template of chronology or common sense elements that you used in the opening statement.[3]

Once you have finished your advice on how the jurors should resolve the factual disputes, you should turn your attention to how they should apply the law. Use a written outline, poster, checklist, or computer-generated image to illus-

---

3. *See* chapter five at 5.2.2.

trate each legal step required for the jurors to reach a verdict. Go through every element you were required to prove to support a verdict for your client and review the evidence that supports each. If your opponent had the burden of proof on an issue, review your opponent's evidence and point out how it comes up short. If a point was conceded, state that fact. Where a fact is disputed, tell jurors why the inference you want them to accept is the most reasonable one. If the credibility of witnesses is crucial to a point of evidence, tell them why they should believe your witnesses and discount your opponent's witnesses.

12.4.4   In a Civil Case, Argue Remedy[4]

Do not be afraid to talk about the money. If you represent the plaintiff in a civil case, you must outline the specific elements of damage to which your client is entitled. You must review the evidence supporting each element and suggest an appropriate amount of money for each. If you represent a defendant, you must explain why the plaintiff's evidence on damages is deficient.

Jurors want to do what is fair, so appeal to their innate sense of fairness. When representing a plaintiff, except where prohibited by the governing law, use specific numbers and justify each one. Be sure you believe in the fairness of your position and convince the jurors to agree with you.

12.4.5   Tell Jurors Exactly What You Want Them to Do

Imagine trying to assemble a children's swing set without directions. To accomplish that feat by hit-or-miss or trial and error would be nearly impossible. However, with a clear set of instructions even a person who is technologically challenged can usually fit the parts together correctly and erect a workable piece of playground equipment.

Most people like to get clear directions. It gives us a great sense of security and confidence to follow a reliable path rather than wandering around lost, blindly seeking the correct destination. Like all people, jurors appreciate guidance when they are forced to make difficult decisions. They want someone to tell them the right thing to do.

The consequences of neglecting to tell jurors exactly what you want them to do can be devastating. If you do not share your expectations with them, they may do your client great harm while thinking they are doing her a favor. This point is illustrated by an anecdote told by an internationally acclaimed insurance defense lawyer,

---

4. If there is a conviction in a criminal case, the "remedy" (the sentence) will be dealt with in a separate stage of the trial. Generally, juries do not participate in the sentencing stage of a trial unless the prosecutor is asking for the death penalty.

Alston Jennings,[5] from the early years of his practice. The case involved clear liability, but few damages. The settlement offer was $10,000 and the case may not have been worth that. However, the plaintiff's lawyer had stars in his eyes and refused to accept anything less than $100,000. The case went to trial. The plaintiff's lawyer asked for $100,000. Jennings conceded liability and argued the minimal damages supported by the evidence, but neglected to suggest a figure. The jurors returned a verdict for $50,000—far more than the case should have been worth. Dejected, Jennings boarded an elevator filled with jurors as he left the courthouse. They began congratulating him on how well he tried the case and how persuasive his case had been. One said, "Yep, Mr. Jennings. We agreed with everything you said. We were convinced that the plaintiff was trying to blow this case way out of proportion. That's why we only gave him half of what he wanted."

You absolutely must end your closing argument by telling the jurors exactly what you want them to do, including actual dollar amounts, if appropriate. Make their job easier by suggesting a solution that will assuage their natural hunger to do justice. If you have established yourself as a person who can be trusted, the jurors will reward you for offering the guidance they seek.

If you will be using a verdict form with several questions for the jury to answer, with the permission of the court create a blowup or handout version of the verdict form. Use your visual aid to explain the form and demonstrate for the jury how you want them to fill in the answers.

12.5   Delivering Your Closing Argument

12.5.1   Do Not Read

No preacher ever saved a lost soul by reading the altar call. Even if what you say is important, the substance of your closing argument is solid, and your argument is simple, logical, and fair, the most well-prepared closing argument will likely be for naught if you do not communicate your sincerity and belief in your case to the jurors. Therefore, *do not read*. Throw away your legal pad. If you need notes, write a few key words on a single sheet of paper. Arranging your visual aids before you begin and referring to them as you make your argument serves as a wonderful substitute for written notes. You can use your exhibits to keep you on track and to avoid forgetting to mention a crucial point.

Look the jurors in the eye and talk to them from your heart. Even if you stumble, your sincerity will do more to sell your case than the most eloquent words you could read. Let your humanity shine through. Be yourself. Not all of us can be great, spellbinding orators. Every one of us, however, can be conversational and sincere.

---

5. Former president of the International Academy of Defense Counsel and of the American College of Trial Lawyers.

12.5.2   Use Visual Aids

Seeing is believing. Therefore, you should use exhibits and other visual aids during your closing argument. Because the jury will take the exhibits—the things actually admitted into evidence—into the jury room when they deliberate, you should remind them to examine any important documents, photographs, or diagrams that are in evidence. If a document contains crucial language, read that portion aloud and request that the jurors examine it for themselves rather than take your word for it. Blowups of important questions and answers from courtroom testimony or depositions may be used effectively. Use your closing argument to show the jurors real evidence—guns, knives, and other instrumentalities—one more time.

If the case involved many documentary exhibits, make an exhibit notebook for each juror, with a photocopy of each documentary exhibit that was admitted into evidence. This allows each juror to have equal access to all of the exhibits throughout the deliberations. Individual evidence notebooks have proven to be so helpful to jurors that some courts have recently adopted the practice of giving each juror one as a matter of course in every civil trial.

Do not limit your visual aids to the items in evidence. You may use charts, graphs, computer slides, timelines, and other summaries of evidence that you prepare specifically to be used as visual aids during closing argument.[6] And do not forget the jury instructions. As mentioned previously, use blowups or computerized presentation of key language that may provide a stepping stone to help the jurors find their way to a verdict in your favor. If you represent a plaintiff, do not fail to write the elements of damage and the amount you suggest for each on a chalkboard, PowerPoint slide, or previously prepared chart.

12.5.3   Do Not Be Too Long-Winded

By the end of a trial, the jurors are exhausted. They have been under constant strain, usually in uncomfortable circumstances, and have often been subjected to hours of boring testimony. Every juror is anxious to get on with it and get to the business of deciding the case. If you give a long closing argument, you will probably bore them and may even offend them. If you reiterate too much of the evidence, you will insult their intelligence. If you bore, offend, or insult the jurors, you cannot persuade them. Worse, they may unconsciously punish your client for your failure to consider their feelings. So say what you need to say succinctly and sit down.

Plaintiff's counsel/prosecutor must be particularly mindful of the jurors' patience when presenting a rebuttal argument. Your competitive instincts and fear of leaving any stone unturned will make you want to share all available refutations of points

---

6. You should always obtain the court's permission to refer to these before you give your closing argument. To draw an objection and be instructed by the court not to use the illustrative aid is devastating.

raised in the defense closing. Rather than help your case, a jot-by-jot rebuttal will simply overwhelm already super-saturated jurors, risking that they will forget the guidance offered by your initial closing. Therefore, limit rebuttal to, at most, your three strongest points. To reduce the pressure of having to construct a rebuttal on the spot, you can prepare in advance the final point of your rebuttal, reminding the jurors of a significant fact that defendant cannot, and did not, dispute.

12.5.4   *Choose Your Words Carefully*

Pay attention to your choice of words. Different words to describe the same thing create different images. To say that a defendant "crashed" or "smashed" into the rear of the plaintiff's car raises a more violent mental picture than saying, "The plaintiff's car was struck in the rear by the defendant's." Note also that the words "crashed" and "smashed" are focused on the defendant and are cast in the active voice. When you are emphasizing what a person did or did not do, speak in the active voice. Make that person the actor with your words. Always accentuate the positive. Stay on the offensive. Do not spend all of your limited time defending your client's actions. Avoid qualifying words. Phrases such as, "It is our position that . . . ," "We feel that. . . ," and "We would argue that . . . ," only weaken your argument. When you have a position to argue, just state it as a fact.

12.5.5   *Vary Your Dynamics and Rhythm*

Dynamics refers to volume. Rhythm refers to timing. Variations in volume and timing are essential to maintaining the attention of any listener because too much of the same bores or irritates us.

The necessity of variations in dynamics and rhythm is most apparent in music, where differences in volume and timing are used to make songs pleasing to our ears. A song that never changed in loudness or speed would be insufferably monotonous. It is the same with speech. A closing argument delivered in a sing-song or mono-tone will drive jurors up the wall. On the other hand, if you incorporate changes in volume and timing into your argument, you will keep their attention and maybe even enthrall them.

"Dynamics"—the varying of volume—captures attention. Like good music, good speech gets louder and softer in different places to convey different emotions and feelings. Like music, the loudness or softness with which you speak will affect the impact of your closing argument dramatically.

First of all, if you speak too softly the jurors will not hear you and your argument may as well have been made in an empty pasture. On the other hand, too much sustained high volume is annoying. Speak in a comfortable, conversational voice, loud enough to be easily heard, but not so loud that the jurors feel they are being shouted at.

Having found your comfortable level, vary that volume, because if you speak at the same level all the time, you will bore the jurors. Raise your voice to convey passion. Lower your voice to draw their attention to your next statement.

Start low. Go slow. Strike fire. Climb higher.

—*Martin Luther King, Sr.*

"Rhythm" refers to the speed with which you speak. If you speak too rapidly, the jurors will have difficulty understanding you. If you speak too slowly, you may lull them to sleep. The key here, as with volume, is to vary your tempo. Use slower delivery to emphasize points.

Silence is golden. It is a valuable tool you should employ to emphasize crucial points. Use it to create contrast and drama in your argument. After a crescendo, just stop. Stand there silently. When you do, everyone's attention will be focused on your next sentence. Wandering minds will return. Then, after a pregnant pause, you can whisper the words that drive your point home.

For example:

> The defendant knew his patient, Flora Jones, was in critical condition after the surgery. He knew Flora Jones's life hung in the balance. Yet he left the hospital while Flora Jones was struggling for her life in the recovery room.
>
> [*Begin slowly building volume here.*] Did he go to attend another patient?
>
> Did he have another emergency surgery to perform? Why, ladies and gentlemen, did he leave her?
>
> [*Climax.*]
>
> [*Pause.*]
>
> [*Whispered.*] Because he had a date for a golf game at the country club.

12.5.6 *Some Rhetorical Devices*

Many standard techniques are routinely employed by master orators, trial lawyers, preachers, and writers to increase the effectiveness of their messages. Many of these have been used since ancient times. Here are a just a few of the many rhetorical techniques most widely used by trial lawyers.

Rhetorical Question

A rhetorical question is one asked for rhetorical effect or emphasis and not intended to be answered. It is a question whose context provides its own answer by suggestion. A few examples of rhetorical questions are:

> Can we give little Johnny his leg back?

> Was it mere coincidence that the man seen running from the scene fit the defendant's description? That he wore a shirt the same color as the shirt the defendant had on that night? That the defendant was seen only fifteen minutes earlier in a bar only a half-block from where the robbery occurred? That the defendant was carrying a switchblade just like the one used in the robbery?

> Why would the defendant have been speeding? Was it because he was late for work and had been told he would be fired the next time he was late?

Using a rhetorical question can be a marvelous technique when there is a key question to which you know your opponent has no effective answer.

The "Rule of Three"

The "rule of three" is a venerable rhetorical tool, employed by speakers and writers since ancient times. The "rule" states simply that you should organize words and ideas into groups of three because we humans tend to remember things in threes. Whether or not the validity of the "rule of three" can be proven empirically, it has been used by most of the greatest writers and orators in history, and if it has worked for so many others, it will probably work for you.

We hold these truths to be self-evident, that all men are created equal, that they are endowed by their creator with certain unalienable rights, that among these are life, liberty, and the pursuit of happiness.

—Thomas Jefferson, Declaration of Independence

Listen to the words of Abraham Lincoln, a great trial lawyer before he was a great statesman, in his Gettysburg Address:

> But, in a larger sense, we cannot dedicate—we cannot consecrate—we cannot hallow—this ground. . . .

> . . . and that government of the people, by the people, for the people, shall not perish from the earth.

Repetition

To repeat a key word or idea emphasizes its importance. The more we are exposed to an idea, the more likely it is that we will recall the message contained in that idea. Those in the advertising industry and those who run political campaigns understand and use this tool effectively. As a trial lawyer, so should you.

We shall go on to the end, we shall fight in France, we shall fight on the seas and oceans, we shall fight with growing confidence and growing strength in the air, we shall defend our Island, whatever the cost might be, we shall fight on the beaches, we shall fight on the landing grounds, we shall fight in the fields and in the streets, we shall fight in the hills; we shall never surrender.

— Winston Churchill

Comparison and Contrast

The arrangement of contrasting idea in pairs, thesis and antithesis, can be an extremely effective way of bringing a point home. This technique is particularly useful in a personal injury case when you can contrast the plaintiff's life before and after the injury:

> Two years ago, Mary Jacobs was a healthy, athletic, young woman. Today, she must spend every day in a wheelchair.

> Two years ago, Mary won the local tennis tournament. Last week she could only watch from her wheelchair on the sidelines.

> Two years ago, Mary started every day with a two-mile run. Now, she lies in bed each morning and struggles to make one foot move.

12.6 Things You May Not Do in Closing Argument

There are few restrictions on closing argument. You may wax as eloquent as you please. You may regale the jurors with stories, anecdotes, analogies, and metaphors. Nevertheless, closing argument does have its boundaries and you must not cross them. The basic rules are that every argument you make must be supported by evidence in the record, and the result you argue for must be justified by the law.

12.6.1 *You May Not State Your Personal Belief as to Credibility*

You may not state your personal assessment of the credibility of witnesses. To say that you personally believe or disbelieve a witness's story, sometimes called vouching for the credibility of a witness, is ethically improper.[7] For example, when discussing the credibility of one of your witnesses, you may discuss all of the reasons reflected in the evidence that his testimony should be accepted as true, such as lack of motive to lie and consistency of his statements. You can exhort the jurors to accept or reject the witness's testimony.

You Can Say	You Cannot Say
"Believe him."	"I believe him."
"Billy is a liar."	"I believe Billy is a liar."

The distinction may seem silly, but the rule is designed to avoid a lawyer's directly vouching for a witness.

The extreme example of impermissible vouching would be, "I've known Billy for years, and I've come to know him even better while preparing this case, and I can tell you, ladies and gentlemen, this boy is telling the truth."

12.6.2 You May Not Ask Jurors to Decide the Case on an Improper Basis

Cases are supposed to be decided logically, based solely on the law as instructed and the evidence as presented. This ideal, of course, flies in the face of all history and human experience and we know that prejudice, bias, sympathy, and anger are always important factors in any decision made by human beings. Although we recognize the inevitability of improper considerations, we also recognize the desirability of their elimination from the trial process. The rules of evidence, procedure, and legal ethics, therefore, do everything possible to minimize the intrusion of improper influences into the sanctity of the jury room. Likewise, you may not overtly appeal to the jurors to decide the case in your client's favor because they feel sympathy or because they feel anger or disdain toward the opposing party.

12.6.3 You May Not Make a "Golden Rule" Argument

The so-called "Golden Rule" argument is simply one form of asking the jurors to decide the case on an improper basis—to "do unto others as you would have them do unto you."[8] You may not ask the jurors to place themselves in the shoes of your client (or the victim in a criminal case) and to find for your client because

---

7. *See* Craig Lee Montz, "Why Lawyers Continue to Cross the Line in Closing Argument: An Examination of Federal and State Cases," 28 Ohio N.U. L. Rev. 67, 108 (2001–2002).
8. The "Golden Rule," from the Gospel According to St. Matthew 7:12.

they would want a jury to find for them in similar circumstances. You must ask the jurors to find for your client because the facts and the law justify a verdict in your client's favor.

12.6.4   *You May Not Invade the Defendant's Constitutional Rights in a Criminal Case*

The prosecutor must continue to respect the constitutional rights of the accused. You may not invade the defendant's privilege against self-incrimination by directly commenting on the defendant's failure to take the stand. The prosecutor also must be cautious not to refer to evidence as "uncontradicted" where the defendant is the only person who could have contested that evidence. You also must ensure that you do not invade the defendant's right to remain silent following arrest and delivery of *Miranda* warnings by commenting on the defendant's silence.[9]

---

9. *See* Douglas v. Ohio, 426 U.S. 610 (1976). *But see* United States v. Robinson, 485 U.S. 25 (1988) (permitting prosecutor to make a "fair response" to defense counsel's argument about defendant's silence).

CHAPTER THIRTEEN

GETTING READY FOR TRIAL

He tried to smile as he answered the phone. "Hello," he said.

"John, it's your Aunt Betty. I hear that you are starting a trial tomorrow. What's it about?"

John was about to begin speaking when he remembered that Aunt Betty had really good critical skills. He trusted her. He took a deep breath and thought about the key facts in the case. He took a moment longer and thought about why he took the case. Then he began a three-minute synopsis of the case, knowing that whatever Aunt Betty said in response would help in his final preparation.

13.1 Marshal the Evidence

After analyzing the facts and law and choosing a case theory, you must marshal the evidence. The phrase "marshaling the evidence" simply means arranging its presentation in a way that will be both logical and forceful. The nuts and bolts of successful case presentation are:

1) Determining what facts establish the chosen legal aspect of your case theory and factual aspect of your case theory[1];

2) Arranging and presenting that evidence in a logical way; and

3) Communicating your reasons for winning to the jurors.

The ability to assemble evidence and disseminate it to the jurors in a way that will both enable them to understand the evidence and persuade them what to make of it, is the sine qua non of the trial lawyer's skills. The case must be presented as an integrated, consistent whole. To present it persuasively, arrange the facts in an order that will enable the jurors to grasp their significance and fit them into your legal and factual case theory.

Facts come to your attention in a number of ways. If you represent individuals, you will usually have an initial interview with your client. If you defend cases for a

---

1. *See* chapter two.

liability insurance company, you will probably receive the complaint and investigation file in the mail with a request to defend. If you are an associate with a large law firm, a partner may toss the case file on your desk and tell you to handle it. However the first facts come to you, they will usually be jumbled and disorganized. Long before you begin your final trial preparation you will have reviewed the facts, sorted them out, analyzed them, determined whether they support any legal causes of action or defenses, and decided your overarching factual story of the case. Now, during the final stages of preparing the case, you must line up the facts for presentation in a way that will maximize the jurors' ability to understand and appreciate them.

For example, if you are trying to prove self-defense in a murder trial, you know you will have to present evidence on the issue of provocation. You may have many different facts and several different witnesses whose testimony will bear on the issue. One witness may have seen the victim with a knife; another may have heard him make a threat; a third may have seen the victim run after the defendant when he left the bar. Your job is to consider all of the evidence that bears on the issue and decide which evidence you will present to the jurors and in what order. The job is more complex than it first appears, because each of those three witnesses may have testimony that bears on other issues. You cannot always organize the testimony chronologically, or even thematically. Further, witnesses may have weaknesses or credibility problems that make you doubt whether jurors will believe what they have to say.

Ultimately, you must make difficult decisions about the order and manner of proof that allow you to present the facts in the way most favorable to your client's position from the jurors' perspective. Always emphasize your strongest points. Favorable facts that are uncontested, or if contested, are clearly in your favor have the most powerful persuasive effect on the jurors. If your lawsuit was a deck of cards, these would be the aces. Facts such as the opponent's admission of liability, a clearly authentic document, or an unbiased eyewitness's testimony can form the centerpiece of your presentation.

You must also simplify the presentation of evidence to enable the jurors to understand your factual theory. Clear out the clutter. Remember that the jurors will be hearing the information for the first time. Present the most persuasive evidence available to support each element of your cause of action or defense and your factual story of the case.

13.2   Conduct a "Favorable/Unfavorable" Facts Analysis

This is a tool many lawyers find helpful in focusing the mind on the essential facts that must be proved, as well as on the major stumbling blocks. This analysis can be performed at any time during your final case preparation. Whenever more than one lawyer has worked on the case, bring them all together for a brainstorming session. Use a chalkboard. Write the name of each witness on the board and put two columns under each name. Under each witness's name, in one column list facts that are favorable to your case that should be elicited during that witness's testimony. Include in this column any key exhibits that should be introduced as the witness testifies. In the second column, list all unfavorable facts pertaining to the witness—those matters that you anticipate will be brought out on cross-examination. Having listed them, you can decide how to deal with them. Perform the same analysis for every witness—yours and your opponent's witnesses.

13.3   Prepare a Trial Notebook

Your trial notebook is the overall script for presenting your case. It should contain, in one easily accessible location, all of the information that you need to be able to locate instantly during the trial. Every lawyer organizes the trial notebook somewhat differently, but there are several sections that should be included in any trial notebook.

A good way to organize your notebook is to use tabbed dividers or separate folders to create the following sections:

- Story of the Case, Theme and Stakes[2]

- Legal Case Analysis/Proof Checklist[3]

- Pleadings

- Pretrial Orders and Stipulations that are relevant to the trial

- Procedural questions for the judge regarding the trial

- Jury Selection

- Checklist of the Order of the Trial (including motions for judgment and a reminder to check the status of exhibits before resting)

- Opening Statement

- Checklist of Exhibits[4]

- For each of the witnesses you will call, a section containing the outline of the direct examination, exhibits to be identified or introduced through the witness, discovery responses and pretrial statements of the witness, and law regarding anticipated objections

- Motion for Judgment as a Matter of Law/Acquittal at the close of the plaintiff's/prosecution's case

---

2. *See* chapter two at 2.3.
3. *Id.* at 2.2.3.
4. *See* chapter ten at 10.3.

- For each of the witnesses your adversary will call, a section containing the outline of the cross examination, exhibits to be identified or introduced through the witness, discovery responses and pretrial statements of the witness, and law regarding objections

- Motion for Judgment as a Matter of Law/Acquittal at the close of the Evidence

- Closing Argument

- Jury Instructions and Verdict Form

- Posttrial Motions

Whether your case file fills a cabinet or merely one manila folder, you must take it apart and rearrange the contents for trial presentation. You must have certain documents at the ready so that you can lay your hands on them immediately and efficiently when they are needed during the trial. The physical act of going through the file and rearranging it will assure that you are familiar with every important matter that must be included in your trial presentation.

13.4   Prepare to Present the Testimony of Your Witnesses

In your trial notebook, you must have a subsection for each of your witnesses. Under each witness's tab should be either a list of questions you will ask that witness or a list of topics you must cover with that witness (sometimes referred to as "bullets"), or a combination of both. The debate continues whether to write out your direct examination questions. All agree that if you write them out, you *must not* read them when conducting your examination.[5]

A degree of mental discipline and thoroughness is achieved through the act of writing out questions. In the early stages of your career, it is probably advantageous to write out all of your questions. Even in the later stages it wise to do so with witnesses whose testimony is long or complicated. But do not ask the questions verbatim as you wrote them. You must be conversational when presenting your witnesses.

At the least, you should write out key foundation questions that will determine the admissibility of exhibits.[6] Include in the notes for each witness a list of foundation questions regarding exhibits that must be asked of that witness. Also include a list of any exhibits that will be introduced into evidence during that witness's testimony. When the legal significance of an expert opinion depends upon the precise language in which the question eliciting the opinion is phrased, by all means write that question out.[7]

---

5. *See* chapter six at 6.3.1.
6. *See* chapter ten at 10.6.
7. *See* chapter nine at 9.3.2.

National Institute for Trial Advocacy

You must also plan the sequence in which you will call your witnesses. Sometimes you will be bound by restraints of necessity—the convenience or availability of the witnesses. Nevertheless, you should always begin and end your case with the strongest available witnesses. Sandwich your necessary but weak or less credible witnesses in the middle.

Generally, a prosecutor or plaintiff should first call a witness who can give a general overview of essential facts. The final witness for the prosecution is usually one who can nail the defendant (for instance, a DNA expert). In a civil case, the plaintiff's last witness is usually a person who arouses sympathy and who can establish damages.

13.5   Take Your Witnesses to the Woodshed

In the old days, when lawyers and judges rode circuit and courthouses were heated by wood stoves, it was customary for lawyers to meet and interview their witnesses in the woodshed. Thus, the practice of preparing witnesses to testify began to be called "woodshedding." Woodshedding witnesses is absolutely essential to the effective presentation of any case. You may not tell witnesses what to say, but you must help them tell what they know in a convincing way.

You must personally interview all of your witnesses. Do it yourself. Work with them as much as necessary, depending upon their importance to the case and their experience in the witness chair.

Your witness preparation should include the following tasks.

First and foremost, the witness must tell the truth. It is important to bring this up with every witness, not because you expect all of your witnesses to lie, but because many witnesses will come to the woodshed believing that you expect them to lie. You need to dispel any false assumption that they may have about lawyers. Explain that telling the truth is not only required, but it is also the best way to be persuasive. If a witness simply tells the truth there is little likelihood of being caught in an inconsistency.

Second, tell each witness to listen to the questions and answer in a way that the jurors will understand and pay attention to. For some witnesses, this means speaking more slowly or more loudly. For other witnesses, it means being more concise or using less formal language. You should practice with and listen to each witness. Help each witness work with his own communication strengths and weaknesses. Bring in another lawyer to help you practice and to role play the cross-examination. Be sure to stop periodically during the role play and compliment the witness for the things he is doing right. Tell the witness, for example, "Your voice is clear and strong. That's great. It conveys your confidence." Also, stop the witness when he goes astray and give specific suggestions about how to improve. Encourage the witness to maintain eye contact with the jurors, to sit up tall in the witness box, to avoid becoming angry or defensive. Say, for example:

> Fred, when I asked you about how much you had to drink before you got in the car, you crossed your arms in front of your chest. You will be asked that question in trial. You should answer it honestly and in as relaxed a manner as you can muster. I'm going to ask the question again. Try answering it this time with your hands in your lap.

Third, this witness's testimony is important or you would not call him to the stand. Tell your witness why his testimony is important to the case. After your witness has told you all that he knows about the case, explain the theory of the case and allow the witness to ask questions. This is important because witnesses may be asked many things on cross-examination. If he does not understand why his testimony is important, he may become flustered or upset—or even tempted to make something up—if he forgets a detail or misstates a fact. On the other hand, if he knows exactly what is going on, he will feel more confident about the entire process. Your explanation of the legal and factual theory should not lead the witness to change his story. It should, however, improve the witness's ability to communicate the important facts and relax about the parts that do not matter.

You should also explain any aspect of the trial process that the witness is wondering about. Explain, answer questions, practice. As you do these things, be especially aware of the witness's concerns. When the witness feels relaxed and well prepared, he will communicate more effectively with the jurors.

Fourth, rehearse both direct and cross examination.

Direct examination. You should rehearse every witness's direct examination with the witness. Ask the questions you will ask at trial so he will not be caught off-guard by hearing them the first time there. It is particularly important to go over foundation testimony with every witness through whom you intend to introduce an exhibit. But neither you nor the witness should want or expect the actual direct to be a verbatim replay of the examination you prepared.

Cross-examination. Prepare the witness for cross-examination. Explain the difference between your non-leading questions on direct examination and opposing counsel's leading questions on cross. Explain that the cross-examiner will probably be quite courteous, but is nevertheless not the witness's friend.

Warn the witness that the cross-examiner may attempt to arouse the witness's anger. Exhort him not to show hostility. Explain that anger is a tool in the courtroom, and that if the cross-examiner makes him show anger, the examiner has been successful in gaining the upper hand.

Tell the witness to answer the cross-examiner's questions with a "yes" or "no" if that is possible, but explain to the witness that he has the right to give full, complete answers. Inform him that if the cross-examiner's question calls for more than a yes-or-no answer, he should respond fully and accurately. Assure the witness that you will object if the cross-examiner asks an improper question. The witness should answer whatever questions are asked without looking over and inquiring, "Do I have to answer that?"

Point out specific matters that you know he will be cross-examined on, such as prior convictions or bias, and advise the witness how to deal with them. In general, it is best to admit the matter forthrightly and then explain it away, if possible, during redirect examination.

Fifth, reassure the witness that his only job is to tell the truth. The purpose of witness preparation is to make the witness confident about the trial, not to increase his apprehension. You do not want the witness to leave the preparation session concerned about whether he can perform to your lofty expectations. Finish the session by reassuring the witness that his role is quite simple: to tell the truth. If any problems arise at trial, it is the job of the lawyer, not the witness, to fix them.

13.6   Prepare Your Cross-Examination

Have a tab in your trial notebook for each of your opponent's witnesses. List the areas and specific questions you know you will cover with the witness. Include references to page numbers and lines in the deposition or other prior statement of the witness that contain key statements you wish to pin her to, or to use for impeachment if she changes her story.[8] Mark the places in the depositions with little sticky-notes so you can locate them readily and efficiently.

13.7   Prepare Your Exhibits

You should arrange your exhibits in the order in which you anticipate introducing them and place them in folders, a notebook, or a file box. In the case of documents, you must have not only the actual exhibit that will be offered into evidence, but also copies for yourself, opposing counsel, usually the court, and sometimes each member of the jury.[9] If required or permitted by court rule or practice, pre-number your exhibits. Buy some stickers at an office supply store that say "Plaintiff's Exhibit No. _____," "State's Exhibit No. _____," or "Defendant's Exhibit No. _____." Place a sticker on each actual exhibit you will introduce, and be sure all copies are marked.

You must have a Checklist of Exhibits in your trial notebook.[10] It should contain every exhibit in numerical order, a description of each, names of witnesses to whom foundation questions must be addressed, and columns headed "Offered," "Admitted," and "Refused." Your exhibit list should look something like Figure 13-1.

---

8. *See* chapter seven at 7.5.
9. *See* chapter ten at 10.4.
10. *Id.* at 10.3.

Figure 13-1.

EXHIBIT LIST				
NO. AND DESCRIPTION	WITNESSES	OFFERED	ADMITTED	REFUSED
1. Offer letter	Plaintiff			
2. Copy of acceptance letter	Plaintiff			
3. Photo of building	Plaintiff			
4. Photo of water leakage	Janitor Brewster			

Check your list as each exhibit is offered and its admissibility ruled on by the court. In the heat of a trial, it is easy to forget to offer an exhibit. The practice of keeping a checklist ensures that you will not forget. Before resting, review your exhibit list with the court to be sure that everyone agrees on which exhibits have been admitted into evidence.

You should also include in the examination notes for each witness the foundation questions you must ask her with regard to exhibits. You should also list in the examination notes all exhibits you intend to introduce while she is on the stand.

13.8   Prepare Motions in Limine

Now that you have a list of every piece of evidence that you plan to introduce, including witness testimony, documents, and demonstrative exhibits, consider whether there may be evidentiary problems with the admission of any of it.[11] Also consider the evidence that you expect your opponent to introduce. Consider filing a motion in limine seeking a ruling in advance of trial on the admissibility of important items of evidence.[12] An advance ruling admitting or excluding such evidence can have an important impact on your trial strategy. For example, a ruling that allows impeachment of your criminal defendant client with prior felony convictions that could not otherwise be introduced as part of the prosecution's case-in-chief will undoubtedly influence your advice to the client about whether to take the witness stand.

The court's rulings on motions in limine also affect your opening statement. If you know that certain evidence will be introduced against your client, you can deal with it during opening statement. On the other hand, if you know that an item of evidence will not be allowed, you know not to mention it during opening statement.

A third function of motions in limine is educational. They serve to alert the judge to significant evidentiary issues and to present those issues to him in a thoughtful

---

11. *See* chapter eleven at 11.4.1.
12. *Id.* at 11.2.3.

manner at a time when he can reflect (and maybe even look up a little law) and reach a more informed decision.

Where a piece of evidence is particularly prejudicial and you want to prevent the jurors from even getting a whiff of it, a ruling excluding that evidence after a motion in limine ensures that no question will be asked eliciting the forbidden information and that no witness will blurt it out.

13.9   Prepare Voir Dire Questions

After you have analyzed the facts of the case, marshaled your witnesses, obtained rulings on motions in limine, considered credibility problems, and completed the draft of your closing argument, you must decide what questions to ask the jurors on voir dire.[13]

13.10   Prepare Your Jury Instructions and Verdict Form

Although it is not often mentioned in law school (or, for that matter, in CLE trial practice programs), judges rarely draft jury instructions. It is the responsibility of the lawyers to draw up and submit sets of proposed jury instructions and present them to the court.[14] The extent to which jurors are able to follow instructions is a matter of ongoing debate, but there is no question that the instructions, as given to the jurors by the judge, are the law of the case as far as they are concerned. You must draft and submit to the judge a set of jury instructions covering every issue that is of consequence to your client. It goes without saying that your legal theory of the case, as well as your closing argument, must conform exactly to the law contained in the instructions.

So, how do you go about drafting jury instructions? Jury instructions must accurately and without argument state the law. Historically, finding accurate and undisputed sources of law for jury instructions has been a problem for lawyers. To address this problem, many jurisdictions have adopted sets of model or pattern jury instructions for some types of cases.[15] In some jurisdictions, use of applicable model or pattern instructions is mandatory.[16] In addition to officially sanctioned model or pattern instructions, several publications contain instructions that have

---

13. *See* chapter four at 4.3. In some courts, you will instead submit questions to the court to be asked by the judge. *See* Fed. R. Crim. P. 24(a); Fed. R. Civ. P. 47(a).

14. *See* Fed. R. Civ. P. 51(a).

15. *See, e.g., Manual of Model Civil Jury Instructions for the District Courts of the Eighth Circuit* (1992); Ark. Model Instr., Civil (2006).

16. *See* Per Curiam Order of Arkansas Supreme Court, entered April 19, 1965, requiring that when an Arkansas Model Instruction (AMI) is applicable in a case, it shall be used unless the trial judge finds that it does not accurately state the law. If an applicable AMI instruction is not used, the court is required to state in writing the reasons for refusing to give the instruction. *See* Vangilder v. Faulk, 244 Ark. 688, 693–694 (1968).

gained court approval in past cases.[17] Where no pattern or model instruction is available, you must look to statutory or case law. Of course, applicable language from a statute or appellate jurisdiction is ultimately controlling.

However, it is not enough that your proposed jury instruction is accurate. The jurors also must be able to understand the instruction. Appellate decisions are written for judges and lawyers, not jurors. Studies have shown jurors understand half of the pattern instructions included in the charge.[18] While a court will be more comfortable accepting a proposed instruction that follows the language of a pattern instruction or an appellate case, you should carefully consider proposing instructions that, while accurately stating the law, do so using language that will be understood by the jurors.[19]

Prepare each instruction separately, no more than one to a page. Number the instructions in the order you want the court to give them. At the bottom of each page, type three blanks:

Given   **Refused**   **Modified**

Also, at the bottom of each page cite the source of the instruction. If the source is a model instruction, cite the model instruction number; if it is based on a statute, cite the statute; if it has been distilled from the language of a case, cite the case. Prepare enough copies so that the court, each of your opponents, and you can have one. Along with your proposed instructions, submit a proposed form for the verdict.[20] The figure below is a typical proposed jury instruction as it might appear in a set submitted to a court in a prisoner civil rights case.

---

17. *See, e.g.,* Devitt, Edward J. et al., *Federal Jury Practice and Instructions: Criminal* (4th ed. 1990).

18. *See* James Alfini, Bruce Dennis Sales & Amiram Elwork, "Towards Understandable Jury Instructions," 65 *Judicature* 430 (March–April 1982); Walter W. Steele, Jr. & Elizabeth G. Thornburg," Jury Instructions: A Persistent Failure to Communicate," 67 *N.C. L. Rev.* 77 (1988); Peter Meijes Tiersma, "Reforming the Language of Jury Instructions," 22 *Hofstra L. Rev.* 37 (1992), William W. Schwarzer, "Communicating with Jurors: Problems and Remedies," 69 *California L. Rev.* 731 (1981); Robert Charrow & Veda Charrow, "Making Legal Language Understandable: A Psycholinguistic Study of Jury Instructions," 79 *Colum. L. Rev.* 1306 (1979).

19. Both Indiana and California have promulgated jury instructions written in plain English. *See* Indiana Model Civil Jury Instructions (2015); www.courts.ca.gov/partners/juryinstructions.htm.; Tips for writing understandable jury instructions also may be found at Peter M. Tiersma, Communicating with Juries: How to Draft More Understandable Jury Instructions, National Center for State Courts (2006) (originally published in 10 Scribes J. Legal Writing 1 (2005-2006)); James Alfini, Bruce Dennis Sales and Amiram Elwork, Making Jury Instructions Understandable (1982).

20. There are three types of verdict forms: a general verdict form, a special verdict form, and a general verdict form with special interrogatories. *See* FED. R. CIV. P. 49. For a discussion of the tactics underlying what type of verdict form to propose, see Sylvia Walbolt & Cristina Alonso, "Jury Instructions: A Road Map for Trial Counsel," 30 *Litigation* 29, 34 (Winter 2004); Howard M. Shapiro & Amy Krieger Wigmore, "Choosing the Right Verdict Form," www.wilmerhale.com/pages/publicationsand-NewsDetail.aspx?NewsPubId-95254 (last visited May 11, 2016); Mark S. Brodin, "Accuracy, Efficiency and Accountability in the Litigation Process—The Case for the Fact Verdict," 59 *Cin. L. Rev.* 15 (1990); Samuel M. Driver, "The Special Verdict—Theory and Practice," 26 *Wash. L. Rev.* 21 (1951).

Figure 13-2.

<u>**Reliability of Witnesses**</u>

In deciding what the facts are, you may have to decide what testimony you believe and what testimony you do not believe. You may believe all of what a witness said, or only part of it, or none of it.

In deciding what testimony to believe, you may consider the witness's intelligence, the opportunity the witness had to have seen or heard the things testified about, the witness's memory, any motives that witness may have for testifying a certain way, the manner of the witness while testifying, whether that witness said something different at an earlier time, the general reasonableness of the testimony, and the extent to which the testimony is consistent with any evidence that you believe.

SOURCE: Model Civil Jury Instructions for the District Courts of the Eighth Circuit, Instruction 3.03.

GIVEN_____

REFUSED_____

MODIFIED_____

The time when you will actually submit proposed jury instructions to the judge varies. Judges have their own individual rules on this subject, and the time may vary from several days in advance of trial to the close of the evidence.[21] Most judges, however, wait until the close of the evidence to make a ruling on which instructions they will give. At the close of all the evidence, the judge generally holds a conference with the lawyers to review the proposed jury instructions. Where the proposed instructions differ, the court makes a decision. If you object to any instruction the court gives, you must object on the record at that time.[22] You must object both to instructions that the judge gives as well as your proposed instruction that the judge refused to include in the charge.[23]

It makes sense for the judge to wait until the close of the evidence to make a ruling on which jury instructions will be given because the court is permitted to give

---

21. *See* FED. R. CIV. P. 51(a).

22. *See* FED. R. CIV. P. 51(c); United States v. Bornfield, 184 F.3d 1144 (10th Cir. 1999); Yore v. M/V Ling Leo, 2000 U.S. App. Lexis 6899 (2d Cir. April 14, 2000).

23. If the judge advises you of his intended charge in chambers and no court reporter is present, you should ask permission to renew your objections in the courtroom, outside the hearing of the jury, where a court reporter is present. FED. R. CIV. P. 51(b)(2). To preserve your objections for appeal, you should renew your objection after the judge delivers the instructions to the jury and before the jury retires to deliberate. *See* FED. R. CIV. P. 51(b)(2).

only the instructions that are supported by the evidence. For example, suppose there is a murder trial in a jurisdiction where a claim of self-defense requires evidence that the victim provoked the defendant. When the defendant requests a jury charge on the issue of self-defense, the judge must think through the evidence that has been presented at trial and decide if there has been sufficient proof of provocation to support a jury finding on that issue. If the admissible evidence and inferences would not support a finding that the victim provoked the defendant, it would be error for the judge to give the jurors charge on self-defense.

Even though you will not have a definite ruling on which charges the judge will read to the jurors until the end of the trial, it is wise to draft the jury charges once you have completed your initial research into the elements at the outset of the litigation.[24] The draft instructions will guide your pleadings, your informal and formal discovery of the facts, and pretrial motions for judgment. And, as the Protocol for Presenting a Legally Sufficient Case prescribes,[25] the draft instructions will govern your examination of witnesses and introduction of exhibits at trial, ensuring that you present sufficient evidence to establish each and every element at trial during your case-in-chief.

13.11 Prepare Your Opening Statement and Review Your Closing Argument

Preparation of your opening statement should be one of the last things you do. You should save its preparation until last because only then do you know exactly what evidence you will present, in what order, and which issues you will deal with on voir dire. You should also review your closing argument now. You should have drafted it long ago and used it as your guiding star throughout your trial preparation. Ask yourself again why you should win. Be sure you can explain:

1) why you came to the courthouse

2) what are the legal elements of your case

3) what is the admissible evidence that supports each element (or, if your opponent has the burden of proof, the missing pieces of evidence that mandate a verdict in your favor)

4) what is your factual story of the case—character, plot and motive

5) what is the theme of your case

6) what are the stakes

7) what you want the jurors to do

---

24. *See* chapter two at 2.2.5.
25. *Id.* at 2.2.

13.12   Before the Trial Begins

Get one or more objective lay opinions. As you prepare a case for trial, you are in constant danger of losing your perspective. You will almost inevitably lose the forest for the trees. One of the best ways to jerk yourself back to reality is to try out your story on objective lay persons. Your spouse, friends, or relatives can be valuable allies as you prepare your case. However, a few words of caution are in order. You must select people who will be honest and not simply tell you what you want to hear. Furthermore, you must keep an open mind and listen to what these people tell you. Do not get defensive and argue with your critics. Take all of their comments into consideration, but make the final decisions yourself. In the final analysis, it is the mature, independent exercise of your professional judgment that will make you worthy of the appellation "trial lawyer."

Try to get a good night's sleep. Peaceful slumber will probably elude you during the night before trial. Nevertheless, go to bed and try. Do not get up and engage in busy work. Lie in the darkness and think. Review in your mind the order of witnesses, your questions on direct and cross-examination, your voir dire questions, and your opening statement. This quiet, lonely, half-wakeful thought can be extremely productive if you will just sink into it and allow your mind to mull over the case.

Get to the courtroom early. Allow yourself and your client time to settle into the courtroom atmosphere. Get to the courtroom at least forty-five minutes before the trial is scheduled to begin, get your materials set up and organized, walk around, let your client look around, say hello to the court officials. In short, get comfortable.

Practice varies as to who sits where. Each side would usually prefer to sit nearest the jurors. In some courts, the party with the burden of proof gets to sit nearer. In others, whoever gets to the courtroom first gets first choice. Find out what the rule is in the court to which your case is assigned and act accordingly.

A final word—the "butterflies" are natural. Every person whose profession involves performing publicly in pressure-filled situations gets nervous. Stage fright is natural. Ask any professional athlete or entertainer. Butterflies in the stomach are the natural result of the adrenalin rush that precedes highly stressful activity. You should be worried if you are not nervous before a trial. The trick is to channel that energy into positive, productive paths so that it causes your performance to peak. One of the authors vividly remembers a time when he served as co-counsel with a nationally acclaimed trial lawyer. From his vantage point at counsel table, he could see the famous lawyer's back as he stood behind the lectern before cross-examining a key opposition witness. The great barrister exuded confidence and control, but much to the author's surprise, the barrister's hands were trembling violently. After a couple of questions, the trembling stopped, and the lawyer stepped out from behind the lectern and conducted a masterful cross-examination. The point is that the great ones get as nervous as you. Like them, you must just accept it and use it to your advantage.

Subject Index

A

Art of persuasion
Generally, 3.4

B

Bench trials
Jury trials distinguished, 1.5

Business records (See EXHIBITS)

C

Challenge for cause
Generally, 4.1
Exercising, 4.3.3

Closing arguments
Contents of effective, 12.3
Delivering
Choosing words carefully, 12.5.4
Dynamics and rhythm,
varying, 12.5.5
Long-winded, 12.5.3
Reading, avoid, 12.5.1
Rhetorical devices, 12.5.6
Visual aids, using, 12.5.2
Discussing why jurors should accept your
version of disputed facts, 12.3.1
Explanation of how jurors should apply law
to facts, 12.3.2
Jury trial, 1.4
Outline of
Generally, 12.4
Civil case, arguing remedy in, 12.4.4
Liability or guilt, arguing, 12.4.3
Reconnecting with jurors, 12.4.1
Telling jurors exactly what you want
them to know, 12.4.5
Theme and factual theory of case,
returning to, 12.4.2
Preparation of, 12.2
Purpose of, 12.1
Reviewing for trial preparation, 13.11
Things not to do in
Generally, 12.6

Asking jurors to decide case on
improper basis, 12.6.2
"Golden Rule" argument,
making, 12.6.3
Invading defendant's constitutional
rights in criminal case, 12.6.4
Stating personal belief as to credibility,
12.6.1

Courtroom
Generally, 1.1
Demeanor (See DEMEANOR)

Cross-examination
Generally, 7.1
Center stage, taking, 7.3.2
Constructive, 7.2.1
Controlling witness, techniques to
Generally, 7.5
Leading questions, use only, 7.5.2
Not asking questions unless, 7.5.1
Question presenting only one fact to
witness, every, 7.5.3
Temptation to force witness to
voice what jury already
understands, resist, 7.5.5
Witness does not know question,
7.5.4
Destructive, 7.2.3
Expert witnesses (See EXPERT
WITNESSES)
Eye contact, maintaining, 7.3.4
Firm but courteous, 7.3.1
Keeping up questioning pace, 7.3.3
Preparation of, 13.6
Purpose of, identifying, 7.2
Sequence of chapters of, determining
Generally, 7.4
Bring out evidence favorable to your
client's case, 7.4.1
Challenge witness, 7.4.3
Witness acknowledge weak spots in
their testimony, 7.4.2
"Thank you for your honest, albeit
mistaken", 7.2.2
The "really?", 7.2.4
Where to stand, 7.3.2